Empathy in the
Global World

For my mother and father, Idell and Alvin Calloway

Empathy in the
Global World
An Intercultural Perspective

Carolyn Calloway-Thomas
Indiana University

Los Angeles | London | New Delhi
Singapore | Washington DC

For information:

SAGE Publications, Inc.
2455 Teller Road
Thousand Oaks,
    California 91320
E-mail: order@sagepub.com

SAGE Publications India Pvt. Ltd.
B 1/I 1 Mohan Cooperative
    Industrial Area
Mathura Road, New Delhi 110 044
India

SAGE Publications Ltd.
1 Oliver's Yard
55 City Road
London EC1Y 1SP
United Kingdom

SAGE Publications Asia-Pacific Pte. Ltd.
33 Pekin Street #02-01
Far East Square
Singapore 048763

Printed in the United States of America

Library of Congress Cataloging-in-Publication Data

Calloway-Thomas, Carolyn
Empathy in the global world : an intercultural perspective/Carolyn Calloway-Thomas.
    p. cm.
Includes bibliographical references and index.
ISBN 978-1-4129-5790-8 (cloth)
ISBN 978-1-4129-5791-5 (pbk.)
    1. Cultural relations. 2. Empathy 3. Humanitarianism. 4. Intercultural communication. I. Title.

HM621.C355 2010
303.48′209—dc22   2009028257

This book is printed on acid-free paper.

09   10   11   12   13   10   9   8   7   6   5   4   3   2   1

Acquisitions Editor:	Todd R. Armstrong
Editorial Assistant:	Aja Baker
Production Editor:	Astrid Virding
Copy Editor:	Gillian Dickens
Typesetter:	C&M Digitals (P) Ltd.
Proofreader:	Dennis W. Webb
Indexer:	Naomi Linzer
Cover Designer:	Candice Harman
Marketing Manager:	Jennifer Reed Banando

Contents

Preface

There is an urgent need for understanding global empathy. It is the subject of this book, and it is a topic that I have thought a great deal about over the years, as I grappled with variations on a sobering question that Dr. Martin Luther King Jr.'s 6-year-old daughter raised in the 1950s when she was told that Funtown, a public amusement park in Birmingham, Alabama, was closed to "colored" children (Washington, 1991, p. 293). The question is, "Why do people treat others so mean?" I also remember very well a similar incident that happened when I was a little girl growing up in Bernice in Louisiana. As my father and I walked down the narrow main street near a drugstore—with a soda fountain—that served ice cream, I asked my father whether we could go inside for an ice cream cone. As I write these lines, it is still difficult for me to do so without tears welling up in my eyes. I watched the face of my dejected father as he uttered words that wounded my gustatory expectations and placed social consciousness on a shelf where I could reach it. "We cannot go into that store for ice cream," said my father, "because. . . ."

My intellectual and affective world was framed by that painful moment, and in this book, years later, as a result of being studiously attentive to both national and international events, as a result of my intercultural experiences, and as a result of my cognitive engagement with scholarship on empathy, intercultural communication, anthropology, psychology, history, political science, religion, and other areas, I came to see the world in a whole new way. And I set out to understand more fully the role of empathy in public culture.

In 1956, in his address before the First Annual Institute on Non-Violence and Social Change in Montgomery, Alabama, without ever using the term *empathy*, Dr. Martin Luther King Jr. urged human beings "to rise above the narrow confines of our individualistic concerns to the broader concerns of all humanity" (quoted in Washington, 1991, p. 138). And he pronounced the new world to be one of "geographical togetherness" and "understanding goodwill. " Employing the terms *togetherness* and *goodwill*, with implicit echoes of the humanism of his mentor, Mahatma Gandhi of India, Dr. King challenged human beings to craft a compelling vision of a beloved community by defining the basis upon which the communication or sharing of ideas and feelings can proceed.

But it is one thing to identify a set of values out of the shared common ground language of a community; it is something else altogether to vivify a world to the point of comprehending and elevating empathy. A half century later, King's philosophical notions that interplays between goodwill, other-regarding behaviors, and a sustainable life can make a huge difference still resonate. This book is animated by a belief that our significance as human beings stems in a very large measure from how much goodwill we inject into the troubled world of globalization.

The vexing issues explored in this book are at the center of some of the most salient aspects of globalization today, and they play a commanding role in arguing one type of community into existence (one based on inclusivity, peace, respect, and universal human values) as opposed to arguing another kind of community into existence (one based on turmoil, meanness, wretchedness, genocide, and heaps of trouble). The challenge of empathy *is* the great challenge of our time.

Although the last chapter in this book articulates an agenda for change that reflects a common ground approach to understanding and "doing" empathy, I am mindful of the nexus that exists between points of reality and an unrealizable utopian dream. I believe, however, that the last chapter sets forth a realistic agenda for empathetic fluency that contains seeds for deepening intercultural relationships among human beings around the world.

During my travels, I have encountered so many people—children at play, tour guides, bus drivers, store clerks, professors, farmers, villagers, townspeople, city dwellers, the downtrodden, haves and have-nots—and all have reinforced my view that human beings worldwide share both the burdens and consequences of empathy or its absence. For this reason, this book is written not only for undergraduate and graduate students but also for general readers who wish to add more light than shadows to the world.

On June 5, 2009, Nobel Peace Prize winner Elie Wiesel, who was imprisoned at Buchenwald concentration camp as a 16-year-old boy, toured the site with President Barack Obama during the latter's trip to Germany. While standing upon the ground where much misery had occurred during World War II, Wiesel raised a question of piercing proportions, and it also has a special bearing on the subject of this book.

In commenting on the barbarism resident at Buchenwald and in reflecting on other terrible and evil acts that are "meant to diminish the humanity of human beings," from Cambodia to Bosnia, Nobelist Wiesel asked, "Will the world ever learn?" ("Obama, Elie Wiesel," 2009, p. 4). One strong, resonant reply to his question is that an understanding of empathy is sorely needed if we are to turn the world toward a more humane bent and away from global unrest and cruelty. I wrote the last sentence with a full and thoughtful knowledge of the multifaceted, weighty dimensions of human empathy. But we human beings must, in the words of Wiesel, "stop hating the otherness of the other" and "respect it" ("Obama, Elie Wiesel," 2009, p. 4). If we do not follow the way of empathy, then what and who will save us?

Acknowledgments

I am most grateful to my wonderful husband Jack E. Thomas, who, over the years, through his invaluable commentary—both spoken and written—helped me to dissect the workings of empathy. But the charitable record would not be complete without acknowledging my sacrificing, devoted parents, nine sweet siblings, and the caring citizens of Bernice, Louisiana, who taught me to wonder more deeply about the relationship that obtains between empathy and the "other."

In countless ways, as a result of my experiences with so many friends and colleagues worldwide, I am the fortunate beneficiary of their kindnesses and insights that helped to bring this book into being.

My former students have taught me so much about what is good and rich in the world, and I thank them for this gift. I also especially thank the following reviewers for their generous time and comments on this work: Molefi Kete Asante (Department of African American Studies, Temple University), Deborah F. Atwater (Associate Professor Emerita of Communication Arts and Sciences and African and African American Studies, The Pennsylvania State University), Benjamin J. Broome (Hugh Downs School of Human Communication, Arizona State University), Alexia Georgakopoulos (Department of Conflict Analysis and Resolution, Nova Southeastern University), Robert Hariman (Department of Communication Studies, Northwestern University), Fred E. Jandt (Department of Communication Studies, California State University, San Bernardino), Mark A. Pollock (Department of Communication Studies, Loyola University Chicago), Mark V. Redmond (Department of Communication Studies/English, Iowa State University), and Therese Saint Paul (Department of Modern Languages, Murray State University).

Finally, I am deeply indebted to the editors at SAGE and Todd Armstrong for believing in this project.

Carolyn Calloway-Thomas
Bloomington, Indiana

1

A Global Imperative

The Unveiling of Empathy

In her powerful autobiography, *In Search of Fatima: A Palestinian Story,* Ghada Karmi (2002) tells a moving story about her confrontation with difference. Karmi describes what caused her family to leave Jerusalem when she was a child; the family's experience in their new home, the Golders Green area of London, England, where they were exiled; and their attempts to fit into English society. Karmi's mother never quite assimilated into the new culture because the mother's spirit remained in Palestine—rooted to the very spot where she had grown up. Anguished by exile and leaving and contained by a failure to grasp "what it would be like to live by someone else's light," to use Isaiah Berlin's (1991, p. 11) phrase, the mother tried to replicate Palestinian social customs in a London household.

In explaining aspects of her culture, Karmi (2002) writes that Palestinians "had no tradition of going somewhere in order to see what it was like, or simply to get away from our routine, everyday setting" (p. 263). Karmi also reveals that "our mother had little interest in places which had no relation to what was familiar to her, like many Arabs, her concept of enjoyment was being with other people, not gazing at historical monuments which she scornfully referred to as 'piles of stones'" (p. 263).

When Karmi's mother had a chance to visit Spain, her view of the world shifted dramatically, however. Karmi (2002) writes,

The only exception to this position she ever encountered in her life was when once, long after we were grown up, our father took her to southern Spain. There, agog at the splendid Islamic buildings of Cordova and Granada, where she could see the grand legacy of Spain's Arab past, she felt the thrill that piles of stones would impart. "What colour, what lightness!" she enthused. How marvelous the Arabs were. (p. 263)

Karmi's mother's narrative reveals a great deal about empathy and why and how stories give humans good reasons for ordering their lives "this way" and not "that way." And when humans order their lives "this way" and not "that way," whatever THE way is, the very act of ordering can foster a mine/thine split that erodes empathy and creates conflict and anguish in the world. The cold war period, which ended in 1989, was emblematic of a "mine/thine" bifurcated global split. The 21st century, however, ushered in the age of warm globalization that was supposed to unite humans into one grand and harmonious global community following the breakup of the former Soviet Union in 1991.

Promises—both explicit and implicit—that swords would be beaten into biblical ploughshares and that humans would study conflict and no longer engage in war abounded. But there were also strong indications that the road to a new world order would have tracks of America all over it. Ironically, Fukuyama (1995) optimistically declared "the end of history" and the "legitimacy of liberal democracy as a system of government" (p. xi). Today, the "flat world" that Thomas L. Friedman (2005) argues is unfolding before our eyes is also one of anguish, distress, turmoil, and inequality. Throughout the world, in many spaces and places, from Bangkok to Beirut, from Chile to China and from Detroit to Dubai, we find that humans' confrontation with difference too often results in violence and conflict.

A World in Conflict

On September 11, 2001, nineteen members of Al-Qaeda destroyed the World Trade Center in New York City, killing 3,000 people. The aftermath of 9/11, Chalmers Johnson (2004) writes in *The Sorrows of Empire,* "more or less spelled the end of globalization" (p. 257).

In 2004, filmmaker Theo van Gogh, the great-great-grand-nephew of artist Vincent van Gogh, was killed in the streets of Amsterdam in broad daylight, because his film, *Submission,* supposedly contained anti-Islamic images and views and because the film posed a threat to assassin Mohammed Bouyeri, a second-generation Dutchman from Morocco.

In one tiny town in northern Italy, Sabrina Varroni, a Muslim woman, was fined 80 euros (about $100 in 2004) for appearing twice in public wearing a veil that completely covered her face. Her punishment was greeted by cheers from some and scorn by others (Fisher, 2004, p. A3).

On October 27, 2005, in towns and cities, French-Arab and French-African youths rioted, burning cars, businesses, and public buildings (Carreyrou, 2005; Smith, 2004). And in 2006, Danish newspaper *Jyllands-Posten* published a caricature of the Prophet Muhammad that created outrage in Muslim countries (Fattah, 2006; Rose, 2006).

Following publication of the cartoons, Muslims in the Middle East demonstrated in Beriut, Damascus, Tehran, and other places, and much robust discussion ensued over issues of first amendment rights, democracy, freedom of religion, and reciprocal obligations to others.

In 2008, war between Palestinians and Israelis raged on, and insurgents in Iraq continued their battle against American occupation of Iraq. Are these acts isolated and aberrant? What happened to the new world order with its promises of positive social, technological, and cultural changes? And whose and what narratives are unfolding at this moment of great cultural confrontation worldwide? Has the profound transformation of cultures from industrial to information societies and from totalitarianism to other "isms" also transformed the spirit of people and compelled them to be more empathetic toward one another—both near and far?

At a time of crucial cultural, economic, and social change, it is imperative to understand how the practice of empathy influences human affairs. This book argues that studying the nature and zones of empathy is a good way of understanding our complex and various world. I will show that much is at stake culturally, economically, and geopolitically when we fail to refashion the world along the lines of empathy. In the 21st century, when the world is being threatened by the possibility of Al-Qaeda and other terrorist groups gaining access to nuclear weapons, now, more than ever, it behooves us to examine empathy—a significant tool for humanity.

Along the way, I explain under what conditions empathy has succeeded and under what conditions it has failed across a range of topics and situations, including hot contestations over global immigration, the undermining of empathy during the Iraq war, and the role of media in galvanizing empathy toward others. This book is not about solutions to every topic discussed, and by necessity, some issues are not covered. But as we shall see, it is about the interplay among urgent human variables that argue for an empathic imperative. Both explicitly and implicitly, I argue that a major way for human beings to live well and address the myriad of problems that confront us is to replace ugly, messy, and mean conflict with empathetic fluency and understanding. And this leads to the second argument of the book: Empathetic literacy can be crucial in addressing intercultural issues. Otherwise, we run the risk of descending into a world of chaos. Should we risk a day of no return?

We owe it to succeeding generations to understand the role of empathy in human relations—both the local and the global—in the 21st century, break it down into manageable units, and propose solutions. Examining the role of empathy is more significant now than ever before because of the compression of time and space and because in this new age, humans are increasingly drawn together spatially and structurally via film, politics, Internet, worldwide television, iPods, iTunes, blogs, chat rooms, dating Web sites, and other forms of media and technology.

Hume's Concentric Circles

Jagdish Bhagwati (2004), in his book, *In Defense of Globalization,* declares that "thanks to television, we have . . . the paradox of the philosopher David Hume's concentric circles of reducing loyalty and empathy" (p. 18). The concept of concentric circles of empathy is that human beings love and are loyal to their families first, and then their loyalty diminishes as they move from the center to the periphery. "Each of us," in Bhagwati's view, "feels diminishing empathy as we go from our nuclear family to the extended family, to our local community, to our state or county (say, Lancashire or Louisiana), to our nation, to our geographical region (say, Europe or the Americas), and then to the world" (p. 18). Thinkers as far back as the Stoics have posited a doctrine of the relationship between the near and the distant. Stoics called this mode of thinking and behaving *oikeiosis,* that is, the notion that we prefer those closest to ourselves than those farthest away.

Bhagwati (2004) also claims further that "what the Internet and CNN have done is to take Hume's outermost circle and turn it into the inner most. No longer can we snore while the other half of humanity suffers plague and pestilence and the continuing misery of extreme poverty. Television has disturbed our sleep perhaps short of a fitful fever but certainly arousing our finest instincts" (p. 19). But has it? Have human beings finally turned Hume's and Stoics' outermost concentric circles into the innermost? If yes, then this certainly would be a beautiful triumph for humankind and should be met with jubilee by all. And, if yes, have we finally begun to bind our goodwill to the goodwill of others far beyond kith and kin and brought to the foreground sweeter possibilities for diminishing conflict and preventing further human carnage in such places as Sudan, Iraq, Somalia, the Middle East, Congo, Bosnia, and East Timor?

Bhagwati (2004) maintains that despite our feelings of anguish for the downtrodden, our intellectual training is impoverished and in need of fixing. And he devotes 265 careful pages to an explication of the benefits of globalization (not empathy) that detractors of globalization have somehow overlooked. But this is where our purposes diverge—at the water's edge.

Outline of the Book

This book is a story of the salience and substance of empathy and how it is being played out in the 21st century. Of course, the connection between empathy, understanding, and behavior is not new or original but has ancient origins, as I will detail in Chapter 2. Nor is the idea of studying the concept, nature, and uses of empathy new—since scholars have covered such dimensions as the aesthetic, the moral, the therapeutic, and the medical previously. Classic works such as E. B. Tichener's (1909) *A Textbook of Psychology,* E. Stein's (1964) *On the Problems of Empathy,* Tom Kitwood's (1990) *Concern for Others,* Nancy Eisenberg and Janet Strayer's (1990) *Empathy and Its Development,* and Arne Johan Vetlesen's (1994) *Perception, Empathy, and Judgment,* and all have contributed to our understanding of the concept of empathy and the commanding role that it plays in human interaction.

Although such compendiums offer keen glimpses into and understandings of the DNA and functions of empathy, I wish to examine empathy for an entirely different purpose. I have selected empathy as an object of analysis because I wanted to know the extent to which human beings are indeed practicing empathy at this critical juncture in history—the juncture of globalization.

This book offers some answers through an analysis of global empathy today, economics, history, and culture. In this chapter, I set the stage on which empathy lives today, define empathy, outline key components of empathy, and raise the question of why empathy matters. The opening chapter follows with an examination of some ancient and modern promoters of empathy, from Buddha to the Stoics to John Stuart Mill. It looks at the beginning of human beings' attempts to move outside village life and embrace the world of the other.

The historical, precursory journey provides a better understanding of when intercultural empathy entered human consciousness. The chapter also helps us grasp the concept of empathy as a discipline of diversity that informs our world today. Chapter 3 examines the hotly contested war in Iraq and the war on terror. The chapter demonstrates how the linguistic and ideological DNA of President Bush, Vice President Cheney, Secretaries Condoleezza Rice and Donald Rumsfeld, and other leaders framed and, to a great extent, overshadowed the human capacity to empathize with the very people whom they had chosen to liberate—the Iraqis. Readers see how politicians' use of powerful metaphors, groupthink, and the language of virtue and vice intersect with the ideology of democracy to retard the moral resources of humanity.

Drawing on Islamic-Arab-Africa immigration tensions in Europe and the waves of immigrants from Mexico to the United States, Chapter 4 examines challenges to the core values of Western culture and raises such questions as the following: How does immigration shape our national and international conversation about empathy? Has a confrontation with difference at the level of changing demographics helped to deplete our commitment to fair play and harmony? Altered both the salience and substance of empathy?

Looking at the world from the perspective of visual images, Chapter 5 explains circulations, diffusions, and patterns that both promote and retard universal empathy. Storytelling and techniques of television, newspapers, and broadcasting are used to illustrate how the choices we make about others influence how we see them—both instrumentally and symbolically. Chapter 6 explicates the extent to which acts of kindness strengthen human responses and, by extension, cultivate the moral imagination. The recent series of natural catastrophes, whether tsunamis, earthquakes, or hurricanes, provide a striking laboratory for an examination of the concrete humanizing imprints of empathy. The chapter also examines the interplay between charity and justice—raising the question of whether charity is a substitute for justice. That is, whether powerful human beings are really working to change structures so that charity becomes unnecessary or whether they are working for their own spiritual health.

Chapter 7 wrestles with economic disparities of world income and how they implicate the role of empathy in human relations. Although poverty is very challenging and has many tentacles, the chapter nevertheless grapples with the standard issue of who gets what in a borderless global economy and the nonempathetic cost to millions of impoverished citizens. The chapter also raises the following question: To what extent do discourses and practices of a rich global (superclass) trouble the workings of empathy?

The closing chapter of the book focuses on the grammar of empathy and examines factors influencing intercultural competence with an eye toward practical approaches to inferring the feelings and thoughts of others. It also identifies and discusses some of the options and issues we have in handling the challenges of an increasingly global society—one that relies very heavily on shared empathy.

I cannot think of a more significant variable that warrants human understanding than empathy in the 21st century because it is the bedrock of global intercultural relations.

Significance of Empathy

Of all the sentiments that have the potential to alter what we do interculturally, none are more important than empathy or sympathy. Although both sympathy and empathy are crucial in human understanding, above all, empathy is the crucible of intercultural relations. Empathy helps us to understand people whose values, views, and behavior are different from our own. Feeling sorrow for individuals who lose their homes in a hurricane, grieving for children affected by cholera in India, feeling joy over a high school drama team winning a national contest, and cheering when the villain in a motion picture is wounded are among the ways that we express empathy. A feeling of pleasure or distress, then, is not limited to those closest to us. It extends to strangers, animals, and fictional characters in our favorite novel.

Empathy is the moral glue that holds civil society together; unless humans have robust habits of mind and reciprocal behavior that lead to empathy, society as we know it will crumble. Humans are united by the powers and possibilities of empathy. In his book, *Concern for Others,* Tom Kitwood (1990; qtd. in Vetlesen, 1994, p. 9) gives one of the clearest and most concise reasons why empathy matters: "our countless small and unreflective actions towards each other, and the patterns of living and relating which each human being gradually creates. It is here that we are systematically respected or discounted, accepted or rejected, enhanced or diminished in our personal being" (p. 149).

Novelist Alexander McCall Smith's (2004) curious and persistent sleuth, Isabel Dalhousie, provides additional good reasons for why empathy matters in human relations. Losing emotional control after a series of attempts to get her daughter, Cat, to see that her boyfriend, Toby, was really up to no good, Dalhousie finally tells her daughter that her boyfriend, Toby, was being unfaithful to her. Upon realizing what her loose and wayward tongue had done, Dalhousie "stopped horrified by what she had said. She had not meant to say it—she knew it was wrong—and yet it had come out, as if spoken by somebody else. Immediately she felt miserable, thinking: So *are wrongs committed just like that, without thinking.* The doing of wrong was not a hard thing, preceded by careful thought: it was a casual thing, done so easily. That was Hannah Arendt's insight, was it not? The pure banality of evil. Only good is heroic" (p. 172). What is the nature of the heroic and not so heroic as regards empathy in the 21st century? And what is the meaning of this complex term, *empathy?*

The Meaning of Empathy

Empathy is a difficult concept to grasp. That is the great historical and philosophical fact that we must face at the outset. The term we call *empathy* was first coined in the mid-19th century by Robert Vischer (1994), who aligned it with the psychological theory of art. Vischer and others attributed it not to its present usage of feeling for and with others but, more aesthetically, to art. Their observations revealed that a strong empathy must obtain between performer and listener/reader in order for the latter to understand, "feel," or "experience" the aesthetic object, whether a poem, a play, a jazz composition, or a novel. This was a way of experiencing human feelings through the act of transference, that is, by transferring aesthetic feelings to oneself in an involuntary way.

In the all-important realm of philosophy in 19th-century Germany, Kant and Hegel saw *Einfuhlung* (empathy) as a vehicle for the "expression of feelings and emotions" (*Dictionary of the History of Ideas,* 2003, p. 2). By the mid-1900s, empathy was no longer thought of as merely a feeling for an aesthetic object but rather had evolved into the rubric of *empathy,* a term coined by American psychologist Tichener (1909) as a translation of the German *Einfuhlung.*

Part of the difficulty in defining empathy lies in the complex nature of the concept. Another difficulty is that there is "no complete agreement on the purpose of empathy . . . in the literature," as Ridley and Lingle (1996, p. 23) observe. In one sense, empathy means other-regarding and the "generation of concern for the well-being of recipients" (p. 23). In another sense, empathy is not necessarily other-regarding and may serve unkind as well as kind purposes, as Phillipe Fontaine (2001) observes. He argues, for instance, that the "world's greatest scoundrels have been exquisitely and unerringly attuned to grasping the significance of the unconscious or unspoken affective communications of others" and that they "have used that knowledge to achieve base aims" (p. 2). The term *empathy,* as it will be employed here, is the ability "imaginatively" to enter into and participate in the world of the cultural Other cognitively, affectively, and behaviorally.

Having posited this working definition, I also recognize the capaciousness of the term because, as John Holzwarth (2004) points out, "If we can enter imaginatively into the mind of one who suffers, why can we not do the same with one who causes suffering?" (p. 2). Holzwarth's notion is significant for what it reveals about the very nature and uses of empathy: "When we discover in ourselves the emotional capacity to engage the experiences of another, we realize that this capacity can apply almost anywhere" (p. 2).

Despite the fact that the concept does not "appear" to have "natural limits," my purpose is to understand some of the core purposes and practices of intercultural empathy today, ever mindful of both the benefits and burdens of the concept and their implications for human affairs. My goal is to understand the nature and zones of empathy and under what conditions empathetic practices succeed and under what conditions they fail. Furthermore, my purpose is to understand how empathy can be cultivated in order for humans to reach their full potential. If "we are close to the edge in life, always, at every moment," as Smith (2004) reminds us in his novel, *The Sunday Philosophy Club,* then we should open the door to "a world of broader possibilities" (pp. 12, 27). Concern for another's welfare, other-regarding behavior, attentiveness, gaining access to other's experiences, the communication of feeling, empathic skill, and "heightened psychic kinship" all just might incline us more toward a production of empathy.

The many practical uses of empathy have never been analyzed properly, probably because of its complex history. It is a vast subject, and an introduction of this nature can only outline those benefits and costs. But several aspects of empathy cannot easily be overlooked in human relations. These are other-regarding behavior, imaginative participation, understanding, and affect sharing. One of the aims of this book is to illustrate the role, processes, and practices involved in generating empathy, both other and non-other-regarding forms, if need be.

Imagining the Feelings of Others

Let us focus for a moment on what is meant by "imagining the feelings of others." The phrase means that we understand the behavior of others better when we are able to enter their world and "see it" through their eyes. If we accept the proposition that people's behavior and words can be interpreted as intelligible responses to the natural conditions in which they find themselves and seek to understand, we are better equipped to deal with diversity. Of course, attempting to "see through the eyes of others" does not mean that we can duplicate others' actual feelings but rather that we can suspend judgment and seek to enter their minds and feelings through "imaginative participation," which I will develop more fully later.

One argument of this book is that virtuous empathy is a necessary condition for highly desirable human outcomes. Underlying my argument about "desirable human outcomes" is an assumption that Kant (1991) advances in his book, *The Metaphysics of Morals.* Rather than arguing whose "ought" is worthier than someone else's "ought," I agree with Kant that in the moral realm of things, respect for dignity is owed all humans regardless of their standing in the community.

In *The Metaphysics of Morals,* Kant (1991) wrote,

> Humanity itself is a dignity; for a man cannot be used merely as a means by any man . . . but must always be used at the same time as an end. It is just in this that his dignity (personality) consists . . . so neither can he act contrary to the equally necessary self-esteem of others . . . he is under obligation to acknowledge, in a practical way, the dignity of humanity in every other man. (p. 255)

Robbing human beings of their dignity is dramatically revealed in the Amritsar massacre that occurred in India in 1919, when troops under British General Dyer ordered his soldiers to fire into a "peaceful Indian protest" (Glover, 2000, p. 23). Dyer's men killed between 500 and 1,000 individuals and wounded a similar number.

After the dust had settled and people observed the carnage, powerful questions emerged: "How could this have happened?" "How could General Dyer have ordered this atrocity?" Glover (2000) provides powerful insight into why the atrocity occurred: Indians' "protective dignity had . . . already been violated" (p. 24). Everyday, in countless ways, Indians had to salute and "salaam" when they met British authorities; they had to dismount when a British officer approached and even "lie down, rub their noses in the dust and grovel" (Glover, 2000, p. 23). Glover's point is that British authorities had routinized, made common, and added huge doses of ordinary acts to their repertoire of vile behavior. Therefore, when the moment of massacre happened, the British soldiers were merely carrying out "business-as-usual" modes of thinking and acting. Because the soldiers' everyday behavior had become ordinary, mercy in the form of thinking and feeling simply did not enter into their worldview. Weren't these acts supposed to occur? What dignity was owed Indians?

The notion of the "dignity of humanity in every other man" or woman, then, plays a key role in establishing notions of what I mean by "desirable human outcomes." And I also mean by the term what Glover (2000) had in mind when he wrote, "Our inclination to show . . . respect, and our disgust at someone's humiliation, is a powerful restraint on barbarism" (p. 22). The idea of desirable human outcomes is one of the most important arguments in virtuous empathy's favor because empathetic humans "care about the miseries and happiness of others, and perhaps (feel) a degree of identification with them" (Glover, 2000, p. 22). Showing respect for someone's dignity symbolizes that person's "moral standing" in the community.

"Dignity of humanity in every other person" both curtails barbarism and leaves us free to act against what E. O. Wilson (1998) calls "unfettered selfishness." Globalization and the compression of time and space have made us ever more mindful of cultural empathy.

The Concept of Cultural Empathy

Empathy as an explanatory concept for understanding why people behave as they do with certain consequences can be pursued only so far. However, like Italian philosopher Giambista Vico and German poet and critic Johann Gottfried Herder, I believe that although cultures differ in historical content, customs, traditions, attitudes, beliefs, and practices, humans are endowed with faculties that make them capable of understanding others across time and space. The notion of "imaginative placement" or "feeling one's way into" another constitutes the essence of what I mean by empathy.

In 16th-century Germany, Herder called attention to the human potential of "imaginative insight," but it was Vico who helped us understand the importance of empathy in human affairs and as a basis for understanding the cognitions, feelings, and behaviors of others—in a word, a panoply of content that undergirds cultural empathy. Vico had in mind an imaginative process that allows one "aspirationally, to leave one's own world and enter into the world of the other" (Holzwarth, 2004, p. 10). In Vico's (1968) "new science," he had in mind humans' ability to understand visions and values of others across time and space, that is, of humans who lived long ago. He envisioned that succeeding generations would be able to understand the folkways and customs of prior cultures even if the latter were different from the former. As one of Vico's chief interpreters, Berlin (1991) notes that Vico's "deepest belief was that what men have made, other men can understand" (p. 60).

Furthermore, according to Vico,

> If anything is meant by the term human, there must be enough that is common to all such beings for it to be possible, by a sufficient effort of imagination, to grasp what the world must have looked like to creatures, remote in time of space, who practiced such rites and used such words, and created such works of art as the natural means of self-expression involved in the attempt to understand and interpret their worlds to themselves. (Berlin, 1991, p. 60)

Fundamental to Vico's implied notion of empathy (implied because Vico does not use the term *empathy*) is the concept of "a sufficient effort of imagination," which I am appropriating because the term has explanatory power. The imaginative process or "*fantasia*" extends beyond self-knowledge, although it is a beginning point to using such empirical evidence as religion, economic factors, language, art, mythology, philosophy, gestures, looks, aspirations, and the like to understand humans both near and far.

In his remarkable book, *Bury the Chains,* Hochschild (2005) identifies empathy as the key reason why White abolitionists such as Thomas Clarkson, John Newton, William Wilberforce, and others succeeded in ending slavery in the British empire. Said Hochschild, the abolitionists "mastered one challenge that still faces anyone who cares about social and economic justice, drawing connections between the near and the distant" (pp. 5–6). At the time, this was a new, enterprising force in history! Because the abolitionists were able to make "Britons understand what lay behind the sugar they ate, the tobacco they smoked, [and] the coffee they drank, they changed the world in dynamic and elegant ways" (p. 6).

Part of empathy's work, then, is to knit together human and cultural elements of both the near and the distant, so that we will care about other people even if they are an ocean away. This book is about such caring. And the materials out of which the complex concept of empathy is crafted are discussed next.

Some of my arguments about the nature of empathy can be found in the writings of Herder, who is more direct in his employment of the term *empathy.* Herder seems to have in mind an understanding of difference. The key to understanding other humans, he posits, is a kind of "imaginative inquiry." In his work, Herder actually uses the word *Einfuhlen,* which translates from German to mean "empathy." Herder argues,

> The whole living painting of mode of life, habits, needs, peculiarities of land and climate, would have to *be added* or to have *preceded:* one would have first to *empathize* with the nation, in order to feel a single one of its *inclinations* or *actions all together* . . . to *imagine* everything in its fullness . . . go into the age, into the clime, the whole history, feel yourself into everything— only now are on the way towards understanding. (Holzwarth, 2004, p. 13)

The Meaning of Cultural Empathy

In his work, Herder proposes an interesting theory about the meaning of cultural empathy, and it is worth noting several things about his writings on empathy. First, certain historical and cultural factors—evidence—provide the content out of which empathy is constructed. In a word, the totality of human beings, including their life ways, customs, and habits of mind, all fall within the purview of empathy and can be used to further human understanding. By yoking together both physical and social factors, Herder provides a unified agenda. This means that a Beethoven symphony as well as the myths and stories of African griots can be used to construct empathy.

Second, "imaginative placement" is critical. One must be able to "see" through the eyes of others, creating both a subject and an object-oriented focus that can shift, depending on whether the lens of cultural empathy is reflecting one as subject or object. Vital to both Herder's and Vico's idea of imaginative placement is the reciprocal relationship between two interacting individuals, even if one is not physically present. This process, in a practical and tender way, also goes to the heart of both empathy and identification. Gilroy (2000), one of the most important writers on the concept of identity, says that "identity is a critical reflection upon who we are and what we want" (p. 99). This reflection upon who and what we are, according to Herder, provides us with a perspective necessary for understanding why people think and behave as they do.

Finally, the notion of feeling is insinuated in the concept of empathy. "To feel yourself into everything" implies emotional participation in another person's experience. The connection between empathy and feeling is seen as a "bridge to civility," to use Sheldon H. Berman's (1998) term. Ronald Milo maintains that "a lack of concern (or adequate concern) for the interests or welfare of others . . . constitute(s) the essence of immorality" (qtd. in Vetlesen, 1994, pp. 222, 223). He argues that "the truly wicked person is *deliberately* uninterested in avoiding moral wrongdoing, he believes that what he does is wrong, he does it nonetheless, indeed does it willingly" (p. 222). My purpose here is not to debate the pros and cons of morality and immorality; rather, my mission is to drive home the point that feeling is an important component of empathy. Some scholars also argue that empathy can be divided into stages. And I focus on this aspect next to demonstrate the vitality of the concept for understanding global human affairs.

Stages of Empathy

Drawing on Husserlian intersubjectivity, Depraz (2001, p. 172) argues that "lived empathy" has "four different and complementary stages":

1. A passive association of my lived body with your lived body

2. An imaginative self-transposal in your psychic states

3. An interpretative understanding of yourself as being an alien to me

4. An ethical responsibility toward yourself as a person (enjoying and suffering)

The first type of empathy is passive and serves to recognize the Other as a moving, breathing, and living human being. This means that when we first encounter Nicholas Walker, a young Wall Street protégé and friend of Little Mark Johnson Jr., we do not perceive his body as merely an object or physical thing but rather as a lived body like our own. Depraz notes that "empathy is grounded in a much more passive and primal experience lying in both our lived bodies" (p. 172). Although this stage is primal, it is significant in promoting human consciousness because it allows us to identify the Other as belonging to the human species.

Even though this stage is passive, there is a clear connection between one sentient being and another. Thompson (2001) believes that this sort of empathy is manifest in an "immediate pairing or coupling of the bodies of self and other in action" (p. 17). By coupling, Depraz (2001) means "an associative process through which my lived-body and your lived-body experience a similar functioning of our tactile, auditory, visual, proprioceptive body-style of our embodied behavior in the world and of our affective and active kinaesthetic habits and acts" (pp. 172–173).

Thus, one body experiences similar feelings, seeing, hearing, touching, and body movements as another lived body. As a result, we see the other as an embodied subject of human experience. This embodied experience extends to "fields of sensations," to use Thompson's (2001) term, that help human beings identify and observe such matters in others as Idell's passing away; Aunt Velma's gusto; Uncle Ray's health and sickness; Tamarek's liveliness and beauty; Melvin's charitable spirit; Alvin's steadfastness; Loyce's irreverent humor; Porter's sacrifice; Michael's soul; Catherine, Gin, and Boo's devotion; and Dr. Jack's robustness and energy. Stein refers to these fields of sensations as "sensual empathy" or "sensing-in" (Thompson, 2001, p. 17). It is important to observe that empathy can remain at the first level—the emergence of experience, "where it remains tacit and prereflective, a matter of passive association." However, for empathy to do its best work and create a more humane world, with less conflict, cruelty, and misery, more is required.

The second level of empathy, according to Depraz (2001), occurs when one moves from perceiving "global resemblance of our body-style" to being able spontaneously to transpose oneself into the self of the other. This stage clearly relates to Vico's and Berlin's notion of "imaginative placement" or "learning what it is like to live by someone else's light." In this regard, one feels empathy when one is able to call up mental states that are similar to the mental states of the other. Depraz's claim that one must be able to "recall similar experiences" is at odds with my idea of imaginative placement, because I argue that true empathy relies heavily on being able to understand mental states that the other might not have experienced firsthand.

For example, little Adonis and big Keon might be able to think "as if" they understand how rich people behave even though they are not rich. What is critical for my purposes, however, is the notion that humans have the capacity to "transpose" others' feelings into their own. In Smith's (2004) novel, *The Sunday Philosophy Club,* the main character, Isabel Dalhousie, is full of empathy and human understanding. When Isabel witnesses the death of a young man who fell from the upper section of a concert hall in Edinburgh, Scotland, she said, upon seeing the young man on a stretcher,

> To be so beautiful . . . and now the end. She closed her eyes. She felt raw inside, empty. This poor young man, loved by somebody somewhere, whose world would end this evening . . . when the cruel news was broached. All that love invested in a future that would not materialize ended in a second, in a fall from the gods. (p. 9)

In this example, Isabel collapses the first two stages of Depraz's conception of empathy. First, she clearly involuntarily (passively) noticed (visual) the young man's body and felt human sensations ("raw inside, empty"), before moving to the second stage of imaginatively entering the world of the young man's family. This is empathy in a pure form. Isabel's "intersubjectivity of consciousness" demanded that she move to the second stage, to a concrete articulation of empathy, making her intimately aware of what should be the viewpoint of the young man's family upon discovering his body.

Isabel's humaneness also contains other ingredients of Stage 2 empathy, and it is the fact that she moves from her own "first-person point of view" (Thompson, 2001, p. 19) toward empathic openness, to a "second-person point of view." In Thompson's (2001) words, "It is through empathy as the experience of oneself as an other for the alter-ego that one gains a viewpoint of one's own embodied being beyond the first-person singular perspective" (p. 19). Following Husserl, Depraz (2001) sums up the work of Stage 2 empathy insightfully: "I am here and I imagine I am going there to the place where you are just now; conversely, you are here (the *there* where I am going to) and you imagine you are going there, to the place where I am (*my here*)" (p. 173). The message is that at Stage 2, we are exchanging psychic states with the Other—whether person to person or removed in geographic space.

The third step involves understanding and communication. At this stage, one expresses (verbal or not) and interprets others' views, which lead to understanding (and also misunderstanding). This stage involves a human's ability to explain, predict, and describe the sentiments of others.

In the example of Isabel, one sees clearly the impact of interpretation on human empathy. She moved beyond her consciousness and interpreted what the family would surely think and feel upon seeing the dead man's body. Isabel saw him as a being loved by someone and that the world of the family would literally fold in upon hearing of the young man's death. Embedded within Isabel's modes of interpretation is a moral disposition of respect and kindness. We also take from Isabel's interpretation the notion that she also cares about the kind of person she is; otherwise, why the morally resonant human understanding toward people whom she did not know?

The final stage of empathy that Depraz (2001) offers is ethical responsibility. And although she does not offer a full-blown elaboration of what is meant by ethics in all of its permutations, Depraz does suggest that ethics involves "affection and considering the other as having emotions: suffering, enjoying" (p. 173). In this respect, Depraz's fourth stage is in line with other accounts of empathy that privilege emotions. Harry Stack Sullivan (1945), Carl Rogers (1951, 1975), and Heinz Kohut (1997) all argue that empathy is a complex of emotions and feelings. It should be noted that these men were especially interested in ways that empathy could serve the relationship between therapist and client—hence their belief that the successful therapist is one who involves himself or herself in the emotional world of the patient by developing a special kind of empathy.

Although one can imaginatively enter the world of another and might not consciously pause (while doing so) and say, "I am in Stage 1 or 2 empathy," a central key to feeling empathy is an attitude of attentiveness.

An Attitude of Attentiveness

In *Bury the Chains,* Hochschild (2005) tells a gripping story of how and why slavery commanded Thomas Clarkson's attention, and the narrative has a major bearing on this book. According to Hochschild, in 1784, Clarkson competed for an essay prize at Cambridge University and chose the papers of a slave merchant for his research investigation. While sorting through the papers, young Clarkson "found himself overwhelmed with horror." He said, "In the day-time I was uneasy. In the night I had little rest. I sometimes never closed my eye-lids for grief . . . I always slept with a candle in my room, that I might rise out of bed and put down such thoughts as might occur to me in the night . . . conceiving that no arguments of any moment should be lost in so great a cause" (p. 88).

Clarkson's essay won first prize, but his life would never be the same again because the evils of slavery had gained his attention. More to the point, he had experienced one of the critical parts of empathy, a feature that commonsensically precedes all else—an ability to tune in to people, problems, and situations that demand empathy and grasp essential components, using a question such as, "What's wrong here?"

After marshaling his evidence and after winning the essay prize, Clarkson later reflected on the subject of slavery and its evil. His feelings grew in intensity to the point where in June 1785, he literally sat down by the side of a road as he journeyed home after having received the prize: "Coming in sight of Wades Mill in Hertfordshire, I sat down disconsolate on the turf by the roadside and held my horse. Here a thought came into my mind, that if the contents of the Essay were true, it was time some person should see these calamities to their end" (Hochschild, 205, p. 89). This single moment transformed Clarkson's thought and feelings. And as Hochschild (2005) points out, the poignant moment of awakening held echoes of Saul's conversion on the road to Damascus. Like Saul's radical conversion to Paul, Clarkson's attentiveness energized his soul, and he began to "see" the world from the perspective of the slave.

Now, several features of empathic attentiveness are relevant here. First, as Tony Alessandra (http://www.Alessandra.com) observes, "Attentiveness means that [one] is open to outside stimuli, your perception or, if the stimuli, are subtler, entering your intuition" (p. 1). Because we select, organize, and interpret the stimuli we receive through our senses into a meaningful picture of the world around us, the perception process is the basis of our communication with others.

This is also what Depraz (2001) means by "imaginative self-transposal." However, as Singer (1987) indicates, "We experience everything in the world not as it is—but only as the world comes to us through our sensory receptors" (p. 9). In other words, we each construct our own reality. Thus, Liesl's reality may not be the same as Makenzie's.

In terms of empathy and perception, the key is that humans who feel for others are able to interpret reality or incoming data from the perspective of the other. In the case of Clarkson, upon first reading and processing the data of slavery, his psychological state, values, culture, and many other factors arranged themselves such that he immediately recognized that something was "out of kilter," other than what it should have been in the area of human rights. This leads to a second aspect of attentiveness: *access to others'* feelings. Attentiveness in the right order and in the proper frame leads to adjusting our world to the world of the other. In the words of Hochschild (2005), "If there is a single moment at which the antislavery movement became inevitable, it was the day in June 1785 when Thomas Clarkson sat down by the side of the road at Wades Mill" (p. 89).

Hochschild (2005) notes further, however, that had there been no Clarkson, there still would have been an antislavery movement in Britain. By implication, Hochschild is suggesting that another piece of stimuli would have claimed someone else's attention and launched an antislavery movement. Part of the reason for this is that matters of attentiveness are part of human equipment for first making sense of stimuli and then using it for instrumental and noble purposes—and sometimes evil purposes.

Space, Place, Time, and Memory

An ability to empathize with others has roots in historical reality and is also tied to memory. Tuan (1977) notes that "all that we are we owe to the past" (p. 197). Our experiences, actions, attachments to home, family, and nation leave traces that we refer to as historical memory. Whatever we have filled our time with constitutes our past, and at any moment, these things can be "rescued," "called up," or "flashed to the surface," during an intercultural communication exchange and subsequently alter how we interact with others. And here I mean the way in which political and cultural history have yoked together human encounters out of which the art of interpreting others is constructed.

From our past, we develop a personal intellectual history that serves as a cultural storage bin for the interpretation of ideas and events. Into this bin we place knowledge of our ancestors, the old family home, a monument to a common hero, a picture album, a stroll down a country lane, the memory of sights and sounds and smells, and myriad other things. At any point in our relationship with others, we can use cultural data to embellish an argument, offer an example, clarify a point, or make ourselves accessible or inaccessible to others—depending on our proclivity toward empathy and its enmeshment with others. Our historical memory changes depending on whether our memory invites joy, pain, or indifference.

It is worth noting as well that histories of suffering born of sharp divisions among ethnic groups' ideas and theories can spring up and naturalize or normalize how the other is viewed. My point in this section is to highlight the fact that the unfolding of past actions can contribute to a situation in which empathetic moral resources are diminished when humans use history to justify ruthlessness.

In *We Wish to Inform You That Tomorrow We Will Be Killed With Our Families*, Gourevitch (1998) notes the powerful hold that memory has on humans: "We are, each of us, functions of how we imagine ourselves and of how others imagine us, and, looking back, there are these discrete tracks of memory" (p. 71). "Discrete tracks of memory" can be derailed if human responses to others are weakened. Glover (2000) observes that one way of diminishing bonds of friendship is to assign others to "some other, stigmatized group" (p. 35). In some instances, as Glover writes, the "excluding classification may be ideological"; however, in other instances, it can grow from the everyday interactions of people, according to where they are in time and space. In Rwanda, for example, where genocide was committed against the Tutsis by the Hutus, more than 800,000 people were killed. But what set of circumstances caused the Hutus to override human empathy for the Tutsis and eventuate in such horrific deeds?

Gourevitch (1998) describes how the two ethnic groups lived together prior to the 1991 season of genocide. In many instances, according to Gourevitch, when "pressed for how they had lived during the long periods between bouts of violence," Tutsis survivors told many stories: "household stories, village stories, funny stories, or stories of annoyance, stories of school, work, church, a wedding, a funeral, a trip, a party, or a feud," but the answer was always opaque: "in normal times we lived normally" (pp. 71–72).

The Case of Yugoslavia

It is this sense of normality of time and place—the crushingly particulars repeated day after day and over a span of time—that can serve as an incubation site for exploitative politicians. As Glover (2000) notes, "Tribal conflicts rarely just 'break out' . . . people are pushed into the trap by politicians" (p. 123). He notes, for example, that Josip Broz Tito's Yugoslavia fell apart during the country's independence from Russia because Slobodan Milosevic exploited the idea of when the republics were formed. Despite Tito's efforts to ensure that power was distributed equally among the different nationalities, Milosevic saw a weakness and used it to his rhetorical and political advantage. After Tito's death in 1980, the fragile republics began to unravel, starting with the Serbian minority, which felt threatened by the Kosovo majority.

When Albanians in Kosovo demonstrated in 1981 in support of independence from Serbia, the ideas had powerful and deadly impacts on the attitudes and expectations of the Kosovo population. Furthermore, stories "of rape and of being forced to move" circulated at a time when Milosevic was ready to stitch strands of nationalism into cultural grievances. He undermined the old empathetic feelings, which had enabled people of many faiths and nationalities to live together in reasonable harmony during Tito's reign.

Milosevic cunningly appealed to soil and the idea of separate relationship of both the land and the environment. This was, for Milosevic, the key to awakening a species of solidarity and national consciousness that disturbed the status of empathy in the former Yugoslavia. A confining relationship between land and nature would transcend the wellsprings of human kindness with an unprecedented power to mobilize Serbians. Milosevic admonished his compatriots:

> You should stay here. This is your land. These are your houses. . . . Your meadows and gardens. Your memories. You shouldn't abandon your land just because it's difficult to live, because you are pressured by injustice and degradation. It was never part of the Serbian and Montenegrin character to give up in the face of obstacles, to demobilize when it's time to fight. . . . You should stay here for the sake of your ancestors and descendants. Otherwise your ancestors would be defiled and descendants disappointed. But I don't suggest that you stay, endure, and tolerate a situation you're not satisfied with. In the contrary, you should change it. (qtd. in Glover, 2000, p. 125)

Whether these appeals to territory, manhood, ancestors, culture, and the "organicity of nature" were the only reasons for the ethnic conflict that ultimately came in the 1990s can be contested. What is more significant for my purposes, however, is that rootedness, place, and identity can and often are used as vehicles for trumping other-regarding characteristics. Because empathy often is intimately tied to space and place, Milosevic helped the Serbians elevate claims of soil, roots, and territory on a grand scale. In a sense, he tapped into the people's sense of place and memories that isolated the relationships that Serbians had had with Croats and Bosnians.

As Tuan (1977) notes in *Space and Place,* "To strengthen our sense of self the past needs to be rescued and made accessible. . . . Our own past, then, consists of bits and pieces" (p. 187). The "bits and pieces" that Milosevic used caused Serbs to look backward to what Serbs had done together—apart from the Croats: relatives living and dying, people tending their gardens and meadows, and living with honor and integrity.

A resilient hallmark of empathy is its capacity to unite the near and the far. In this instance, Milosevic helped the Serbs to evoke memories of the past as a bridge to the future—a future as it had been, possibly.

Absent from Milosevic's evocations are attitudes toward time and space that included Croats. There were no efforts to construct a relationship based on a shared humanity and a common citizenship, although Yugoslavs had lived together relatively harmoniously for years. Milosevic understood that his discourse was consistent with the basic tenets of empathy. As J. Q. Wilson (1993) observes, "As a rule, we strive harder to protect our own children than somebody else's, that parents seem to make more sacrifices for their children than children make for their parents" (p. 42). This helps to explain Milosevic's cultural practice of pushing the idea that "likes attract likes" and redefining Croats as strangers, foreigners, and enemies. This explanation is consistent with binary notions of inclusion versus exclusion and kin versus nonkin behaviors. The human capacity for empathy with those closest to one in culture, values, beliefs, and folkways becomes even more complex when weighed against the way people respond to their spatiotemporal world.

"The experience of time and space is largely subconscious," as Tuan (1977) reminds us, making it easier in some quarters of the globe for well-intentioned ethnic groups to be bamboozled by the political elixir of politicians of Milosevic's ilk.

But Milosevic had one more trump card to play, one that increased in intensity when fused with elements of soil and ancestry: fear. Following his ancestry/soil speech, Milosevic extended his reach beyond Yugoslavia to other places such as Montenegro. Milosevic forced out the incumbent, took over the Serbian presidency, and participated in the 600th anniversary of the Battle of Kosovo. There, fusing identity with fear and just the proper mix of appeals to courage, forbearance, and memory, he told the gathering, "The Kosovo heroism does not allow us to forget that, at one time, we were brave and dignified and one of the few who went into battle undefeated" (qtd. in Glover, 2000, p. 125).

These attempts to ground identity in courage and strength make a lack of empathy appear to be natural rather than a social phenomenon rooted in language and power. By emphasizing the relationship between time and dwelling places, Milosevic closed kinship bonds between Croats and Serbians; a main consequence of this was a production of anxieties over the boundaries and limits of human dignity. Manliness coupled with history and time became the main devices in Milosevic's mind. And the fact that he could galvanize similar feelings in other Serbs is testament to the human disposition to defend home and hearth. In his rhetoric, Milosevic spoke of the hope of a transformation of the moral will of the Serbs. If taken seriously by the Serbs, his words would lead to an act of warfare! And, of course, his implicit intentions materialized because his words "weakened the human responses" of the Serbs. And war came. As Glover (2000) reminds us, "People slide by degrees into doing things they would not do if given a clear choice at the beginning" (p. 35).

My point is that place overlaid by awful meaning can lead humans to inflict pain on others, denigrate them, and become cruel. If one doubts the role of place in constructing meaning, then consider Werner Heisenberg's and Niels Bohr's answer to the age-old fundamental question, "What is a place?" when they visited Kronberg Castle in Denmark. Bohr said to Heisenberg,

Isn't it strange how this castle changes as soon as one can imagine that Hamlet lived here? As scientists we believe that a castle consists only of stones, and admire the way the architect put them together. . . . None of this should be changed by the fact that Hamlet lived here . . . but "once we know that, Kronberg becomes quite a different castle for us!" (qtd. in Tuan, 1977, p. 4)

Once we know that people respond to time, space, and memory in complicated ways, we also know that our capacity for being decent persons can be changed—based on the nature and quality of history and the environment. And on myths and legends.

Myths and Legends

Conventional wisdom is right in focusing on myths and legends as a precipitating cause of the lack of empathy. The archetype for this notion is how Westerners have dealt with diversity, especially during the 16th century—and later—when Portuguese and other explorers first came into contact with indigenous peoples in Africa, Asia, and the South Pacific. Myths, according to some widely accepted definitions, are stories that attempt to explain why the world is the way that it is. Myths hold that prototypical stories are passed on from generation to generation and are spread by oral tradition. I examine under this definition both the myths that people create to explain their existence and also the narratives that Westerners have circulated to justify their exploitation of indigenous peoples under the rubric of "progress" and the "march of civilization."

Myths, for my purposes, are assertions that serve as a basis for the promotion of what Blake (1979) refers to as cultural warrants. Blake explains that cultural warrants are basically beliefs, laws, and customs that allow people within a given culture to justify their communicative actions and behaviors. Such warrants are found in traditions, religious texts, traditional values, constitutions, important decisions by judicial bodies such as the Supreme Court, and the general norms that guide the relationship between children and parents, the young and old, and authority figures and subordinates.

Of course, myths are not warrants. But I argue that myths are the *substance* out of which warrants are constructed. They become the frame for viewing the other, and humans rely very heavily on warrants to finish the work of myth construction. My focus on myths and legends is not intended to compete with traditional definitions of such terms. I argue that myths and legends work their effects on humans through the process of both persuasion and force. The processes involved in the construction of cross-cultural myths serve as rhetorical vehicles to support atrocities in distant and far-removed cultures. It was the inability of Westerners to picture other cultures as like themselves that largely helped to create mythmaking.

As a cultural warrant, the Bible in a country that is influenced by the Judeo-Christian tradition is a powerful source upon which an argument can be predicated. Cultural warrants are powerful tools we use to justify our myths and actions. Cultural warrants provide the cover. They, therefore, represent, in a nutshell, "knowledge" of ourselves and about others that are derived from our ways of seeing the other disturbingly. Although myths are not the only reasons why empathy breaks down in a confrontation with difference, I argue that a tendency to breed contempt for others occurs because people overemphasize difference and underuse sameness.

A historical example of how myths can be used to view the other in a well-constructed manner can be found in Dutch descriptions of the Khoikhoi of the Cape of Good Hope in South Africa. Because most visitors to the Cape failed to see the indigenous Africans as humans and were repelled by the customs and habits of the Khoikhoi, first came the descriptive rhetorical foundation for the construction of a degraded human being. The Khoikhoi wore animal skins that were coated with "stinking grease" and the "entrails of animals around their necks" (Fagan, 1984, p. 28). Fagan (1984) writes that the expression "They are very priggish in their eating" was a common reaction, a description applied to "pagan" peoples in many parts of the world. They seemed to "eat everything that we find loathsome" (p. 29).

This type of descriptive segmentation was not likely to serve the interests of empathy within the structure of White/Black relations. The ideology of the loathsome Khoikhoi also extended to their language, which heightened the belief that Europeans were superior to the Khoikhoi, who had a "strange click language and primitive way of life" and seemed to represent "the nadir of humankind, the most barbarous of all humans" (p. 29).

Thus, the Khoikhoi were condemned simply for being who they were and for exhibiting cultural habits that were different from the cultural habits of Europeans. And the Europeans became very adept at painting concrete, vivid pictures to justify the fact that the Khoikhoi were ancient in their "savage" behavior. Because difference ran so deeply in Europeans at the time, it was almost impossible for them to eliminate from their mythmaking an image of Khoikhoi as nonprimitive.

The practice of negative description and the circulation of myths by the Europeans of the Khoikhoi erased from history notions of a Khoikhoi cultural heritage of noble genes or language or physiognomy. Descriptions of the magnitude described here were ultimately social killing. The myths grew, were embellished, and became detached from the geographic space that the

Khoikhoi occupied. In such myths, we also receive a glimpse of precisely how and why it is difficult for human empathy to survive in the midst of such common and recurring myths of depravity. There was no diversity of opinion, and there were no counterarguments and behavior to still the human quality of mastering the techniques of "mine" and "thine." One wonders what would have been the response of Europeans had the Khoikhoi at least had some recognizable resemblance to Europeans? And had the Khoikhoi placed the same premium on property held by the former? In relation to encounters that human beings had with the cultural other even earlier? I turn now to ancient and modern promoters of empathy, which should give us a more complex understanding of the interplay between the concept and human relations. When did our ideas about empathy derive across space and time? What set of circumstances and predispositions animated humans to become empathetic toward nonkin? And what lessons can be learned from the emergence of caring about others—both near and far?

2

The Creation of Empathy

From Ancients to Moderns

Beginnings

In Eritrea, there is a powerful story concerning British liberation of citizens from fascist rule in a small town, Keren, that has been passed down from generation to generation. According to popular legend, as reported in Michela Wrong's (2005) book, *"I Didn't Do It for You": How the World Betrayed a Small African Nation,* a British captain "leading his weary men on the march from Keren into Asmara" met an old Eritrean woman "wrapped in the ghostly white shroud of the highlands" (p. 98).

To express her jubilee over her country "being saved from Italian Fascist rule and the start of a new era of hoped-for-prosperity," the old woman ululated in the presence of the captain while extending a warm, traditional greeting. Legend also has it that the captain stopped the Eritrean woman in "mid-flow" and replied, "I didn't do it for you, nigger." And then the captain strove on toward the next town, Asmara (Wrong, 2005, p. 99). Why did the captain not take into consideration the feelings of the Eritrean woman? Why did he behave in a seemingly uncaring way?

Perhaps, as Wrong (2005) notes, the captain was irritated by the Eritrean's ululating sounds. Whether the story is true or not, it is indeed striking for what it reveals about other-regarding behavior and the importance of taking the perspective of the other. Reflectively, the story also raises questions about the beginnings of perspective taking throughout human history. When did a universal respect for understanding the views of others gain prominence? Cultural anthropologists, historians, and sociologists provide some answers regarding when and why humans began to move physically and intellectually outside village walls.

For thousands of years, as hunters and gathers, our ancestors had no great need to consider the behavior and feelings of individuals outside their group since they lived in tight-knit bands of low density. In an agricultural society, hunters and gatherers had to forage for roots, berries, nuts, and other foods, and they were fairly dependent on individuals close to camp for their survival. Although in their habitat, hunters and gathers "laid down the mental matrix necessary for thought and reason, language and culture," as Burke and Ornstein (1995, p. 11) note, "it is the case that their communication skills were not only rudimentary, but also highly localized. And the longer they stayed in one area, all across the planet, the more they developed different local characteristics, depending on the environment their tools made livable" (p. 23).

Later, as humans became more sophisticated and turned to tool making—puny by 21st-century standards—the tools enabled them to adapt and inevitably placed them in contact with other members of the human species as they entered what historians term the Axial Age (800–200 B.C.E.). In the Axial Age, the beginning of humanity as we know it, people began to migrate away from scattered, isolated, and lonely hilltops to more densely concentrated areas. The social situation was changing, old rules were breaking down, a new urban class was emerging, and power had begun to shift from kings and temples to the merchant class. These great transformations ushered in three important social, spiritual, and economic changes that had a crucial bearing on empathy.

First, it was a time that led to great advances in the spiritual foundation of humans with the creation of the world's major religions, which we still practice today. Buddhism, Janism, and Hinduism in India; Confucianism in China; Monotheism in Israel; and Greek rationalism (more philosophical than spiritual) in Europe all made their appearance in the Axial Age. It is important to note that great advances in philosophy, religion, and cultural change occurred almost simultaneously in both Asia and the Middle East. In each instance, the founders of the specific religion did so in reaction to social upheaval and political turmoil, paving the way for compassion and empathy to enter the world, as we shall see later.

Second, and most significantly, in the course of the Axial Age, especially disturbing agonistic and aggressive impulses were evident in India and other parts of the world, fostering and sustaining violence, carnage, and exclusion. In India, the Brahmin class clung to principles that benefitted the few rather than the many, employing secrecy as a modus operandi, which Buddha later aptly characterized as "close-fistedness" (H. Smith, 1958, p. 94). In the very ancient civilization of China, states warred with each other, and in searching for a way out of the confining spaces of violence and brutality, a different type of human being emerged who grappled with such large human questions as the following: What are the sources of violence? How can humans change a cruel world? And are human beings utterly impotent in the presence of a suffering world?

That self-questioning was especially critical given the rise in urban populations and a movement away from an agrarian world to the circulation of basic market goods, a third transformation. Such changes offer a proper explanation for the backdrop out of which compassion and empathy appeared. By definition, competitive markets serve as a means of moving information and goods from place to place, inducing people to become more inclined toward commercialism and the psychology of possession. In the Axial Age, rudimentary markets came into being primarily because of the diminishing influence of the priestly and kingly classes, but markets and their accompanying human misery also animated people to develop consciousness and to seek ways of alleviating pain.

Buddhism

In response to militarism, warring, and in the presence of much violence and grief, augmented by the development of markets, what human being would adroitly use his cognitive and relational skills to reach people at the highest level of human consciousness? Into this world stepped Siddhartha Gautama, better known today as the Buddha, the "Enlightened One," offering a compelling way of grappling with human misery and social relations. In the 16th century B.C.E., in the foothills of what are now the Himalayas, 29-year-old Gautama lived with his wife and son in a splendor befitting a comfortable existence in Kapilavatthu in Nepal (Armstrong, 2001, p. 1). Even though Gautama's father's house was elegant and he lived in a manner that paralleled the luxury of well-to-do families of the day, Gautama began to ponder why the world was so brutally indifferent to suffering, and he "found himself longing for a lifestyle that had nothing to do with domesticity, and which the ascetics of India called 'homelessness'" (Armstrong, 2001, p. 1).

It must have been physically exhausting for Gautama as he searched for a new way of viewing human consciousness, meandering for 6 years through the plains of the Ganges River listening to other sages' accounts of compassionate and altruistic modes of living. While searching for a new way of dealing with humanity, a trance-like state revealed to Gautama the essential content and substance of a path away from a terrifyingly brutal world. Gautama was never the same again, and in his account, at the point of transformative rapture, "The whole cosmos rejoiced, the earth rocked, flowers fell from heaven, fragrant breezes blew and the gods in their various heavens rejoiced" (Watson, 2005, p. 117).

The Four Noble Truths and Eight-Fold Path

The jubilant way that Gautama described what the trance produced, after 49 days of bountiful concentration, undoubtedly speaks to the joy he felt over the possibility of plumbing the depths of human potential and consciousness. As a consequence, Gautama came out of the trance with a keen insight into the agony of pain and an approach to eliminating it, resulting in an enlightened way of understanding the human psyche. The enlightened way consists of four noble truths, which comprise the substance of Buddha's teachings: (1) Man's (humans') existence is full of pain, sorrow, and suffering (*dukkha*); (2) suffering is caused by man's selfish desire; and (3) emancipation is a way out of suffering and (4) a way to liberation, which is an engaged way of "living a life of compassion for all living beings, speaking and behaving gently, kindly and accurately and by refraining from anything like drugs or intoxicants that cloud the mind" (Watson, 2005, p. 117). Thus, an empathetic and compassionate person has all the right values as far as "honoring the sacredness in others" is concerned. The fourth noble truth lays down the Eight-Fold Path, which details a general treatment curriculum for fostering a trio of compassion: benevolence, loving-kindness, and generosity.

But why Four Noble Truths and an Eight-Fold Path? There is one significant respect in which the truths and the path should be regarded. By emphasizing both process and substance, Buddha forcefully signaled that compassion requires a vigorous analysis—placing it in a philosophical and practical realm that stoutly says that compassion is an urgent and serious business! The Eight-Fold Path includes the following:

1. Right View—a set of beliefs with an intellectual orientation; a focus on what meaningfully constitutes life's problems.

2. Right Intention—a passionate investment in what one's heart really wants.

3. Right Speech—a commitment to speak the truth, using charitable discourse, omitting from life's curriculum such negative traits as gossip, slander, and idle talk.

4. Right Action—understanding one's behavior and aligning it with an eye toward human improvement. After right action is achieved, one should not kill, lie, or be unchaste, virtues that mirror the Ten Commandments.

5. Right Livelihood—choosing an occupation (life's work) that promotes compassion instead of destruction. Although, according to Buddha, a caravan trader would not be regarded as an empathy-generating profession, Buddha left no reasons for omitting this profession from the mix.

6. Right Effort—a robust match between exertion and outcome. One must carefully choose the passions that lead to human compassion.

7. Right Mindfulness—the power of thought to bend humans toward the good. Right thought leads to right action.

8. Right Concentration—a sufficient focus that leads to enlightenment—one of "cosmic import."

In Buddha's plan for an empathetic and compassionate approach to humanity, one sees not just a way of eliminating suffering but rather, and this is most crucial, how to understand and relate to other people—an interpenetration between self and others—capable of generating empathy. In this way, Buddha appealed to the best that is in humankind, a pretty radical idea for the time.

This awakening of self and relationship to others also marked the beginning of human consciousness, creating a sharing impulse and a sense of solidarity with others outside village walls. But how was this seemingly special act of compassion to be accomplished? First, as was noted, Buddha responded meaningfully to a world that was changing and insisted, with a spiritual reflection upon both self and others, that one must look around, with powers of huge observation, and realize that something is wrong; only then, could humans become emancipated for the greater good. Focusing on the "something is wrong" aspect of human consciousness parallels the philosophy of the Stoics with their dynamic diagnosis, which I will detail later.

Second, Buddha saw human compassion as something deeply and abidingly obligatory in the areas of social and cultural relations—extending to all living beings. Of course, the strong animating notion that society had gone awry, attentiveness to the chaos of the human situation, and interest in the world of people also echo in the teachings of Confucianism, Janism, and Taoism.

Buddha's approach to human consciousness and his emphasis on a "livable life" alone are worthy of emulation because it is not a provisional way-station between self and others but rather a generative mechanism for changing human souls in several domains of experience and behavior—hence, Buddha's stress on right talk, gentleness, and kindliness. Emphasis on such qualities leads not to a detachment from others but instead to a certain competency in empathy and in skill building. Buddha was much moved by an all-consuming need for human beings to be mindful of and nimble toward others, to get one's mind moving in a cooperative manner.

We have seen how rapture changed the world of Gautama and, by extension, others. But he was not alone. Other prophets and moral philosophers also emerged in the Axial Age, including Confucius (Kongfuzi, 551–479 B.C.E.), China's most influential philosopher and teacher who also espoused a philosophy of moral conduct through emphasis on righteousness, justice, harmony of mind and thought, gentleness, and consideration of others. Confucius rebelled against the dreadful suffering of ordinary people in China, and his moral teachings dominated that ancient civilization for over 20 centuries—an iconic symbol of what happens to human consciousness when it bends toward compassion.

The key significance for the future of empathy, however, is that brainy species exercised their smarts and became curious about how others lived and why. Many classical scholars, among them Martha Nussbaum (1997, p. 55), argue that paying attention to other cultures also appeared in early to mid-fourth century ancient Greece. Although Greeks contributed largely to a narrowing of the lens through which we view the other, it was not always the case in ancient Greece. Prior to the appearance of Alexander the Great, Greeks' attitudes toward foreigners were, by today's standards, insensitive; indeed, their appellations revealed much about how they viewed culturally diverse people.

To a Greek, one belonged to one of two worlds: the Greek and the Barbarian. Indeed, Greek historians were fond of seeing the whole world as either Hellenes or Barbaroi. Rollo (1937, p. 134) maintains that the term *barbaroi* included old and brilliant civilizations such as the Persians and the Egyptians, as well as such "wild primitive tribes" as the Thracians and Sicilians.

Alexander the Great

In the all-important realm of politics and expansion, in 334 B.C.E., one man would help to change the landscape of diversity, and his name was Alexander the Great. It was a practical necessity that made all the difference in the spread of empathy, however narrowly viewed during that period. As a result of his conquests, Alexander the Great began to yearn for a kind of world unity that first began to make the transmission of empathy possible.

Alexander the Great played a pivotal role in establishing a structure for empathy to flourish, whether he was mindful of this or not. This is one of the most important arguments in empathy's historical favor. Because Alexander the Great opposed the creation of his conquered areas into small provinces, he ushered in something akin to a universal or centralized government. Such a system therefore helped to ensure that people at least experienced the consequences of contact with one another. Rollo (1937, p. 134) believes that Alexander the Great's march toward unity helped to explain why he chose a Persian wife. In the society of the time, other army officers were expected to follow the model of the general.

My point is that in the case of Alexander the Great, structure and modeling were greatly intertwined. Not only did Alexander the Great marry a Persian wife, but he also brought offerings to the Egyptian god Apis and then proceeded to stage a Greek Sports Tournament, "in order to show the possibility of the union of two different conceptions in one and same person and therefore in the world" (Rollo, 1937, p. 134). This penchant toward empathy helps to explain why, as Rollo observes, Alexander the Great resisted Aristotle's advice to be gentle and kind toward Greeks and both despotic and unkind toward the *barbaroi,* who were not considered Greek. This connection, between structure and modeling, went a long way toward demonstrating how the good can be elevated and put into practice.

Because Alexander the Great could do such things, he eventually achieved a better outcome despite the fact that many of his trusty Macedonians refused to heed his goodwill. Later, however, his successors "adopted his ideas in the world of culture and put them into practice" (Rollo, 1937, p. 134). Underlying everything said here is an assumption that Alexander the Great placed into the ancient theater of ideas some fundamental attitudes toward how people were viewed. These attitudes, in turn, helped to extend empathy's reach, even though the shift was not extensive.

But there was a shift from categorizing non-Greek based on race as opposed to defining humans based on whether they were perceived as cultured or uncultured. And although this view also has imitations, it furthered the human dialogue on empathy as well as served as an explanatory device for changing attitudes of Greeks toward non-Greeks. The semantic and however slight attitudinal shift offered incentives for others to follow, including Herodotus.

Herodotus the Traveler

One of the first great excursions into the way of empathy began with Herodotus, a name that is synonymous with the word *traveler.* Although people have "always been travelers, riding beasts of burden from settlement to settlement, carrying bits and pieces of other worlds to barter for local surplus" (Crossen, 2000, p. 51), Herodotus was one of the first persons to travel the world and become interested in why some people live one way while others live another. As a result, as some scholars argue, Herodotus "at once creates and disperses meanings and interpretations, a pluralizing methodology that anticipates contemporary literary and cultural theory" (Herodotus, 1921, p. 4).

In the process of circulating meanings, Herodotus (1921), through his signal work, *The Histories,* and with a zest for investigating and paying attention to other cultures in the then "known world," turned his local gaze outward to others. It is the connection that Herodotus makes between those who lived near and those who lived far that is of interest to us because he was one of the first persons to seriously entertain the idea that cultures beyond the shores of Athens might have something to offer the world (Nussbaum, 1994). Herodotus's orientation and streams of interest also undergird a powerful principle: The effective use of empathy requires the marriage of attention and "caring enough" about others to ensure a steady improvement in human development.

One wonders what made Herodotus turn his gaze outwardly. Did the fact that he grew up with tales of the exploits of the Greeks' triumph over Persia ringing in his ears cause him to travel? To become interested in encounters between Greeks and Egyptians? In an effort to identify aspects of Herodotus's cross-cultural inquiry, we can look at his push toward empathy in terms of observation/process, interactions/interpretations, and circulations.

Observations and Interpretations

Over many years, Herodotus traveled to Persia, Egypt, Scythia, and most of the cities in Greece. In the process of traveling, he managed to do what "no one had ever done before, put down a coherent story, with a beginning, a middle, and an end, and with an explanation of why things happened the way they did" (Van Doren, 1991, p. 53). As Nussbaum (1994) writes, Herodotus "examined the customs of distant countries both in order to understand their ways of life and in order to attain a critical perspective on their own society. Herodotus took seriously the possibility that Egypt and Persia might have something to teach Athens about social values" (p. 53).

Herodotus's observations of other cultures are built on the premise that other humans are worthy of attention and not all humans are the same, creating an extension of the argument that can be rendered thus: We should not expect to treat all humans the same. But what did Herodotus observe about other cultures? And how did he do it?

As a "foundational figure," Herodotus investigated geographic and cultural differences in human societies, using the descriptive method that is related to but not identical with current ethnographic techniques or practices. Herodotus's method comes closest to Wolcott's (1995) notion of "a study of human beings in social interaction" (p. 19), using a less than perfect objective system that involves "the process of forming links between ideas in the observer's mind and what one has observed"; this is a dialectical mission because "ideas inform observations and observations inform ideas" (p. 163). This distinction is crucial for our understanding of Herodotus's empathic mission because he is often accused of being not only the "father of history" but also the "father of lies" (Redfield, 1985, p. 100). But I will not take this detour; rather, I will focus on what Herodotus observed and how his observations furthered the ends of empathy.

Customs, Geographic, and Cultural

One thing about Herodotus's *The Histories* is clear: He provided foundational descriptive work in three major areas: customs, geographic, and cultural. In the area of customs, Herodotus described etiquette, food, religion, bathing rituals, kinship, burial rites, hair, clothing, language, kinship, and differences in various cultures stretching from Egypt to Scythia. His keen devotion to the language of description, concreteness, contrasts, and similarities and his penchant for seeing the other led him to some pretty vivid renditions of Scythian customs. They cooked their food. "When they flayed the victims, they strip the flesh from the bones and throw it into the cauldrons of the country," and their process of bathing involved using the "seed of hemp" cloth onto red-hot stones. "This was better than a Greek vapor bath!" (Herodotus, 1921, vol. 2, p. 259). Moreover, Scythians "never wash their body with water" (p. 259).

In the domain of clothing, Herodotus compared the Neuri, "who are nomads wearing a dress like the Scythian, but speaking a language of their own; they are the only people of all these that eat men." But the Budini "are nomads," "native to the soil," and "eat fir-cones." Herodotus (1921) also took pains to comment on the sartorial practices of Libyans, who "follow Egyptian usages for the most part" and whose women "wear bronze torques on both legs; their hair is long; they catch each other's own lice, then bite and throw them away." In terms of diet, Libyans "eat meat and drink milk for the same reason as the Egyptians," but "they will not touch the flesh of cows" and "rear no swine" (p. 260).

The Everyday and Cultural Borrowing

When describing how customs and traditions operate in these ancient cultures and how and why people used certain products or did specific cultural things, Herodotus appears to have appreciated differences in people's environments. Admittedly, the previous passages are pretty raw and brutal descriptions of ancient cultures, and admittedly, Herodotus seemed a bit obsessed with strange behavior, but it is worth noting that as far as I can tell, Herodotus refrained from passing harsh judgment on the Scythians, the Neuri, and the Egyptians. Nor was he concerned with the "functional, structural coherence of the cultures he describes"; rather, "he had much interest in the daily life rituals and customs of the people, and by implication, their standard of living" (Redfield, 1985, p. 97).

The people ate, fished, dressed, held feasts, greeted one another, were interested in astrology, practiced very specialized medicine, embalmed their dead, and placed emphasis on beauty and reputation. As a result of the detailed descriptions of Herodotus, we know that Greeks took from the Egyptians (cultural borrowing). Despite the limitations of Herodotus, the "wandering stranger," his study of ancient cultures made possible great advances in cultural knowledge—particularly in not only knowing the content of cultures but also giving us a "way of seeing things" and a "knowledge of cultural particulars" (Van Doren, 1991, pp. xviii, xix).

Prior to Herodotus, humans had very limited views of how other people lived. And most of their interest and attention were driven by who was within visual range—in face-to-face encounters. When the conditions of life are geographically isolated, not much is known about whether the Nile overflows the land, who worked linen cloth, whether "saucers are full of salt and oil," or whether there is a "feast of lamps," as Herodotus vividly informs us with regard to Egyptian culture (Book 2). Understanding Herodotus's penchant for sailing fairly long distances to encounter other people and to confront new ideas also takes on added significance. His curiosity about other cultures suggests that he wanted to understand and record firsthand as much as possible about Scythians, Persians, Libyans, and Egyptians. One has to note, however, that in the process of transmitting his stories, Herodotus likely also circulated many stereotypes.

As military historian and professor of classics Victor Davis Hanson (2001) has remarked, "In the past Western historians have relied on Greek authors such as Aeschylus, Herodotus . . . and Plato to form stereotypes of the Persians as decadent, effete, corrupt and under the spell of eunuchs and harems" (p. 39). Although restraints on stereotyping the other are crucial, Hanson also warns us that we should not go too "far in the other direction," that is, in the direction of being dismissive of using information to understand "a complete alternate universe to almost everything Greek" (p. 39).

Clearly, because of Herodotus, humans extended their knowledge and learned a great deal about cultural particulars such as how people ate, what they wore, how they wove cloth, and how to clear the land. Herodotus's *The Histories* also reveals that he took careful notes wherever he went regarding observations and that he interviewed people (Van Doren, 1991, p. 53). Despite the persistence of commentary concerning the authenticity of Herodotus's reports, evidence suggests that he tried to be objective—at least he used language that many scholars would consider to be as free of bias as possible.

Herodotus and the Language of Description

Throughout Chapter 2 of *The Histories,* in describing the Egyptians, for example, Herodotus uses language such as, "I also heard other things at Memphis," "they said," "by this reckoning," " I believe that," " I credit those who say it," "now if we agree with the opinion of the Ionians, who say that," and "I heard from the Theban priests," to signal to the reader that he was not only in the realm of cultural discovery but that he was also driven by a reflective method of investigation.

Of course, as Wells (1907) notes, one has to assume that Herodotus is "a trust-worthy witness, that he reports truly what he has heard, without exaggeration or suppression, and that he had some idea of the differing values of various witnesses" (p. 37). However we read Herodotus's motives and means, there is a payoff in terms of his ability to make cultures more intelligible to humans, even though in the case of Egypt, he was concerned with "both the strangeness of Egyptian culture, as well as insights into Greek culture that an understanding of the religion and history of Egypt could bring" ("Herodotus on Ancient Egypt," 2002). Although Herodotus's descriptions and insights into other cultures have been subjected to some criticism, his observations still were in the spirit of trying to understand others. Being an adventurer into other cultures, Herodotus summoned humans to the cultural enterprise, giving ultimate purpose to curiosity and to some linguistic constraint.

For my purposes, this linguistic temperament suggests that Herodotus brought some of the habits of mind that we typically associate with the Enlightenment to his study of cultures. Moreover, Herodotus by his own accounts, employed language that was at least rooted in the cultural soil of an *is* world, despite Redfield's (1985, p. 97) claim that Herodotus was ethnocentric. According to my reading of Herodotus's work, he rarely passed from an *is* world into an *ought* world. By an *is* world, I mean a world constructed from observable facts—the way things in sheer actuality are.

Of course, the words "the way things in sheer actuality are" are culturally determined. By an *ought* world, I mean a coercive, value-laden world.

Even when Herodotus issues some pretty rough-hewn, unflattering descriptions of different cultures, one is rarely, if ever, in the presence of harsh, indicting language. For example, when Herodotus (1921) claims that the Scythians "flayed" their victims or "laid the dead in the tomb on a counch" with "plant spears on each side of the body and lay across them wooden planks," as well as other such renditions, as far as I can surmise, Herodotus's language rarely is fortified by divisions into good and evil, the sacred and the profane, and virtue or vice. Of course, one could be on safe grounding by alleging that such dark descriptions come with their own value-laden tendencies.

Despite these cognitive possibilities and this caveat, it is important to remember that Herodotus was inspired to study and visit other cultures. Scholars have not determined for certain why Herodotus was curious about so many things because history does not speak specifically and informatively to his individual motives, that is, whether he was motivated by A or by B. We do know that he was the son of Lyxes and Dryo—a prominent family— and that he had a brother, Theodorous.

Records also indicate that Herodotus traveled to Samos and that his *Histories*—a book extraordinary by most standards—made people aware of a whole new world in which one could view non-Greeks as well as Greeks. He also welcomed strangers! In this regard, he made culture available to a rich group of people, including mathematicians, merchants, scientists, philosophers, and other renowned individuals.

Herodotus's Influence

Oswyn Murray (1972) notes, for example, that Herodotus was popular during the Hellenistic age and that his influence was "at the basis of the whole tradition of Hellenistic historical ethnography." Murray argues further that Herodotus influenced the historians of the court of Philip of Macedon, inspired Theopompus, and shaped Hecataeus's standard narratives of Egypt under Ptolemy. In a similar vein, Nearchus took Herodotus's accounts of India very seriously.

Together, these influences suggest that Herodotus had a galvanizing effect on other writers and leaders and provided them with some of the intellectual and explanatory tools necessary for "seeing" the other and, by extension, what it means to be human in a world divided between Greek and non-Greek and between barbarians and nonbarbarians. This means that Herodotus's work was soon circulating throughout the Greek, African, and

Asian world. There is a parallel here between British abolitionists drawing connections between the near and the distant and Herodotus's ability to draw connections between the near and the far.

Hochschild (2005) notes, for instance, that by challenging British and European order in the 19th century, "The abolitionists' first job was to make Britons understand what lay behind the sugar they ate, the tobacco they smoked, the coffee they drank" (p. 6). By extension, Herodotus's first job was to try to make individuals in the Hellenistic world understand the minds and customs of others in an effort to move people away from a Greek-centric approach to people and cultures. Without the venturesomeness of Herodotus, the world would have evolved more slowly from the local to the global and thus retarded the progression of empathy.

Herodotus is important for still another reason. He gave ultimate purpose to curiosity; he believed in adventure, "a go there and find out" type of world that surely inspired elites to move beyond their shores in search of diversity—however narrowly defined at the time. Herodotus's nosing about also led him to use the comparative method of acquiring knowledge and understanding others. As Jared Diamond (2005) observes, "The comparative method allows one to compare natural situations differing with respect to the variable of interest" (p. 17). And compare Herodotus did! In fact, Martin Bernal (1987), in his groundbreaking work, *The Afroasiatic Roots of Classical Civilization,* maintains that Herodotus saw the relationship between Greece and Asia and Africa "as one of similarities and differences, contacts and conflicts" and that "he asked many questions on these topics during his wide travels in the Persian Empire from Babylonia to Egypt, and on its northern and western fringes from Epirus and Greece to the Black Sea" (p. 98).

The results were stunning because Herodotus's zeal to, in the words of Isaiah Berlin (1991), "learn what it was like to live by someone else's light," led Herodotus to turn his gaze from Greece to other human beings. In the process, Herodotus imbued others with a kind of universal respect for humanity in general. In *Histories,* for example, in discussing the names of gods in Egypt, Greece, and Libya, Herodotus notes, "These customs (religious) and others besides, which I shall indicate, were taken by the Greeks from the Egyptians" (Herodotus, 1921, chap. 11, p. 14).

Moreover, in explaining such differences, Herodotus (1921) is very careful to avoid the polarities of good and bad. Redfield (1985), one of his most vocal critics, admits that Herodotus did not "treat the foreigners as inherently inferior." And he ultimately became "explicitly conscious of the relativism of other cultures"—a precursor to human understanding. Perhaps this helps to explain why Herodotus simply states, with regard to religious practices, "These came from the Pelasgiams, from whom the Athenians were the first Greeks to take it, and then handed it on to others. For the Athenians were then already counted as Greeks when the Pelasgians came to live in the land with them and thereby began to be considered as Greeks" (Herodotus, 1921, chap. 2, p. 15). Once again, one sees in Herodotus's passages a keen mixture of geography and perceptions of other people. This is not to say, however, that Herodotus was blind to notions of good and bad. Rather, it is to say that he toed the line in terms of veering into one direction as opposed to another.

As Wells (1907) aptly observes, Herodotus reported "truly what he . . . heard without exaggeration or suppression" (p. 37). Allan Bloom (1987) reminds us that "Herodotus was at least aware of the rich diversity of cultures. But he took that observation to be an invitation to investigate all of them to see what was good and bad about each and find out what he could learn from about the good and bad from them" (p. 4). In sum, Herodotus provided materials on which judgments can be made, even though there is scant evidence, if any, that Herodotus tried explicitly to move his readers in direction A instead of in direction B.

Well's (1907) and Bloom's (1987) analyses lead ultimately to the point that Herodotus did research and tried to understand foreign cultures and distant regions. And in doing so, he set ideational boundaries, making it possible for a range of competing discourses and ideas to circulate in the Hellenistic age, and for people to entertain the possibility of becoming global citizens, as typified so well by Stoics.

Stoics: Citizens of the World

Herodotus set the intellectual stage for the coming of the Stoics. Whereas Herodotus contributed to empathy by giving us a sense of the ecology of human beings by commenting on the ingenuity of people, the new versus the old, and comparison and contrasts, the Stoics reached even further into the "worldly art of grappling with human misery" and focused their attention "on issues of daily and urgent human significance" (Nussbaum, 1994, pp. 3–4), hewing closely to the way that Buddha diagnosed human situations.

In the process of grappling with "issues of daily and urgent human significance," history tells us that Stoics gave to the world something even more significant, according to Nussbaum (1994), one of the most authoritative scholars on the subject of the Stoics. They gave humankind the gift of "universal respect for the dignity of humanity in each and every person regardless of class, gender, race, and nation—an idea that has ever since been at the heart of all distinguished political thought in the Western tradition" (p. 12).

Although belief in the possibility of cultivating humanity had not yet been codified in the way intercultural scholars view and study it today, the Stoics provided content, methods, and procedures that are central to understanding empathic human behavior. Given that humane action is rarely impervious to behavior that requires careful and responsible everyday sensibilities about what one ought to do, how, with whom, and under what circumstances, Stoics gave ultimate purpose to things that one can do to create a just and humane society. For the purposes of empathy, the Stoics expressed explicitly a technique of bringing about a happy condition that prepares the human soul for acceptance of the other.

Stoics and the Psychology of the Soul

To do this, the Stoics entered the realm of human psychology and adopted strategies of "self-shaping." Chrysippus, for example, observed that Greek philosophers were quite adept at providing cures for the body but not for the soul. For this reason, he developed an art that centered on a "diseased soul." In explaining this hugely important empathetic focus, Chrysippus and other Stoics turned their attention to "modes of doctoring" the soul. To demonstrate the urgency of the activity of soul doctoring for humane interaction, the Stoics persuasively drew parallels between medical doctors and doctoring the soul. Seneca notes that a good doctor will not offer a prescription to a patient before examining him or her. Rather, the doctor must feel the pulse of the patient, take his or her temperature, and become keenly aware of the patient's personal history. So, too, must this be done in matters of the soul.

By recommending a course of action with regard to matters of the soul, a way of "toning up the soul," and by declaring that human beings must grapple with anger, for example, Stoics were fully in the realm of not only self-analysis but also audience analysis—an interactive way of shaping self for philosophical and practical receptivity to others. In striking contrast to old Hellenistic philosophers such as Plato and Aristotle, who were dry, the Stoics saw philosophy as therapeutic, and as such, the latter became "key popularizers" (Gottlieb, 2000, p. 284).

Although Stoics, with their emphasis on ordinary people and ordinary modes of thinking and doing, met with criticisms, they extended human understanding by making ideas and precepts comprehensible to everyone so inclined. Following their founder, Zeno the Stoic (c. 335–263 B.C.E.), who taught his students in the Stoa Poikile, or Painted Colonnade, Stoics, as Seneca suggests, implicitly offered a prescription for behavior in the public sphere by stressing that one should observe the deficiencies in his or her own soul first (Van Doren, 1991, p. 71). I will talk more specifically about Seneca's contributions later, but for now it is important to observe that his and the Stoics' meanings were crucial for creating pathways for empathic understanding.

In this domain, like Buddha, Stoics offered the world an answer to a vexing question: How is it possible for one to know and understand others without knowing and understanding oneself? The notion of knowing self contains the seeds of a humanizing and other-directed orientation. Seneca's insights remind us that we have multiple selves, such as student, parent, gardener, niece, doctor, lawyer, plumber, and teacher. Despite our multiple selves, the Stoics remind us that we must know not only who we are but also how who we are affects our interaction with others, including the moral choices we make, our strengths and weaknesses, our sense of our own roots, our communication style, and our prejudices, as well as the emotions that guide our behavior.

At least, that is what I think Stoics meant, after reading them, with some care. In other words, Stoics were deeply interested in *how* virtue is cultivated in the world (Nussbaum, 1994). However, the most important point here is that by recognizing the naturalizing effects of nurturing humane virtues, the Stoics were onto something mighty powerful for the reign of empathy. From these fundamental but compelling premises and elaborations of soul nurturing have come a wealth of information about such virtues as justice, the nature of the good, compassion, communal connections, affiliation, and identity, as we shall see. It is possible to examine critical aspects of Stoic philosophy by studying what modes of thinking and language emerged from the tenets of specific Stoics and how their activities interacted with other events to change the course of cultural empathy, as I will now explicate.

Cicero on Duties and Empathy

By the time Stoics arrived on the scene, everyone from Julius Caesar to Brutus to Antony was caught up in the intrigues of political life in Rome. Someone who observed the capricious and ambitious happenings of the day would surely be curious about matters of friendship and where such roads should lead. A lawyer and orator named Cicero was just such a person. He was one of the first persons to make the case that we should treat humanity with respect and imbue our talk with hospitality and graciousness (Nussbaum, 1994, p. 59). His philosophy of care extended to those on foreign soil and offered an alternative to the violent civil discord of his day.

Although Cicero was deeply affected by the goings-on in Roman political life, he soon found himself embroiled in turmoil, especially in conflict between Caesar and Pompey for "world domination" (Van Doren, 1991, p. 73). Because of his striking legal acumen and his famous orations in defense of his clients, Cicero attracted the attention of both Caesar and Pompey and was forced to make a choice between the two highly political men. By embracing Pompey, Cicero chose the wrong side. He also made another ill-advised decision when he verbally attacked Mark Antony and Octavian for their encroachments on Roman freedoms (Van Doren, 1991).

For his truth-seeking-upholding behavior, Antony, known by some to be a brutal man, had Cicero murdered. History records that after Cicero was murdered, Antony cut off the hands of the corpse and had them nailed to the senate rostrum as a vivid reminder to others of what could and might happen were they to follow the teachings of Cicero. Fortunately for history and for empathy's sake, Cicero turned to literary issues during the last decade of his life—prior to his untimely demise. A member of the educated class and son of a wealthy family, Cicero (2000), through his treatise, *De Officiis,* or *On Obligations,* turned his attention to a monumental challenge that confronted humankind: how to sustain freedom. Cicero's answer was service to the community through the distribution of duties and responsibilities.

Empathy, Reason, and Communal Responsibility

He was instrumental in setting in motion principles of how one should behave toward others in civic culture, and he played a commanding role in defining attributes that are fundamental to obtaining and practicing empathy, although he does not specifically use the term *empathy.* Walsh (2000) argues that from the fourth century on, Cicero played a unique role until the end of 18th century in the "formation of ethical values in the world" (p. xxxv). One of the most important ways that Cicero elevated empathy is through his keen emphasis on natural endowment—reason—what separates human beings from animals.

Humans' capacity for reasoning allows them to "visualize consequences, and to detect the causes of things," according to Cicero (2000, p. 6). This stipulation, plus men's inclination to form "gatherings and meetings," to "lay in adequate supplies of clothing and food, not merely for themselves but also for their wives, children, and the others dear to them whom they should protect," all "kindle men's spirits, and develops them for the performance of task" (p. 2). Thus, Cicero (2000) suggests that humans come into the world with a chromosomal imprinting mechanism that inclines them toward a healthy concern for others.

By insisting that "search and scrutiny" into truth are also important, Cicero (2000) placed himself solidly in the company of those who see human beings as seekers after a truth that ultimately leads to noble "designs and actions" (p. 7). Because no other creature shares this orientation, Cicero reminds us to "do nothing which is unsightly or degenerate, to do or to contemplate nothing capricious in all our actions and beliefs. These are the qualities which kindle and fashion that honorable conduct which we seek" (p. 7).

Four Essential Virtues

Cicero maintains that if we have knowledge and wisdom, then we are clearly equipped to safeguard the community by cultivating habits of mind that lead to right behavior. Right behavior involves four essential virtues: wisdom, justice, beneficence, and magnanimity.

The lessons learned from the practice of such virtues in turn points in the direction of empathy. Justice, for example, rests on the principle that no one should harm another and on principles of communal and private interests. Cicero's insistence on the importance of justice in promoting empathy caused him to call it the "brightest adornment of virtue" (Cicero, 2000, p. 9). The primary function of justice is "to ensure that no one harms his neighbor unless he has himself been unjustly attacked" (p. 9). This rule is essential for managing both intrapersonal and intercultural interactions with others. Through this bent, Cicero believes that people will be inclined to be good toward others, and in this regard, he gave humankind a way of dealing with others.

For Cicero, munificence and generosity are adjuncts to justice, but these do have pitfalls, even though they are in some sense natural. "Nothing more accords with human nature than munificence and generosity," according to Cicero (2000, p. 17). Here he places constraints on our intentions because we must ensure that generosity or altruism does not do harm to recipients in the name of "kindly gestures" (p. 17). If we apply Cicero's theory of generosity to humans, it implies as well that the giver will not give at the expense of his or her own survival. In other words, generosity must not "go beyond our means," and it must be "apportioned to each recipient according to his worth" (p. 17). This way of reasoning is consistent with the fact that, as a rule, when one gives, one ought to strive toward justice. Cicero insists on such principles partly because such rules are the basis of or "the touchstone of all transactions" (p. 17).

What is striking is that Cicero's analysis ultimately moves into rules for determining how to evaluate empathic behavior. He came to believe that understanding empathy was a necessary precondition for acting in social relations with others. Anticipating that some humans can and do use generosity as a hedge against abuses of fame, Cicero also wanted to ensure that humans do not rob one person to be generous to another in a quest for fame and distinction. In this regard, Cicero tries to ensure a parsimonious use of empathy.

We can see then that Cicero was most concerned about cardinal virtues that undergird principles of empathy. Following Stoic ideals, he believed that "greatness of soul" was itself a virtue. Although he wrote *On Obligations* after his life in politics had ebbed, he had always shown a strong interest in philosophy, starting in his teen years.

Seneca: Cultivating Humanity

Seneca on Anger

Seneca was one of the first persons to make the case that it is wrong to be hostile, cruel, and angry. Thus, when we talk about activities that thwart rational thought, calm decision making, and general concern for the well-being of others using norms of empathy, we think mainly of Seneca and his treatise, *De Ira* or *On Anger* (in Seneca, 1995). Written as an extended treatise to his brother, Novatus, *On Anger* is a guidebook for understanding what counts as anger, whether it is natural, when it is appropriate, how to check one's anger, and, most critically, how to cure it. Seneca argues that anger has three parts: an explication of anger that shows it to be "nonnatural" and "nonnecessary," an element of rationality and reason, and a curative dimension (Nussbaum, 1994, p. 410). Although these three main elements are present in his work, they are not organized sequentially.

Seneca (1995) argues that what counts as anger is "not with those who have harmed us, but with those who are about to harm us; which shows you that anger is not generated by being wronged" (p. 20). Like other Stoics, he believed in norms of cooperation by members of the human community. To Stoics' way of thinking, wayward emotions such as anger deflect from elevating communal bonds of friendship. Seneca says that humans differ considerably from wild animals, which are "subject to impulse," because we are reasoning beings who have been "granted prudence, foresight, scrupulousness, deliberation" (p. 21). He asks, "What is the need for anger when reason serves us well?" (p. 28). Seneca implies that these are key traits that humans have been granted for checking the passions of anger, which can lead to ugly behavior. For this reason, he warns against anger, which is "out of accord" with humans' nature.

According to Seneca (1995), "Human life rests upon kindnesses and concord; bound together, not by terror but by love reciprocated, it becomes a bond of mutual assistance" (p. 23). He talks about the terrible effects that anger can have on human behavior. And he believes that we have the ability to project ourselves into the feelings of others through proper conduct that involves being a good person, using "gentle words," and avoiding punishment since the latter "goes with anger" (p. 24). As far as possible, one needs to act in such ways that generate empathic well-being for other people and society. Although Seneca praises empathic behavior, he acknowledges that there are messy issues surrounding the directionality of anger, and for this reason, he interrogates whether a person should become angry if she sees a mother, sister, or brother maimed by a ruthless enemy or tortured in excruciatingly painful ways.

Seneca's answer is no. He answers in the negative primarily because he makes a firm distinction between punishment and protection. In the former instance, Seneca argues that one should "avenge" the wrongdoer not because one is angry but because "one should." To that end, Seneca places vengeful behavior in the category of duty and honor and not in the province of anger; it is "fine and honorable to go forth in defence of parents, children, friends and fellow-citizens under the guidance of duty itself, in the exercise of will, judgment, and foresight" (Seneca, 1995, p. 30). The clear distinction between anger and duty is faithful to Seneca's notions regarding reason and rationality. After all, animals exhibit raving behaviors, not reason-giving humans. This helps to explain why Seneca grants humans permission to act vengefully in the name of duty and honor: The behavior is governed by the cerebral cortex and not by impulses.

This theory is consistent with Hume's concentric circle of radiating loyalties, as I noted in the introductory chapter. At the same time, however, Seneca rescues behavior aimed toward revenge from behavior that generates anger. He remains devoted to the proposition that anger is destructive and injures the very fabric of human society because it diminishes both tranquility and the human soul. A crucial dimension of Seneca's position on anger is the extent to which he believes anger is justified. Toward this end, he believes, as do many Stoics, that "in circumstances where evil prevails, anger is an assertion of concern for human well-being and dignity; and the failure to become angry seems at best slavish (as Aristotle put it), and at worst a collaboration with evil," as Nussbaum (1994, p. 403) observes.

As I have attempted to show, Seneca distanced himself from situations that invite anger and urged that this sensibility operate in much of our dealings with other human beings. In Seneca's view, the highest good emanates from a life free of anger. At the end of On Anger, after advising his brother Norvatus that "life is too short to waste it being angry" and after admonishing Norvatus that we should concentrate our empathetic attention on "virtue alone," Seneca writes one of the most moving comments in the annals of cultural history that should serve as a guide for universal respect: "At any moment now, we shall spit forth this life of ours. In the meantime, while we still draw breath, while we still remain among human beings, let us cultivate humanity." But would economics, property, and wealth test the resources of empathy?

Adam Smith

In 1776, the same year that America gained its independence, a man named Adam Smith published a seminal treatise on systematic economics titled *The Wealth of Nations*. By many accounts, he became the preeminent economist of all time because his work provided an ideological and philosophical basis for nations embracing unfettered economics. Although Smith's name is most synonymous with economics, his most humane contribution was the notion that moral sentiments are founded on "the near universal human attribute of sympathy" (Wilson, 1993, p. 31). When he advocates that "there are evidently some principles in his (man's) nature, which interest him in the fortune of others, and render their happiness necessary to him, though he derives nothing from it except the pleasure of seeing it," Smith opens up a fascinating insight into human behavior and the way we perceive others (Wilson, 1993, p. 1).

But Smith is not, as Wilson notes (1993), advocating a special type of benevolence, that is, promoting an ideology of helping others. Rather, Smith argues that there is symmetry between our natural inclination to both admire and to want to please others. This explains the role of imagination and fellow-feeling in Smith's conception of empathy.

Smith points out, "As we have no immediate experience of what other men feel, we can form no idea of the manner in which they are affected, but by conceiving what we ourselves should feel in the like situation" (Wilson, 1993, p. 1). The logical sequence of Adam Smith's (1790) insights leads to a powerful point about empathy: Since we cannot know what others feel, we must imagine it! "This is the source of our fellow-feeling for the misery of others, that is by changing places in fancy with the sufferer, that we come either to conceive or to be affected by what he feels" (p. 2).

Smith (1790) uses this example to illustrate this point. "Though our brother is upon the rack, as long as we ourselves are at our ease, our senses will never inform us of what he suffers. They never did, and never can, carry us beyond our own person, and it is by the imagination only that we can form any conception of what are his sensations" (p. 1). This means that through the instrument of the imaginary, humans can feel empathy for individuals who lose their loved ones in a massacre, cheer when the villain in a motion picture is wounded, and grieve for children affected by cholera.

Most of us would agree with Smith that the imagination is a stupendous key to "fellow-feeling." However, it would be wrong for us to interpret Smith's analysis of moral sentiments to mean that all feelings are universal and therefore equal. Quite the contrary, Smith's entire analysis embodies the concept of an inequality of sentiments—that is, an evocation of judgment. Thus, we not only feel certain emotions for others but also judge the goodness of fit between our fellow-feeling and the content of the passions expressed. Smith (1790) carries his analysis further: "There are some passions of which the expressions excite no sort of sympathy" but "serve rather to disgust and provoke us against them" (p. 3). For instance, the thought of billionaire Bill Gates being upset at the loss of a penny would arouse no empathy but derision because "we cannot bring his case home to ourselves" because we cannot imagine ourselves in such a position.

"Bringing the case home to ourselves" or using a principle of proportionality is a most important standard for judging what excites or does not excite empathy, according to Smith (1790). Empathy, therefore, "does not arise so much from the view of the passion, as from that of the situation which excites it" (p. 3). While we might not empathize with Bill Gates in the previous example, it would be difficult indeed for most people not to be distraught by the following story. At the height of one of the most brutal moments during the Iraq War, a doctor and his family were literally marooned in their house because of violence. To protect themselves from stray bullets, all family members huddled in a bathroom for several days— father, mother, daughter, and two sons. As time passed, the doctor said to his wife, "We need food, please cook!"

To accomplish a basic task such as cooking, the wife literally had to hunch her back as she approached the kitchen because she did not dare place her body in front of the window. We are likely to approve of this conduct because the empathy is sensible, and it meets Smith's tests. Smith (1790) notes that in empathy-producing situations, we ask, "What has befallen you?" and it is only after we have answered this question that we can begin to "feel for another" because we put ourselves in his or her case, causing passion to "arise in our breast from the imagination" (p. 3).

Reciprocal Empathy and Pleasure

Not surprisingly, Adam Smith (1790) also gives attention to "mutual" or reciprocal empathy. "Whatever may be the cause of sympathy, or however it may be excited," Smith argues, "nothing pleases us more than to observe in other men a fellow-feeling with all the emotions of our own breast; nor are we ever so much shocked as by the appearance of the contrary" (p. 5).

Mutual empathy is a special kind of sympathy. It invites "correspondence of sentiments," fair exchanges, and a beautiful expectation that favors granted will be favors returned. In this regard, we find a keen understanding of the moral sentiments of fairness in Smith, who probably knew that in the context of empathy, fairness plays a central role.

If Amaj and Amorion, who have to work and live together in a community, share the rule of fairness, doing the work of empathy costs less. By contrast, people who do not invoke the rule of fairness will end up void of much fellow-feeling and unable to form a community based on common empathy. Thus, by extension, Smith sees in fairness the source of healthy cultural environments. In other words, fairness is motivated by something broader than pure individual self-interest.

Pleasure is another plane that shapes and gives empathy vivacity and beauty. To Adam Smith (1790), empathy is also a mirth-making enterprise derived from good company, enlivening moments, and the sheer joy of knowing that a "correspondence of the sentiments of others with our own appears to be a cause of pleasure" (p. 5). And so an inclination toward pleasure grows organically out of mutual empathy. On a practical level, Smith sees the meaning-making pleasure-giving arm of empathy as a way of alleviating grief by "insinuating into the heart almost the only agreeable sensation which it is at that time capable of receiving" (p. 6). Translation: When empathy giving and seeking human beings find another who is burdened by afflictions, evoking in their "memory the remembrance of those circumstances which occasioned their affliction," they produce a mighty work of restoration. For example, Smith notes that when we take the grief of another seriously, we excite empathy in him or her. The idea of restorative empathy is based on the notion that there are specific things that all humans can do to bring joy to others, such as the empathetic pangs of a mother who learned that her child had been killed by a crazed individual at Virginia Tech, where 32 individuals were gunned down by Seung-Hui Cho on April 16, 2007. For Smith, empathy is a universal human potential, a capacity that all humans share.

Empathy, Property, and Principles

Despite Smith's injunction that humans be good to one another and despite his writings on empathy, his ideas are forever linked to his famous book *The Wealth of Nations,* published in 1776. In fact, most educated people have probably never heard of Smith's (1790) work, *Theory of Moral Sentiments.* And yet, there is much fascination worldwide with his principles about the relationship between property and principles. To understand what led Smith to write the influential *Wealth of Nations,* one must know that he marveled at the wondrous workings of the humble pin factory. For this reason, I quote portions as follows:

> One man draws out the wire, another straightens it, a third cuts it, a fourth points it, a fifth grinds it at the top for receiving the head; to make the head requires two or three distinct operations; to put it on is a peculiar business; to whiten it is another; it is even a trade by itself to put them into paper. . . . I have seen a small manufactory of this kind where ten men only were employed and where some of them consequently performed two of three distinct operations. But though they were very poor, and therefore but indifferently accommodated with the necessary machinery, they could, when they exerted themselves make among them about twelve pounds of pins in a day. There are in a pound upwards of four thousand pins of a middling size. Those ten persons, therefore, could make among them upwards of forty-eight thousand pins in a day . . . but if they had all wrought separately and independently . . . they certainly could not each of them make twenty, perhaps not one pin a day. (A. Smith, 1776)

Although some scholars read *Wealth of Nations* as a treatise on greed and self-interest, one should remember that the passages above with which Smith opened his work speak powerfully to another view. Notice, for example, that our eyes are drawn toward the following words in the moving story of the pin factory: "though they were very poor," "but if they had wrought separately and independently," and "they certainly could not each of them make twenty, perhaps not one pin a day." Notice further that the entire passage contains a clear measure of empathy in it. In elevating aspects of classical economics, Smith is concerned about demonstrating empathy and concern for others. Fukuyama (1995) writes, "Adam Smith, the premier classical economist, believed that people are driven by a selfish desire to 'better their condition,' but he would never have subscribed to the notion that economic activity could be reduced to rational utility maximization" (pp. 17–18).

Bethell (1998, p. 97) believes that, as a starting point, the narrative of the pin factory left much to be desired in a work on economics. However, if one adds Smith's impassioned interests in society, as revealed in *The Theory of Moral Sentiments,* one can understand his enthusiastic empathy for the common laborer. One must also remember that Smith's visit to a pin-making factory and his empathy for the common person inspired him to write his economic book. Smith's insistence on what he called the "self-interest" of the marketplace (meaning that the marketplace governed the rise and fall of prices such that when prices were high, "the attraction of profit meant that more goods were made" [Burke & Ornestein, 1995, p. 193]) and his idea of an "invisible hand," guiding everything, have caused some scholars to lose sight of his interest in the common good.

Another way of viewing Adam Smith's (1776) *Wealth of Nations*, then, is to argue that he saw property, economics, and empathy as compatible enterprises. In other words, economic interests need not cannibalize humans' march toward cooperation, which is crafted from empathy. Smith's views of property and economics are central to the promotion of empathy because they demonstrate that cultural views can shape economic views. Although Charles Murray (2003) delights in the fact that "Smith changed forever the age-old assumption that wealth is a limited pie over which governments and men fight to get the biggest piece" (p. 51), it is also the case that Smith encouraged acts of benevolence.

John Stuart Mill

The Public Good

Sixteen years after the death of Adam Smith, John Stuart Mill, another influential economist, also carried good news about the very notion of other-regarding behavior. Born in London in 1806 and educated by his father, with educational assistance of Jeremy Bentham, Mill contributed to our understanding of empathy through the creed of the "Greatest Happiness Principle," which holds that "actions are right in proportion as they tend to promote happiness, wrong as they tend to produce the reverse of happiness" ("Mill," 2009, p. 3). By happiness, Bentham meant pleasure and "freedom from pain," the only "things desirable as ends" ("Mill," 2009, p. 3). But one should not construe Mill's idea of happiness with doctrines of hedonism, idleness, the choice not to work, profligacy, and a quest for unrestrained motivation. Rather, happiness is a "directive rule of human conduct," "not the agent's own greatest happiness, but the greatest amount of happiness altogether" ("Mill," 2009, p. 7). Mill drives this point still further by appealing to the golden rule of Jesus of Nazareth, "the complete spirit of the ethics of utility," "to do as you would be done by, and to love your neighbor as yourself" ("Mill," 2009, p. 12). For Mill, this Christian orientation constitutes "the interest, of every individual, as nearly as possible in harmony with the interests of the whole" ("Mill," 2009, p. 12).

The purpose of happiness is not merely to satisfy oneself, and this can be done by making other people happy because the "world in general is immensely a gainer by it." According to the Greatest Happiness Principle, the end of human action is also a standard of morality, which is governed by other-regarding principles and can be distributed to the "whole sentient creation," to use Mill's own words. One should have a sincere interest in the public good, declared Mill. The very notion of the public good—of the inter-connections of the will of others, human care and effort and the elimination of what Mill terms "indigence, disease, unkindness, and worthlessness" and, by implication, the links that exist among health and legal systems, "noxious influences," and physical and moral education—can be reduced by sustained empathetic attentiveness. It is worth remarking, in this connection, that implicitly Mill offers a problem-centered approach to his principle of happiness. In reality, one can increase the amount of happiness in the world by focusing not on "what men can do" but on "what they should" do ("Mill," 2009, p. 11).

In the long run, "the best proof of a good character is good actions," and in fact, Mill believed that conduct that resulted in bad behavior deviated from the good. By promoting the "general interests of society," it is possible to multiply human happiness, but not necessarily out of sheer duty, since to do so would be to pervert the utilitarian mode of thought. Let me give an example of what Mill meant. He says that one who saves a fellow human being from drowning does what is "morally right," whether her or his motive for doing so is driven by duty or the hope of being paid for the trouble. This can be put another way. It is the doctrine of the multiplication of good actions. Mill argues that by paying attention to specific individuals in time and place, one extends good deeds outwardly in a radius-like fashion. By fixating in an individual way, one ends up helping society at large, whether the intent is "so wide a generality as the world" ("Mill," 2009, p. 13).

Thus, it makes no difference whether a person's inner, radiant beam shines as an individual light; she or he still has the power to be a "public bene-factor" ("Mill," 2009, p. 13). Mill maintained that the interests of a few people can be extended to the many—in the public interest. In this way, a person's powers of empathy can be exercised from the specific to the general.

Morality and Utilitarianism

Mill also argues in a strong Kantian sense, when invoking Stoics. He observes that all humans should be accorded "a sense of dignity" (Kant, 1991, p. 255). This is the very spirit of what Kant meant when he said, "Humanity itself is a dignity; for a man cannot be used merely as a means by any man . . . but must always be used at the same time as an end" (p. 23). Mill's appellation regarding human dignity is spacious in its reach since it touches those in war-weary Darfur in Sudan as well as those in rich Dubai in United Arab Emirates. Thus, the belief that one should be empathetic toward one another is a central tenet of Mill's philosophical work.

Although Mill came under particular scrutiny for his utilitarian views, he believed that "the moral and intellectual development of individuals is of the utmost importance," as William R. Patterson (2005) notes in his critique of Mill, Thomas Henry Huxley, and Social Darwinism (p. 79). In industrial Europe, one protest against Mill is that utilitarianism is "complicit with social Darwinism" (p. 79). While I will not lean on this fact, it is noteworthy that Mill's philosophy had its critics. The point is that Mill was influential during the 19th century and that his views found sway not only in the ethical domain but also in the area of economics.

Mill's (1884) *Principles of Political Economy* reveals a great deal about the meshing of economics and empathy. Some of his strongest views are evident in his commentary on Karl Marx and communism. Bethell (1998) and others assert that as an economist, Mill was more interested in the distribution side of economics as opposed to the production side. Mill believed that production was already "fixed" by "the laws and conditions of the production of wealth." Moreover, he claimed that unlike production, distribution was not subject to iron-clad laws. For my purposes, it is significant that Mill believed that the distribution of wealth "depends on the laws and customs of society. Rules of distributions are what the opinions and feelings of the ruling portion of the community make them, and are very different in different ages and countries" (Bethell, 1998, p. 111). Using his brand of logic, Mill reasoned that long after laws had been made for the production of goods, "once there," they would benefit the whole of human society. Put another way, Mill made a careful distinction between the laws of production and modes of distribution; the former are "real laws of nature," while the latter are "subject to certain conditions" and "dependent on human will" (Bethell, 1998, p. 111). An important extension of Mill's reasoning is this: A progressive change would occur in "the character of the human race" (Bethell, 1998, p. 112). This worldview would also necessitate a change in humans' mental and moral makeup in a push toward good ethical behavior.

My point is that Mill believed that the economic state of 19th-century Europe would eventually bend toward an elimination of suffering and injustice—placing his ideology in the camp of communism—where humans would be working "under the eye, not of one master, but of the whole community" (Bethell, 1998, p. 112). The uppermost point is that public consciousness is a way out in the troubled world of both Mill and Marx. What matters further is that human thought and action should serve the province of humankind.

But Mill and Marx were a long way from the geopolitics of specific events that would hover around empathy in the 21st century, starting with the destruction of two architectural edifices in the city of New York on September 11, 2001. I now turn to a discussion of that event and others to

3

Geopolitics

The Spoils of Empathy

Whirlwinds: 9/11, Iraq, and Al-Qaeda

The 19 men from Saudi Arabia, Egypt, and other places in the Arab world who attacked the U.S. World Trade Center and the Pentagon on September 11, 2001, gave human beings worldwide an opportunity to witness both the best and the worst of what it is possible for individuals to do. For one exceptional moment, diverse individuals from Africa to Asia tried to process the enormity of the situation. Ever mindful of horrific images of plunging debris, tornadic-like rings of billowing smoke, and fresh memories of lives taken, goodwill for Americans stood at unprecedented levels. Empathy reigned. And people vied for ways to express their fellow-feeling for Americans despite the powers of empire, "a new Rome, the greatest colossus in history" (Johnson, 2004, p. 3). The sad, ugly event clearly demanded human sympathy, and world opinion stood with Americans and went to the very core of humanity.

British Prime Minister Tony Blair sent condolences on behalf of his people and noted empathetically, "There have been the most terrible, shocking events taking place in the United States within the last couple of hours. We can only imagine the terror and carnage there and the many, many innocent people who lost their lives" ("International Reaction," 2001, p. 1). Egyptian President Hosni Mubarak called the attacks "horrific," and Palestinian President Yasser Arafat said, "I send my condolences, and the condolences of the Palestinian people to American President Bush" ("International Reaction," 2001, p. 2).

Libyan leader Moammar Gadhafi, whom the United States had once accused of supporting terrorism, also expressed sadness; he called the events "horrifying" ("International Reaction," 2001, p. 3). Iranian President Mohammad Khatami also expressed "deep regret and empathy with the victims" and said that "it is an international duty to try to undermine terrorism" ("International Reaction," 2001, p. 3).

After September 11, I recall pausing at the entrance to my neighborhood to collect stray pieces of paper that the wind had gently tossed about when a gentleman stopped his car and asked whether I needed help picking up the paper! The point is that both emotions and deeds meshed well during that fateful time in the United States.

Comments regarding the great rupture suggest that 9/11 occurred at a crucial psychical and political moment, one that members of the George W. Bush administration might have used for the moral uplift of humanity. However, because President Bush, representatives of his administration, and others later pushed ideological discourse and action too far, the goodwill that had been abundant internationally soon was spent. And the spoils of empathy came, as this chapter will detail later. To understand how ideas, ideology, and zeal later coalesced in the absence of abundant empathy, one has to consider the events and discourse that led to America's involvement in Iraq. Such variables as an inattentive gaze, nonempathetic versus empathetic inscriptions in structures, a split between value and fact, and a disjunction between analysis and practice all played interactive roles. An examination of such matters reveals that an intertwining chromosomal cultural imprinting mechanism was at work in Iraq. For this reason, it is almost impossible to discuss any one of the aforementioned variables without implicating another.

An Inattentive Gaze

In his book *After Theory,* Eagleton (2003) offers trenchant comments about the nature of sameness and difference and what happens when one's gaze is fixed on one body as opposed to another. "How much more peaceable human history would almost certainly have been," writes Eagleton, "if cultural differences had never sprung on the scene, and if the world had been almost exclusively populated by gay Chinese" (p. 158). But it is not, and historically, at least since the 16th century, humans have become accustomed to a "subjective looking" that too often assumes a White elite subject, although clearly perceptions in this regard are changing. The notion of gaze in the case of empathy reveals that the first Bush administration officials' customary way of looking inward was such that they acted upon themselves and, by extension, ended up directing discourses to themselves.

For an understanding of the phenomenon, it is necessary to provide a synopsis of how and why the Iraq War "started as a war of ideas" during the first Bush administration (Packer, 2005, p. 13). George Packer (2005) dates the beginning of ideas that would become inscribed in the first Bush political structure as March 8, 1992, almost the precise time that an Iraqi exile named Kanan Makiya shed his anonymity and urged the overthrow of Saddam Hussein, the president of Iraq. Earlier, Makiya (1998) had written a book titled *Republic of Fear* under the pseudonym Samir al-Khalil that captured poignantly the subjective life of millions of Iraqis who lived a nightmare of perpetually deep fear of Hussein and Baath Party rule. The book was published anonymously because Makiya also feared for his life. Against this historical backdrop, Makiya emerged after the first Gulf War of 1991, and his ideas regarding the overthrow of Saddam became inscribed in the structure of the Pentagon in the form of a 46-page document called the *Defense Planning Guidance*. The document served as a foreign policy primer for military and political strategy after the cold war (Packer, 2005, p. 13).

To see how early seeds were planted that would have far-reaching consequences for what eventually took place in Iraq, starting in 2003, we need to note that a cast of characters emerged who shared a similar constraining worldview. The members included Secretary of Defense Dick Cheney; Lewis "Scooter" Libby, who would later become Vice President Cheney's chief of staff; Paul Wolfowitz, a former head of the World Bank; and a few lower-ranking men, among them, Zalmay Khalilzad and Abram Shulsky—men who would also reappear during the second Bush administration. The *Defense Planning Guidance (DPG)* document is significant because it left cultural and political imprints that would define not only how members of the Bush administration viewed the world but also how and under what conditions their ideology would become vivid on the world stage.

Defense Planning

Under the auspices of then Defense Secretary Dick Cheney, the *DPG* document outlined a political and military post–cold war policy for the United States. It set forth three major points regarding the preeminence of America following the fall of the former Soviet empire in 1991. "Our first objective," wrote the neoconservative authors of the *DPG*, is "to prevent the re-emergence of a new rival" (Packer, 2005, p. 13). This objective is important because of its ironic nature.

At a crucial moment when the world was supposed to be moving toward Marshall McLuhan's global village, Cheney, Wolfowitz, and others saw potential threats to America. In the process of anticipating grand shifts that would occur in transition from a bipolar world to a unipolar world, members of the Bush administration already had begun intellectually and potentially to redivide the globe into multipolar attitudinal worlds, despite the discourse that the planners articulated at the time. Conservative planners reasoned that elevating the spending levels of the defense budget would keep American rivals safely at bay, including allies in Europe, Asia, and other international places.

Second, according to *DPG* planners, Americans must "safeguard U.S. interest and promote American values." America should aim "to address sources of regional conflict and instability in such a way as to promote increasing respect for international law, limit international violence, and encourage the spread of democratic forms of government and open economic systems." With this articulation of democratic values, the *DPG* planners, by extension, reasoned that terrorism, culture clashes, and other ills did not bode well for the United States and the world. The paradox of the *DPG* discourse, however, is that it contains within it both explicit and implicit moral responses to humankind that simultaneously masked America's economic and political interests. *The New York Times* employed the words *benevolent domination* to describe the Bush administration's perception of its global role in the new post–cold war world order. The *DPG* document is a rejection of "collective internationalism" and virtually pushes the collective will and decision making of others to the sideline. As *The New York Times* notes, "The Pentagon document articulates the clearest rejection to date of collective internationalism, the strategy that emerged from World War II when the five victorious powers sought to form a United Nations that could mediate disputes and police outbreaks of violence" (Tyler, 1992).

The third and final major feature of the *DPG* document urged America to "act independently when collective action cannot be orchestrated" to grapple with quick and compelling responses to global affairs. *The New York Times* said that Bush officials' efforts to "develop a one-superpower World" were a way of ensuring no rivals to America's hegemony (Tyler, 1992). Glover's (2000) statement that "narrow self-interest is also limited by the way we care about being one sort of person rather than another" (p. 26) is clearly implicated in how the *DPG* planners viewed others—those who had virtually no say in the course of action that the United States ultimately would take in Iraq in March 2003.

Because *The New York Times* and *The Washington Post* leaked information about the *DPG* document to the public in May 1992, the first President Bush released a "toned-down" revision and smoothed the language by pledging a more cooperative world stance (Packer, 2005, p. 14). But by that time, the ideological map for the second President Bush had already been drawn. And the ideological framing would become reinscribed in structure, and a defining discourse, dubbed the Bush doctrine or the second President Bush's National Security Strategy of 1992, would become influential with "uncanny accuracy, down to the wording of key sentences" (Packer, 2005, p. 14).

Thus, a small circle of men within an enclosed conceptual system of interests had begun to develop both the ideology and the techniques that would eventuate in the Iraq War, a cadre of men who saw the world through the lens of people like themselves, people who fixed their gaze on how America should behave in the world with little regard for congressional or popular oversight primarily because the discourse circulated largely in secret—in stealth-like form.

The Joining

Following the publication of the *DPG* document, other men and women who saw the world similarly both joined in and supported the second President Bush's team, including Secretary of State Condoleezza Rice; history professor Robert Kagan; Kagan's friend, William Kristol, then editor of Rupert Murdock's magazine, *The Weekly Standard;* Richard Perle; and James Woolsey. All brought to the scene a conception of "benevolent global hegemony," which translated as looking away from humanity and chiefly to an enclosed American mind-set that virtually disconnected planners from the constraints and obligations of others.

Through the publication of articles in academic journals and through the dissemination of freshly painted ideas about how the world should be constructed, well-connected, enthusiastic neoconservatives continued to craft national policy that framed the world in their image, a crafting that ultimately posed a challenge to the art of generating empathy. From the world of ancient Greece and Rome to philosopher Hobbes, politicians have grappled with both the salience and substance of this thing called "the people" and what it means to act on their behalf. Allen (2004) argues, for example, that "democratic politics cannot take shape until 'the people' is imaginable" (p. 69).

And I argue that the Bush administration did serious political work on behalf of "the Iraqi people," but in the process, the "idea" of *with what authority* became heavily implicated precisely because the wills of Iraqi citizens were undermined. Despite this undermining, neoconservatives continued to act "in the name" of Iraqis.

In 1997, Kagan and Kristol created another structural apparatus for the promotion of neoconservative views in the form of a second ideological mechanism—the Project for a New American Century or PNAC (Packer, 2005, p. 23). The members consisted of Rumsfeld, Wolfowitz, and Perle. Once again, like-minded men promoted the organization as a means of generating ideas for the overthrow of Saddam Hussein. It is meaningful, politically, that the PNAC planning occurred during President Clinton's term in office. In fact, Rumsfeld, Wolfowitz, Perle, and a few others went to the Clinton White House to discuss Iraq with Sandy Berger, Clinton's national security adviser (Packer, 2005, p. 23). At that point, there were few details about how Saddam was to be overthrown but rather a key emphasis on the fact that this *should* occur.

Packer (2005, p. 24) argues that President Clinton's preoccupation with the Monica Lewinsky affair pretty much ensured a policy outcome that resulted in the passage of the Iraq Liberation Act of 1998, which President Clinton reluctantly signed. In signing the act, President Clinton said, "This Act makes clear that it is the sense of the Congress that the United States should support those elements of the Iraqi opposition that advocate a very different future for Iraq than the bitter reality of internal repression and external aggression that the current regime in Baghdad now offers" (Mylroie, 1998). More than $8 million was "made available for assistance to the Iraqi democratic opposition" (Mylroie, 1998, p. 2).

In these ways, plans for the overthrow of Saddam were codified and disseminated, and a new and different foreign policy came into being—one that many Americans had very little knowledge of.

The Fate of Iraq

The second Bush administration's newly minted vision of the world stretched further and further and underscored the fact that the fate of Iraq was largely tied to a few men "who lacked the baseline belief in the public sphere" and who systematically devalued popular transparency, as Naomi Klein (2007, p. 354) observes. And most critically, a policy devoid of support from the Iraqis themselves, even though admittedly, it would have been most difficult for forces to foment rebellion in a country ruled by fear, as was the case in Iraq. In part, this explains why members of the second Bush administration developed plans to employ an exile from Iraq named Ahmad Chalabi to help them devise a regime change in Iraq.

As plans for the overthrow of Saddam developed, the second Bush administration crafted a discourse of reasons to justify why removing the Iraqi dictator would be a practical idea. Packer (2005) claims that justification was based, in part, on America's intricate relationship with the state of Israel. The communication took on a "it would be good for Israel" cast, a point that many neoconservatives well understood, according to Packer (2005, p. 30). Douglas Feith, who had served as an aide to Perle in the Reagan administration, and David Wurmser, the author of the paper, informed Benjamin Netanyahu, the prime minister of Israel, of plans to oust Hussein, according to Packer (2005, p. 30).

According to the narrative, Netanyahu was instructed to rearrange the coalition forces in the Middle East to ensure the security of Israel. There was even talk of restoring the Hashemite family of Jordan to the throne (the family had been deposed from the Iraqi throne in 1958, the year of the coup and Chalabi's departure) to rule in Iraq. These elements were also resources for nonempathetic inscriptions into the structure of discourse surrounding the coming 2003 war in Iraq. The robust belief circulating was that such events would isolate and, by implication, force the Palestinians to concede to Israeli demands for peace in the Middle East (Packer, 2005, p. 30). Many involved in the decision making argued that they had the authority and obligation to decide what was in the best interests of America and the world without necessarily consulting other cultures, with the possible exception of Israel. Such thinking promulgated the notion that ideas have consequences in favor of those in a position to both define and dictate the course of human events.

The sheer nature and magnitude of the planning implied inattention and an appearance of outright indifference to the lives of those who ultimately would be affected in significant ways. The role of those involved not only created an infrastructure for the circulation of nonempathetic attitudes but also fostered a sense of arrogance. The second Bush administration exploited the wave of "humanitarian intervention" that was cresting at the time (Packer, 2005, p. 33). Humanitarian intervention policies promoted the idea that sovereignty was no excuse for the abuse of human rights on the basis of nationalist grounds—the "nation-state trap" (Glover, 2000, p. 143). In particular, according to this line of reasoning, internal governments should no longer be given a green pass when it came to rape, torture, harsh imprisonments, and other sordid acts that were practiced within some nationalist borders.

Interventionist Measures

Armed with this seemingly empathetic global orientation, the Bush administration was free to exercise its own brand of interventionist measures mixed with right-seeming and "right-oriented talk." Who could fault the United States for protecting other world citizens on the grounds of human rights and democracy? Even though the term *humanitarian intervention* was not quite in vogue during the South African apartheid period, governments from the

United States to Great Britain stood in opposition to the brutality of the P. W. Bota government. As a result, 31 million Black South Africans were freed.

But was the Bush administration rhetoric and morality cut from the same empathetic cloth? Or, did structures further implicate empathy's ability to stand stalwart? With a specific way of looking at foreign policy and the world, structures favored neoconservatives who worked in the Bush administration and distanced empathy. Working through the structure of the Future of Iraq Project, the Bush administration relied very heavily on stories of massacres, tribal tribulation, and other acts of cruelty meted out by Saddam's men and women. Chalabi—aided by such men as Kanan Makiya, author of *Cruelty and Silence;* Rend Rahim, director of the Washington-based Iraq Foundation; and Salem Chalabi, a London lawyer—produced most of the narratives (Packer, 2005, p. 68).

Chalabi and other exiles fed the White House a daily diet of narratives that supported America's belief in universal principles of democracy. In essence, the discourse of exiles provided neoconservatives with an ideology that aligned beautifully with Bush's plans to oust Saddam. Chalabi had good reasons for encouraging the overthrow of Saddam because of what had happened to his family in the 1950s. As a scion of a wealthy middle-class family in Iraq, Chalabi and his family were forced into exile in 1958 and, as a result, lost a great deal of power and property. Exiles also reported that Saddam had weapons of mass destruction (WMDs) and that there were solid links between Saddam and Al-Qaeda. In June 2003, in an interview with NBC newsman Tom Brokaw and after it was evident that no weapons of mass destruction had been found in Iraq, University of Chicago Dr. Chalabi still declared that "the weapons of mass destruction are in Iraq. The way to get them . . . they've gone about getting them in, I don't think, [in] a very impressive way" (http://www.williambowles.info/ini/2006/0106/ini-0382.htm1, p. 5).

Much of what Chalabi reported about human rights violations and WMDs in Iraq was circulated through *The New York Times* reporter Judith Miller. A key point about the expansive paradigm and transformative stories is that Chalabi's repetitive narratives—many of them hidden from public scrutiny—supported the Bush administration's reasons for going to war with Iraq. Although it was exceedingly difficult at the time for everyday Iraqis to talk about the situation in Iraqi space, the organizational structures of the White House ensured that "othering" was a good mile from Iraqis. Indeed, in 1998, when a panel of academic experts at New York University who were opposed to the Iraq War issued consensus statement after consensus statement, Makiya, the last speaker, reminded the panelists—academic scholars, journalists, and a British diplomat—that the discussion "had been a selfishly

American one." "The other panelists had failed to take into account the Iraqi people themselves, who would pay the highest price in the event of war, and whose organized opposition overwhelmingly wanted one" (Packer, 2005, pp. 82–83).

Makiya's statement is strategic and instructive for what it reveals about humans' penchant for excluding others. It also highlights how universal abstractions can become so entrenched in formal structures such that human beings are unmindful of real, concrete, living, breathing individuals. Other organizations participated in producing reports that also led to the overthrow of Saddam and collectively functioned in exclusive nonempathetic ways. The National Defense University, the RAND Corporation, the Army War College, the United States Institute of Peace, the Center for Strategic and International Studies, and the Council on Foreign Relations—all issued reports that "were striking for their unanimity of opinion," according to Packer (2005, p. 113). Packer maintains that "where it mattered and could have made a difference, the advice of experts was unwelcome" (p. 113).

L. Paul Bremer's Role and Groupthink

A chief obstacle to the antiexpert phenomenon was L. Paul Bremer, who ultimately became the head person in charge of operations in Iraq under the auspices of the Coalition Provisional Authority, which I will discuss later. For now, however, it is relevant to underscore the point that initial planning, selection of officials, ideology, and narrowness of focus contained within them aspects of groupthink—and groupthink (Janis, 1972) usually coalesces around uniform ideas that become the centerpiece for all else. Because individuals who engage in groupthink concentrate so much on mission and virtually think alike, it is almost impossible for independent, fresh ideas and thoughts to emerge from outside the group.

We have seen how the formulation of groups can have morally limiting effects on decision making. This was especially the case under the Future of Iraq Project, and several features of the organizational workings of the group are hugely important for understanding constraining instrumental uses of empathy.

First, Bremer, the person selected to lead the organization responsible for helping Iraqis make a successful transition to democracy following the demise of Saddam, had "never served in the Middle East," nor was he a "Middle East Expert." According to Thomas E. Ricks (2006), author of *Fiasco,* Bremer members of the coalition forces lacked the language skills and cultural expertise necessary for nation building. An old friend of Scooter Libby, who was Vice President Cheney's chief of staff, Bremer came to the job fresh and without any "nation-building experience," according to Michael Gordon, chief military correspondent for *The New York Times*. Rajiv Chandrasekaran (2006), author of *Imperial Life in the Emerald City*, claims that Bremer wasn't even "a noted post-conflict guy" ("The Lost Year," 2007, p. 1),

And Jared Diamond (2004) observed that "throughout the occupation the coalition lacked the linguistic and area expertise necessary to understand Iraqi politics and society, and the few long-time experts present were excluded from the inner circle of decision-making in the CPA" (p. 43). As a result of the strong bestowal of power, Bremer was free to follow his and the Bush administration's interests rather than the specific, tangible interests of the Iraqi people or even the collective interests of the American people, for that matter. The latter had earlier been amputated from the process of decision making because policy making was conducted almost entirely behind closed doors and within a small circle of people. Jeff Faux (2006) maintains that a management of messages was evident, that "lies and misrepresentations" circulated, and that through a program of linguistic abstractions, the Bush administration was able to "use nationalist feelings to morph support for the troops into support of the war" (p. 51).

Second, Bremer selected a group of young people who were "largely . . . ideologically sympathetic" to him. This, in effect, meant that first-timers likely would be more loyal to Bremer and not to a broader ideological constituency. Thus, by forestalling the possibility of transparency, Bremer was free to plan, organize, dictate, and disregard others in limiting ways, especially the Iraqis who were having decisions *made for them,* but without due, rigorous consultation. And plan Bremer did, in very narrow and controlling ways. Moreover, Bremer dictated that everything regarding Iraqi operations go through him instead of through the White House or even the State Department. Chandrasekaran argues that even if the White House was free to offer directives to others—for example, to Bremer's senior advisers—"they couldn't do it unless Bremer signed off on it." Furthermore, Chandrasekaran claims, employing iron, cage, and tool metaphors that Bremer would say to people, "I don't want to deal with the Washington squirrel cage. I don't want somebody in Washington with an 8,000-mile screwdriver interfering with what we do here" ("The Lost Year," 2007, p. 2).

Although Bremer's comments also speak to fear of the dreaded Washington bureaucracy, his words are telling for what they reveal, or at least suggest, about his mind-set at the time. First, he cut off lines of inquiry from others; second, the use of the term, "interfering with what we do here," is pretty exclusive and self-focused. Bremer not only exhibited dismissive attitudes toward the Iraqis but also systematically worked against the sending of cables about happenings in Iraq to the White House, the State Department, and the Pentagon. By cutting these popularly constituted governmental organizations out of the loop, Bremer almost single-handedly directed the affairs of Iraq. Bremer's modus operandi, however, had an even more devastating consequence because he instructed Stephen Hadley, Secretary of State Rice's deputy at the National Security Council, to amputate the decision-making process so that he could avoid the usual vetting process that cabinet officers typically employ, according to Chandrasekaran ("The Lost Year," 2007, p. 2). In this way, Bremer narrowed further the already scrupulously narrow interest of those in charge of the war in Iraq—decisions what would later have serious consequences for the Iraqi people and for America's image abroad, as I will discuss later.

Second and equally concerning is the fact that Bremer refused to "assemble a team filled with all of the smartest Arabists and post-conflict specialists in the U.S. government." He didn't want people who were more senior, according to *Frontline* ("The Lost Year," 2007). Bremer didn't want a resilient line of communication flowing from "some ambassador level person" in Iraq to Colin Power or Richard Armitage ("The Lost Year," 2007, p. 3). The danger, of course, of this type of reductionism is that the interests of the Iraqi people receded in the background while the wishes and agenda of Bremer and the United States commanded the foreground.

Career diplomat James Dobbins ("The Lost Year," 2007), in an interview with Bill Moyers on *Frontline,* depicted Bremer as "a very competent, decisive, articulate, very funny, very amusing person with a sharp sense of humor" but also as a person with no "actual experience in nation-building." Here, if we accept Dobbins's view, we see the expansion of American interests in the directorship of Bremer, who was selected to head the Provisional Authority with little hard thought about whether he knew enough of the right things to support and uphold Iraqi interest. In this regard, one is forced to ask whether the strongest power in the world placed little emphasis on specific, expert credentials for the man who would lead major nation-building efforts in Iraq. There was more going on here, and it was the fact that the historic transformation of Iraq was constructed out of both ideology and hubris.

A Narrower Focus

Because the Bush administration was certain that Plan A would be operational, other, more substantive things were managed cavalierly, in addition to selecting a man with no prior experience in nation building. Plan A was that "the Iraqi government would be quickly decapitated, security would be turned over to the remnants of the Iraqi police and army, international troops would soon arrive, and most American forces would leave within a few months. There was no Plan B" (Packer, 2005, p. 118). To what extent was this rose-color, "shock-and-awe" mentality invisible to the very people who were supposed to be rescued in the first place?

Dobbins believes that one of the central reasons why the Bush administration failed to address doubts about success of the military operation was because "they short-circuited the interagency process" ("The Lost Year," 2007, p. 5). The usual way that a president communicates with senior staff—weighing and considering evidence, vetting alternative proposals, using an open and fair exchange of ideas, and arguing robustly—was compromised in the Bush administration. And, of course, a central flaw in the structural proceedings was that Bush "made his mind up early, before he had fully heard all of the arguments" ("The Lost Year," p. 5).

Furthermore, as Dobbins observes, "Responsibility for preparations for the post-conflict phases were transferred from State and the (U.S.) Agency for International Development (USAID) to the Defense Department." This meant that the thrust and parry of debate, or the "process of adversarial debate between advocates and critics of Iraq policy," was increasingly more difficult to sustain ("The Lost Year," 2007, p. 5).

Another dimension of the narrowing of the lens on Bremer's watch also comes into play in this way: Lt. General Jay Garner had been in charge of operations previously and took a slower, more inclusive approach to the multitudes. Garner was mindful that the sovereign will of the United States and the sovereign will of Iraqis were not necessarily congruent in all instances. According to Chandrasekaran, Secretary of State Rice had to think of creative ways to get information about what was going on in Iraq under the leadership of Bremer. Chandrasekaran notes, she had "somebody reading the CPA Web site trying to see what decisions Bremer made that day" ("The Lost Year," 2007, p. 2). The fact that so much power over the lives of so many people accrued to one man boggles the mind precisely because of empathetic inattentiveness.

Intensification of Inattentiveness

Berman (2006), in his book, *Dark Ages America: The Final Phase of Empire*, offers one further possible implicit explanation for why Bremer was selected to head the Provisional Authority in Iraq. "Part of imperial psyche," according to Berman, is "utter contempt for Third World peoples" (p. 223). This is a serious but indicting way of saying that in the eyes of some diplomats and governmental officials, Third World people don't really count because elites know what is best for them—hence, inattentiveness and the absence of abundant other-regarding moral behavior. It is hard to imagine Secretary of State George C. Marshall going into Germany after World War II with a mission of rebuilding Europe after Hitler's murderous reign of terror with "very little planning, very little staffing . . . having to improvise and make things up as he went along," as was the case with Bremer, as Dobbins indicates in his *Frontline* interview with Bill Moyers ("The Lost Year," 2007).

Still another dimension of empathetic inattentiveness is revealed in the leeway that Bremer was given in the Green Zone—the place of refuge for upper echelon officials responsible for the day-to-day operations of the war in Iraq. This is indeed a complex enterprise, and I cannot do it justice here; however, a few examples should suffice. Because Secretary of Defense Rumsfeld and other members of the Bush administration had high, exhilarating hopes for the outcome in Iraq, one of the first things that they did was to secure the oil fields in Iraq. In all fairness to Bremer and his cadre of men and women, despite the "exercise in heroic amateurism" and the fact that everything in Iraq was "improvised," "hundreds of dedicated, courageous Americans went and filled positions for which they had not the slightest preparation," as Dobbins argues ("The Lost Year," 2007, p. 9). However barren the preparation, it is important to note that empathy characterized some aspects of Bremer's organizational men and women.

But consider what happened in the Green Zone that contributed to a lack of proper empathy in Iraq. First, the people who were responsible for making the decisions that would affect the eventual outcome of the war lived in barbed wire–enclosed spaces and places, apart from the very people they had gone to Iraq to help—for whatever ideological and, understandably, security reasons. The pristinely walled-off concrete compound dubbed the Green Zone led Mahmud Ahmed, an Iraqi citizen "with thick black hair and a thin mustache," to say of the zone, "This doesn't feel like Iraq. . . . It feels like America" (Chandrasekaran, 2006, pp. 22, 23). In Ahmed's observations, one sees the close association between "an archive of roots and place" an "archive of fond memories and splendid achievements that inspire the present" (Tuan, 1977, p. 154). As Yi-fu Tuan (1977) notes, "Place is permanent and hence reassuring to men, who see fragility in himself and chance and flux everywhere" (p. 154).

The intimate connection implicit in Ahmed's comment and the geographic separation—despite security risks—spoke volumes about closeness and proximity, sameness and difference, and caring and not caring. Dobbins paints a pretty lackluster picture of the goings-on inside the Green Zone. Some of the workers "didn't know where their home office was," while others "didn't know who the person at the next desk was." Furthermore, workers "weren't sure exactly what they were supposed to be doing, who they were supposed to be working for" ("The Lost Year," 2007). The absence of consideration of Iraqis is further dramatized by a numerical imbalance in Iraq. According to Naomi Klein (2007, p. 347), Bremer's staff consisted of only 1,500 people to govern 25 million Iraqis. By contrast, Haliburton had "fifty thousand workers in the region, many of them lifelong public servants lured into the private sector by offers of better salaries" (p. 347). These numbers are striking for what they reveal about inattentiveness and about an imbalance between U.S. means and purposes.

But perhaps stretching empathy to its limits, according to Dobbins's testimony, American workers did not have an office in Washington where they could call and say, "How did we do this last time? Remind me, how do I fill out this form? How do we train a police department? What are the mechanisms that we have for building political parties? What are the options for getting electricity back on?" In fairness to the process that Bush followed, perhaps there was insufficient time for advisers to scurry throughout a piercingly charged political and emotional climate so near the aftermath of 9/11. History should judge this ("The Lost Year," 2007, p. 9).

Despite this caveat, Dobbins's striking questions go to the heart of human kindness and concern. They illustrate convincingly how isolation, distance, elite ideologies, ineffective structures, and the psychology of human interactions can blind individuals to the good and create a moral vacuum that even extended to the food that was served in the Green Zone. "The fare was always American often with a Southern flavor" (Chandrasekaran, 2006, p. 9). It is most telling that Iraqis had to "handle food that they deemed offensive," as Chandrasekaran (2006, p. 12) observes. Apart from these concerns, there is an equally significant issue. And it is how Ambassador Bremer responded to the first burnings that he observed in Baghdad. Reports suggest that once Bremer was driving around the city (Baghdad), and he "sees burning everywhere and says, 'Oh my God, what is this?' And his people reply: 'It's the looting.'" Then, Bremer recommended a solution: "Let's shoot the looters" ("The Lost Year," 2007, p. 10). Stories of Bremer's seemingly callous disregard for the people of Iraq are also supported by other observers and pundits.

According to Packer (2005), when he asked Eli Pariser, a 22-year-old contributor to Moveon.org, whether the wishes of the Iraqi people should be considered, Pariser replied tellingly, "I don't think that first and foremost this is about them as much as it's about us and how we act in the world" (p. 85). This is an incriminating but astute observation from a 22-year-old from Maine because evidence clearly tilts in that direction, especially when one considers the interplay among personalities, organized thought, geography, and an absence of sufficient input from Iraqis.

Split Between Fact and Value

Pariser made his comments in February 2003—at a time when the Bush administration was carefully orchestrating matters about Iraq that would result in a big split between fact and value. Because Al-Qaeda struck the World Trade Center on September 11, 2001, and because Bush officials were keen to justify toppling Saddam, they began to fashion arguments that would sustain both their ideology and their claims. In this way, as we shall see, one can get a sharper understanding of how claim-making behaviors can drive human beings at the expense of the other and at the expense of empathy. Clearly, as evidence overwhelmingly reveals, there were no WMDs in Iraq. But what pattern of ideas and events led to the ultimate decision to go to war in Iraq? I have already discussed the extent to which Iraqi exiles played a role in the events leading up to war. What remains is for me to outline some key reasons why a president of the United States was willing to go to war with little visible regard for Iraqis—the very people who would suffer greatly, from restrictions on electricity (in some instances 6 hours of access per day) to the amputation of their middle-class livelihood to an inability of people to go about their daily business in free and undisturbed ways in cities and towns, especially in Baghdad. By October 18, 2006, electricity levels in Baghdad were at the lowest since the U.S. invasion ("Think Progress," n.d., p. 22).

Obsession with a big idea about the virtues and value of democracy, as well as capitalism and freedom, served as key reasons why advocates of war in Iraq turned a blind eye to the relationship between fact and value. Bush and his men and women were driven by a messianic cast of mind. By messianic cast of mind, I mean that they were imbued with the idea that they must go forward and save the world from itself, starting with Iraq. A messianic cast seizes the minds of advocates, gives them a single-purpose orientation, and imbues them with heady ideas of inclusion and exclusion—all tailor-made to place the object of change in the background because purpose becomes the overarching motive that drives the messianic mind. This helps to explain why the other can be short shrifted at such seemingly beautiful moments; it also explains how and why universal abstractions can lead people astray—away from the path of moral uplift.

In their zealotry, the Bush administration separated fact from value, starting with the issuance of the October "Joint Resolution to Authorize the Use of the United States Armed Forces Against Iraq" (2002). In the joint resolution, Bush argued that Iraq had "large stockpiles of chemical and biological weapons" and "demonstrated its continuing hostility to the United States." Bush also maintained that Congress had "taken steps to pursue vigorously the war on terror" against "members of Al Qaeda, an organization bearing responsibility for citizens and interests, including the attacks that occurred on September 11, 2001," and that Iraq was responsible for concealing "international terrorist organizations that threatened the lives and safety of American citizens" ("Joint Resolution," 2002, p. 2). In this way, the administration created the impression that Iraq had worked universally against the interests of the United States and concealed the fact that America was instrumental in bringing Saddam to power (Johnson, 2004, p. 223).

While it is not within the purview of this book to detail specific ways that this happened, it is valuable to point out, as an aside, that the Central Intelligence Agency (CIA) orchestrated events in Iraq and "supported the anti-Communist Ba'ath Party's efforts to bring Kassem's (General Abdel-Karim Kassem) republic to an end" (Johnson, 2004, p. 223). This led to the rise of young Saddam Hussein. Such events occurred in large part because the United States was involved in an active cold war with the Soviet Union. But a crucial point is that in Bush's "Joint Resolution" and in the war against Al-Qaeda, it was necessary for proponents of the Bush doctrine to suppress such matters and create a tie-in between Al-Qaeda and Saddam's regime, despite America's past involvement in CIA-sponsored activities.

Bush's naming of the enemy as "terrorists" and "terrorist parasites"— his claim that Iraq had "plotted to develop anthrax, and nerve gas, and nuclear weapons for over a decade" and that the "regime" had "something to hide from the civilized world," that North Korea was a country "arming with missiles and weapons of mass destruction while starving its citizens," and that Iran "progressively pursues these weapons and exports terror, while an unelected few repress the Iranian people's hope for freedom" ("President Delivers," 2003, p. 2)—led him to the following conclusion: These three countries constituted an "axis of evil" aiming to threaten the peace of the world. Bush's depiction of the political enemy and construction of the Other are examples of how governmental practices and narrative framing of the enemy, backed by cultural heritage and a compelling vision, can elide focus on real human beings—making possible war, whether just or unjust. Of course, employing the enemy as a foundational element in the relationship between values and war is an ancient one. From Greek city-states in the 4th-century B.C.E. to Nazi Germany in the 20th century to the war in Sudan in the 21st century, governments have skillfully employed the common and recurring theme of the enemy as reasons for organized killing. Such strategic ideological framing, augmented by a compelling vision of what the world "ought" to be like, has rarely elevated the standards of empathy. Evidence indicates that Bush and his supporters rarely stopped to ponder what the Iraqi people wanted at their moment of freedom, despite the monstrous acts of Saddam.

Bush's constant demonization of the enemy serviced by technology, weaponry, war making, and a cleansing of the body politic diminished the moral fiber and magnified the clear-cut clash between totalitarianism and democracy and between good and evil. After all, Saddam was a "brutal dictator," was producing "germ warfare agents" and "methods of enriching uranium for a bomb." These alleged facts were corroborated by the International Atomic Energy Agency and the British government. Bush also used testimony by three Iraqi defectors to support his argument regarding the production of germ warfare ("President Delivers," 2003, p. 2).

In March 2003, at a National Press Conference and using the weight of science and logic, Bush again maintained that Saddam was hiding "biological and chemical agents." He also suggested that the CIA, Federal Bureau of Investigation (FBI), and other security organizations had proof positive that Saddam was a bad guy with wicked intent, which was a very real threat not only to America but also to the world. Of course, we now know that the January statements were forerunners of his March 18, 2003, declaration of war speech against Saddam. He claimed that "events in Iraq have now reached the final days of decision"; outlined a temporal grid regarding the long, arduous efforts of other nations to disarm Saddam; alleged that Saddam used "diplomacy as a ploy to gain time and advantage"; noted that "the regime has a history of reckless aggression in the Middle East"; and declared that Saddam was a threat to the United States. These claims are significant because they demonstrate that words repeated often enough can take on a "fact-like" aura and undermine other-regarding behavior, but not necessarily because the users of such ideology are evil incarnate. Rather, because at the symbolic level, this is a powerful guise or way that political capital is transferred from leaders to the multitudes, creating asymmetry between the real and the ideal and between life and death.

Democracy for Iraq

Bush's political worldview is also valuable for what it reveals about his thinking. First, Bush suggested, loosely and in a tangential way, that there was a connection between Al-Qaeda and Saddam, but he is very clear about his concerns; they are for "the American people and our friends." He was transparent about the "terrorist threat to America and the world" but not specifically to the Iraqi people. Later, however, he is mindful of the Iraqi people who are "deserving and capable of human liberty" and who can "set an example to all the Middle East of a vital and peaceful self-governing nation." But Iraqi interests seemed peripheral and secondary to American interest.

We see, in this regard, that a biopolitical agenda-setting mission on the part of Bush and members of his administration created a new genealogy of action, which, to their way of thinking, was a condition necessary for realizing democracy in Iraq. Thus, it was vital for Bush to employ such universal abstractions as "the just demands of the world," "the power and appeal of human liberty," and "the greatest power of freedom is to overcome hatred and violence" because they created the impression that this is what all people want! And while it is generally true that people seek freedom over tyranny, Bush's political matrix operates at a consultative level—that is, his words suggest that a poll had been taken in Iraq and elsewhere and that the overwhelming majority of people in Iraq and worldwide had signed on to his brand of peace and democracy. Separation of fact from fiction largely omits valorizing Iraqis.

Widening Circles

In the previous section, I argued that the Bush White House used inattentiveness and a disjunction between fact and fiction to construct a landscape of action for the Iraqi people. These conclusions lead to three crucial questions. Where did Bush White House habits of mind lead? To virtue? Or to newer and more robust forms of terrorism and insurgency?

Straight away, it should be noted that the integrated primary assumptions underlying Bush's universalistic abstract values with their rendering of the world in such contrastive, bipolar terms as good and bad, virtue and vice, and democracy versus tyranny produced generous amounts of optimism. And nowhere was this optimism more evident than in the expressed belief that following the toppling of Saddam Hussein, Americans would be welcomed throughout Iraq. Three days before the start of the Iraq War, Vice President Cheney declared on NBC's *Meet the Press,* "We will, in fact, be greeted as liberators" (Daalder & Lindsay, 2003, p. 153). The sheer force of a simple line, "we will, in fact, be greeted as liberators," cast the Iraqis "in the role of awed spectators, first by U.S. military technology and then by its engineering and management prowess" (Klein, 2007, p. 347).

Of course, many Iraqis assumed that "having suffered through the sanction and the invasion . . . that they had the right to benefit from the reconstruction of their country—not just from the final product but from the jobs created along the way" (Klein, 2007, p. 355). But that was not to be. Klein (2007) maintains that rather than reconstructing Iraq, Bush policies resulted in "wiping of the country's industry," a potent symbol of cultural pride for Iraqis (Klein, 2007, p. 355). Furthermore, according to Klein, "Only fifteen thousand Iraqis were hired to work for the U.S. funded reconstruction during Bremer's tenure, a staggeringly low figure" (p. 355). Such neglect fostered ill will between Americans and some Iraqis, including insurgents from neighboring countries. Although Iraqis gained a great deal of freedom following the removal of Hussein, they soon confronted a harrowing local situation. There was no electricity to cool the homes and cook the food, security was soon disappearing, and there was no gasoline for their cars.

A huge consequence of a messianic narrowing of views was military and policy planners' focus on the end result of the mission rather than on both process and product, or the end game. Daalder and Lindsay (2003) argue that the Bush administration made mistakes because it believed that "its goal was to remove a regime, and the postwar problems would all be America's" (p. 152). But this was not the case, however, as General Garner soon found out. "We thought we would be walking into functioning ministries, that we would fire the Baathists in the top jobs, and get the trains running again in a couple of months," said Garner (Daalder & Lindsay, 2003, p. 152). Statements such as these suggest a deep, robust optimism in America's notion of how progress should occur and a belief that the Iraqi landscape was something to be written upon—much like Rousseau's tabula rasa. In other words, things would redound to America's good—a prototype for American business as usual in Iraq. Ministries would function, trains would run on time, and the Iraqi army would be put to work cleaning the surly streets of Baghdad.

But the mission of Baghdad took on an entirely different cast from that imagined by the ideology in which it was rooted. Instead, looters ransacked government offices, destroying the files and data central to governing, as Daalder and Lindsay (2003, p. 153) note. Iraqi policemen also reverted back to what their culture and mores dictated, including the taking of bribes and the use of arbitrary force.

Terrorism and Insurgency

So, instead of being greeted as liberators, Bush planners confronted a deteriorating situation in the form of Sunni Arab resistance, most especially in and around Baghdad. This opened the way for a widening circle of insurgents who began the work of terrorism. By January 17, 2004, five hundred U.S. soldiers had died in Iraq ("Think Progress," n.d., p. 5). Despite the Bush administration's insistence that America was winning the war in Iraq, both guns and ideas misfired, and Al-Qaeda and insurgencies enlarged the circles of attack. When the regime collapsed, "a large power vacuum naturally emerged," and a "festival of cruelty" ensued. Never had the absence of moral sense resounded more loudly in the world than in Al-Qaeda's and insurgencies' widespread use of sectarian violence. Much of the violence was directed against the Shi'a population of Iraq. Abu Musab al-Zarqawi and his followers demonstrated precisely how far extreme brutality and spectacular cruelty can extend. On February 28, 2005, a suicide car bombing in Hilla killed at least 122 people and wounded 147 more. On October 24, 2004, Iraqi police recruits were ambushed at a false checkpoint, and 49 people were killed. On May 17, 2004, suicide car bombings killed Governing Council President Izzedin Salim (Anti-Defamation League, 2009).

Vicious beheadings and burnings also occurred. Glover (2000) observes that "the instrumental uses of torture and other kinds of cruelty are not enough to explain their prevalence or the artistry with which they are carried out" (p. 33). "Deep in human psychology, there are urges to humiliate, torment, wound and kill people," avers Glover (2000, p. 33).

Nowhere is the import of Glover's words clearer than in the beheading of American journalist Daniel Pearl. Pearl wrote for *The Wall Street Journal* and was murdered in 2004—at the height of unspeakable violence in Iraq. He was kidnapped in Karachi, Pakistan, in January 2002. The murder and the brutal way in which it was carried out held appeal for those who love violence and abhor empathy for other human beings' suffering. Furthermore, appeals to violence lie in the special urgency that such acts can symbolize. In a twisted way, the horrifying drama and descriptions of cruelty surrounding the beheading of Pearl functioned as some sort of curious sanctification for adherents to both the brand of Islam and the followers of such men as Khalid sheik Mohammed, who carried out the beheading. To demonstrate the specialness of the cruelty, mixing hatred with religious symbolism, Mohammed bragged, "I decapitated with blessed hand the head of the American Jew."

In the final days of Pearl's life, his throat was cut, and a shocking video of Pearl's murder was circulated around the world. Ritualistically, the murder of Pearl was reenacted by a camera operator who had not recorded it earlier, according to the British *Telegraph* (Ansari, 2004, p. 1). That was part of the ritualistic appeal of violence in the name of Allah. Two of Pearl's Pakistani bodyguards witnessed the cutting. "Before he was murdered, they forced him to relate his Jewish background and sympathy with detainees in Guantanamo Bay before putting the knife to him, then again, a second time, owing to the faulty camera," one of Pearl's bodyguards said (Ansari, 2004, p. 3). One of the persons present at the beheading recalled his feelings: "When they were slaughtering him in front was a bad dream. I had seen the cutting of a goat or chicken many times, a human being slaughtered in front me" (Ansari, 2004, p. 3).

Embedded in the symbolism is also a manifestation of power not only over Pearl but over other victims as well. In effect, Mohammad and his cohorts turned the murder of Pearl into a lesson in the genealogy of killing. This is indeed the lesson embedded in most beheadings and violence carried out by Al-Qaeda. In one instance of unspeakable horror, to teach lessons to humans who might be inclined to confront its authority, Al-Qaeda "cut their face (family members) off with piano wire in front of their family and then murdered everybody except one child who told the tale afterwards," according to Lieutenant James Danly of U.S. Military Intelligence. On February 21, 2007, five people were killed and more than 55 were injured in a car bomb explosion in Baghdad. And on July 9, 2007, the death toll from a suicide truck bombing in a small village in northern Iraq was 150, "one of the deadliest single bombings, if not the deadliest, since the 2003 invasion" (*The New York Times*, July 9, 2007).

Embedded in these killings was a message based on Koranic and Islamic teachings and on a warped interpretation of what it means to be a human being living within the freedom and limitations of civil society. The savagery of Al-Qaeda and other insurgents can also be understood against the canvas of religion and a zeal for the enactment of one brand of Islam. Al-Qaeda believed that it was, in some fashion, representing the wishes of Islamic people and opening up the way for a means of identifying themselves in contradistinction to what America and the West are not. Hence, the typology of evil.

Like Saddam Hussein, then, Al-Qaeda's acts of violence were designed to change the grand narrative of history in the service of ideological goals and not in the service of empathy. And the consequences of a lack of empathy extended further and deeper across the historical landscape.

Trouble Sites: Israel, Iran, and Hezbollah

By all accounts, Israel, Iran, and Hezbollah played and continue to play a central role in shaping human perceptions of empathy in global affairs. Violence in Iraq, the beheading of Pearl, and discourse related to Iraq all are intertwined with Israel. In this section, I want to show how competition among memory, space, and place can undermine the primacy of humans' decent obligations to one another and simultaneously become a natural complement to violence and ugliness. Israel, Iran, and Hezbollah will be used to demonstrate the undermining of a central content of morality: "to be effectively other-regarding we must, at some crucial point, where the fate of persons is decided, directly perceive and appreciate them" (Selznick, 1992, p. 201). In the case of Israel, Iran, and Hezbollah, other-regarding behaviors are tested precisely because competing memories exist regarding who owns the state of Israel. While this clearly is not the only reason, and there are many complex and various things associated with such trouble sites, memory space and time play commanding roles. As Bernard Lewis (2004) observes, Palestine "is a region of ancient civilization and of deep-rooted and often complex identities" (p. 154).

Let us consider briefly how British policy in the Middle East is implicated in the tensions among Israel, Iran, and Hezbollah, as well as the consequences that flowed from it that greatly undermined other-regarding conduct.

After World War II (in reaction to Hitler's reign of terror in Europe and in response to British and French imperial systems that still were intact in Libya, Syria, and Lebanon),"in . . . Palestine, British withdrawal led to a defeat for the Arabs when the state of Israel was created," Hourani (1991, p. 351) explains. A result of the resolution of conflicting interests created "lasting relations between the Arab peoples and the western powers" (Hourani, 1999, p. 358). Much of the conflict in May 1948 occurred as a consequence of Britain's unsuccessful attempts to quiet Jewish demands for a state and the potential opposition that would emanate from the Arabs, who "were fearful of being subjected or disposed," Hourani (1999, p. 359) argues. Furthermore, according to Hourani, "Britain's close relationship with America, and American pressure from its larger and politically active Jewish community, tilted matters in favor of Jewish immigration and statehood" (p. 359).

These series of associations and attitudes also ensured that Palestine would become an important issue on the world stage, creating a fragility of empathy. Because Arabs and Jews could not resolve the matter of statehood for Israel and for Palestine, Britain decided to turn the issue over to the United Nations. As a result, the United Nations produced a plan of partition on terms "more favourable to the Zionists," according to Hourani (1999, p. 359), at least that was and still remains the perception of many Arabs.

These attitudes and actions paved the way for Israel to declare its statehood on May 14, 1948. From 1948 to the time of this writing, huge conflicts between Israel and its Arab and Islamic neighbors continue. For a number of reasons that are fraught with competing narratives about what happened, how, and under what circumstances, about two thirds of the Arab population left Palestine and became refugees. Lewis (2004) points out that "the failure of Arab states and armies to prevent half a million Jews from establishing a state in the debris of the British Mandate for Palestine—all the more of a shock" (p. 154).

Furthermore, almost 75% of Palestine became a part of Israel, stretching from Gaza to the Egyptian frontier. According to Hourani (1999, p. 360), what was left of Palestine was annexed by the Hashimite Kingdom of Jordan, under the auspices of a treaty with Great Britain. The annexation had a huge impact on human relations in that part of the world. Finally, Jerusalem was partitioned between Israel and Jordan.

Hezbollah

Struggles over national genealogies were much affected by these political and cultural events, extending to the founding of Hezbollah, the "party of God," in 1982 following Israeli occupation of Lebanon. War occurred in Lebanon in 2006 primarily because the Palestine Liberation Organization (PLO), which had been expelled from Jordan, had moved into southern Lebanon. This led to Hezbollah's suicide assaults against the Israelis, rearticulated through the metaphor of "occupation." Murders, tactical suicide bombings, assassinations, and other acts of violence occurred under the leadership of Sayhed Hassan Nasrallah, its secretary-general. Using fragments from Arabs' historical relationship with Israel, Hezbollah turned to the land, a common ground theme around which other Arabs acting in solidarity could rally. Literature suggests that one aspect of "The Hezbollah Program" is to put "an end to any colonialist entity on our land" and to "stop imperialistic infiltration onto our country," as Hezbollah discourse reflects ("Hezbollah," n.d.).

Hezbollah's original 1985 manifesto is replete with the religio-cultural dynamics of formations between land and people. "We are," the manifesto reads, "linked to the Muslims of the whole world by the solid doctrinal and religious connection of Islam." Elevating its Islamic Shi'a ideology, the manifesto also states that "the party of God" was "made victorious by God in Iran." In this way, evoking Ruhollah Musawi Khomeini, leader of the Islamic Revolution of Iran, Hebollah constructed a bridge-like common human link among Shisim and with many who identified with Islamic culture, lands, and people. The manifesto recognizes the poetics of "either soil or blood," to use Gilroy's (2000, p. 111) instructive language, as techniques for fostering solidarity with one group and setting up boundaries for lessening empathy for others. Hezbollah's founding manifesto also cuts a large swath across Muslim land and people from "Muslims in Afghanistan and Iraq to the Philippines and elsewhere" that "reverberates throughout the whole Muslim umma of which we are (Hezbollah) an integral part" ("Hezbollah," n.d., p. 4). Forging linkages of common solidarity is thus essential to Hezbollah's waging of a jihad against Israel.

To demonstrate the ferocity of commitment to the destruction of Israel and the maintenance of what is regarded as Arab land, Hezbollah's leader Nasrallah said, "I am against any reconciliation with Israel. I do not even recognize the presence of a state that is called 'Israel.' I consider its presence both unjust and unlawful. That is why if Lebanon concludes a peace agreement with Israel and brings that accord to the Parliament our deputies will reject it. Hezbollah refuses any conciliation with Israel in principle" ("Hezbollah," n.d., p. 5). Nasrallah's words locate a powerful nexus among memory, place, and space and why people are willing to sustain strong attachments to soil and rootedness at a great cost to humanity.

More significantly, through a mastery of the language of attachment, Nasrallah manages to create cultural warrants to justify both communicative and violent actions against Israel. By cultural warrants, I mean "beliefs, laws, and customs that allow people within a given culture to justify their communicative actions and behavior" (Calloway-Thomas, Cooper, & Blake, 1999, p. 42). Speaking violence into existence, Hezbollah, according to some reports, has been responsible for the hijacking of TWA Flight 847, the kidnappings of Americans, and the killing of Israeli civilians, and it also has been accused of the 1983 Beirut barracks bombing that killed more than 300 American and French peacekeeping troops. Hezbollah was helped by the efforts of Iran, which sent about 1,000 Islamic Revolutionary Guard Corps into Syria and the Bekka valley of Lebanon to aid war efforts against Israel.

Other Connections

Connections to land also have a special meaning for Israel because the state of Israel is a physical embodiment of a memory shared by Jews throughout the Diaspora. Like Dr. Martin Luther King Jr.'s metaphorical promissory note of a promise of freedom for Black Americans, Jews believe that they are heirs to a land that led to their expulsion from Palestine by the Romans more than 3,000 years ago. Friedman's (1989) idea that "the Jewish people's reconnection with their land and their building of a modern state there have opened up a whole new set of options for defining oneself as a Jew—some of which were totally unknown in the Diaspora" (p. 285)—is clearly applicable.

Despite the four major schools of thought associated with the Diaspora, from "being back in the land of Israel" to "the ultra-Orthodox, non-Zionist Jews filled with the awe of God," all feel a closeness to Israel, as Friedman (1989, pp. 285–287) observes. The land of Israel as an important symbol helps to explain the Israeli invasion of Lebanon in 2006. Acting in self-defense and in defense of soil, nothing better dramatizes the resilience of a defense of land and country than the number of cluster bombs that Israel dropped on Lebanon. Regardless of the geopolitical reasons for the cluster bombs, in such instances, "human responses are weakened" (Glover, 2000, p. 35). Amnesty International reported that "hundreds of thousands of children in Lebanon did not start school on time" in November 2006 because "theirs had been destroyed or because they had fled their villages after losing their homes" (http://web.amnesty.org/wire/November2006/Lebanon, p. 1).

Commenting on damage that can occur as a result of the use of "indiscriminate weapons," Kenneth Roth, executive director of Human Rights Watch, reported on the killing of 60-year-old Maryam Ibrahim inside her home and a taxi driver's loss of both legs caused by the cluster munitions and the wounding of his five children, ranging in age from 3 to 12 years of age. Furthermore, according to Human Rights Watch (2006), Israel's "use of cluster munitions in populated areas may violate the prohibition on indiscriminate attacks contained in international humanitarian law" (p. 3).

Bombs rained down on the Lebanese people, entailing human misery and wretchedness on largely innocent women and children. The point of these stories is to illustrate that rival narratives can cause humans to use tit-for-tat behavior that frees the actors to show disrespect for others' dignity. In the presence of Hezbollah and Israeli violence, how can empathy assert itself? Regardless of the reasons for who owns what land, the soil wars between Israel and its neighbors are implicated in America's occupation of Iraq. The moral erosion deeply affected the empathy that the world extended to America in 2001.

America's Image Abroad

"In Iran, 60,000 soccer fans and players held a minute of silence. In Germany 200,000 expressed sorrow at the Brandenburg Gate—where the Germans came together after the Berlin Wall fell." And "in Nairobi, site of a 1998 bombing of the American Embassy, the word *pole* (Swahili for "sorry") [was] on the lips of many Kenyans" (Marquand, 2001). Such was the outpouring of sympathy for Americans after 9/11. Not since post–cold war times had Americans been interlocked so well with what had happened to them. There was almost universal solidarity—spiritual and figural—with America as a towering giant that had been attacked in a brutal manner by Al-Qaeda. In keeping with our moral sense, we are appalled by acts of horror and instantly identify with those who have been wronged. A good deal of evidence suggests that leaders, countries, and people who disliked American foreign policy in specific ways were willing to embrace the United States because, as Daalder and Lindsay (2003) argue, "The United States is a uniquely just and beneficent great power" (p. 80). At least that was where the perception of things stood in 2001.

Later, however, because of America's involvement in Iraq, because of Bush's "go it alone" policy, and because of America's antiterror actions, the U.S. image abroad began to decline. By December 2002, Pew Research Center reported that "despite an initial outpouring of public sympathy for America following the September 11, 2001 terrorist attacks, discontent with the United States has grown around the world" ("Public Diplomacy," n.d.). By March 2003, on the eve of the Iraq War, global surveys from nine countries revealed that "anti-war sentiment and disapproval of President Bush's international policies" continued "to erode America's image among the publics of its allies" ("Public Diplomacy," n.d., p. 19).

Such attitudes coincided with and followed Bush's neglectful attitudes toward the larger global community. In his January 2003 "State of the Union Address," Bush used the metaphor of an "axis of evil" to refer to Iran, Iraq, and North Korea. America had stared in the face of evil, and for Bush, there was no turning back in efforts to overcome "the diabolical evil" of North Korea, Iran, and Iraq. For this reason, as evidence suggests, it appears that Bush and members of his administration were keen to remedy the messiness of the world that had been, in their minds, created by an "axis of evil."

By invoking the metaphor of evil and by reaching for what members of the Bush administration viewed as high watermark values in pitting—both explicitly and implicitly—civilization against barbarity and evil against nonevil, Bush did two things that robbed America of the feelings of goodwill that had been evident after 9/11. First, the metaphor, "an axis of evil," marked both a real and a symbolic change in the events of human history. A new period had begun in terms of how the world would view America, in large part because Bush had pressed human attitudes too far. It is hard to scramble from hard ground to soft ground when no alternatives are apparent in such socially pacifying but ossified talk about the nature of evil.

Second, the Bush administration applied visions of good versus evil, civilization versus barbarism, and bad people versus good people directly to the global scene. The single-purpose messianic perspective, as I noted previously, shaped America's worldview, but in the instance of image breaking, the tough stance that Bush took almost simultaneously exposed a cultural chromosome that would have grave implications for America geopolitically. In this instance, the idea of deviltry in Iraq and other places contributed to Bush's belief that he had inherited a mandate from the American people to search to the ends of the earth for Osama bin Laden and Al-Qaeda. Emboldened, Bush set loose an "America is an imperial power" mentality capable of slaying any dragon—but one that excluded other nations. But how far would fire from the dragon reach? And what risks were involved in the mobilization of war? Let us consider the implications of Secretary of State Colin Powell's political theater.

Survey Data and America's Image

When Secretary Powell gave his groundbreaking speech before the United Nations in 2003, it was clear that the United States was imparting information and setting the record straight. Accordingly, Powell's role before the United Nations was to "tell" nations what was "going to be" and what America "was going to do" to ensure America's course of action ("U.S. Secretary of State," 2003). This meant, then, that the goodwill and social capital that earlier had accrued to America were turned upside down and inside out. Thus, in June 2004 (15 months after the invasion of Iraq), "a fundamental change in transatlantic relations" was likely under way, according to "Transatlantic Trends" ("Public Diplomacy," n.d., p. 17).

The survey also showed that "while Europeans and Americans still shared many common values, Europeans remain[ed] very skeptical of a strong U.S. leadership role in the world." According to the report, 58% of Europeans wanted "a more independent approach for Europe on international security and diplomatic affairs" ("Public Diplomacy," n.d., p. 18). By April–May 2005, the image of America was "up slightly," but a Pew Global Attitudes Survey revealed that countries still held negative views of America. America was "broadly disliked in most countries surveyed," most especially in Europe, the Middle East, and Asia ("Public Diplomacy," n.d., p. 16). By June 2006, America's image had declined even further. The Pew Global Attitudes Survey reported that the war in Iraq accounted for many damaging opinions of America, not only in predominantly Muslim countries but also in Europe ("Public Diplomacy," n.d., p. 13).

The same poll noted that a year earlier, anti-American images had begun to abate somewhat because of the benevolent contributions North Americans made to tsunami victims in Indonesia and Thailand. James Q. Wilson's (1993) observation that "our sense of another's feelings and of their appropriateness given the circumstances—is the basis of our judgment. More bluntly, to sympathize is to judge" (p. 32). It was precisely this type of sweet generosity that elevated others' perceptions of America after 9/11. At the same time, the charitable giving on the part of Americans is part of what Selznick (1992) refers to as moving from the "significant other" to the "generalized other, "from the 'we' of affinity to the 'we' of humanity—all are expressions of a quest for community *that looks outward rather than inward*" (p. 196). This aspect of empathy will be dealt with in Chapter 6, but for now, it is useful to observe that Americans' embrace of strangers in Indonesia and other places symbolized dramatically that the former not only was a part of humanity but was willing to bring others into their precious orbit.

Nowhere does a less than sunny negative outcome of America's image abroad show itself more lucidly than in falling perceptions of the country. In 2006, favorable opinions of America had fallen in most of the 15 countries surveyed. For example, America's image fell from 71% to 56% in India and from 38% to 30% in Indonesia ("Public Diplomacy," n.d., p. 14). Plummeting positive regard for America in 2007 surely mirrored the way in which Bush administration officials imposed their views on the world, and 2006 was undoubtedly "one of the bloodiest" years of the war with Iraq. Most critically, the credibility of America regarding Iraqi possession of WMDs was seriously eroded.

Newspapers, television pundits, military officials, and former governmental officials all corroborate the fact that Hussein did not possess weapons of mass destruction. And as a consequence, President Bush's rationale for why America went to war slipped away, resulting in a sorely damaged credibility. America itself was revealed in the way these events unfolded, even as Bush proclaimed that the Iraq war had reached "a turning point" and even as Rumsfeld elevated his decibel level by declaring that war critics were "quitters" who "blame America first" for giving "the enemy the false impression Americans cannot stomach a tough fight" ("Think Progress," n.d., p. 20).

The undermining of the Bush administration's credibility and the very contradiction that accompanied it go far in explaining the persistence of the incantatory discourse that was most non-other-regarding. I mentioned this great contrast between the said and the done before, and I emphasize it here again because it goes so far to explain why trust in America waned even more precipitously. Echoes of Rumsfeld's sure-fire confident and discordant discourse undoubtedly echoed and reechoed worldwide. Three years earlier, in March 2003, Rumsfeld had uttered in very specific, confident terms, "We know where [the weapons of mass destruction] are. They're in the area around Tikrit and Baghdad and east, west, south and north somewhat" ("Think Progress," n.d., p. 1).

By January 2007, according to a BBC World Service poll of more than 26,000 people in 25 different countries, more than 73% disapproved of how America dealt with the war with Iraq. Even more critically, more than two thirds of those surveyed felt that America's presence in the Middle East created more conflict than it had resolved. Seventeen percent said that U.S. troops had a destabilizing force in the Middle East. A year later, the *International Herald Tribune* said, "The ebbing of positive views of the United States coincides with a spike in feeling that the war in Iraq has made the world a more dangerous place" (Knowlton, 2009, p. 1). The 2006 statistics also demonstrate a great contrast between America's image before it went to war with Iraq and its image after the war, and the statistics also reveal how a non-other-regarding U.S. foreign policy helped transform America as a moral force in the world for good into an almost exclusionary world policy on the part of the Bush administration.

Based on an interpretation of statistical data, the key symbols of America as a rich, balanced mixture of social practices that elevate democracy, notions of freedom, liberty, and rationality were being compromised. This waning of America's image, to be sure, has its concerns. Most explicit, this damage is manifest in comments from Andrew Kohut, president of the Pew Research Center: "Obviously, when you get many more people saying that the U.S. presence in Iraq is a threat to world peace as say that about Iran, it's a measure of how much Iraq is sapping good will to the United States" (Knowlton, 2009, p. 2). The crucial question, however, is whether Bush administration officials had a sufficient effort of imagination to grasp the impact of the war on people worldwide but most especially on the people in Iraq. Failure to do so led to spoils of empathy. But how is the world grappling with others in our midst, across borders and in areas of immigration? How are we managing the multitudes who are occupying geographic spaces that challenge such factors as resources, attitudes, population, and other factors?

4

Immigration

Empathy's Flickering Flames?

The Coming: Before Global Immigration

"Our ancestors . . . never had to deal with all of humanity as a factor in their daily lives," write Burke and Ornstein (1995), "because for most of history they only knew a small number of individuals going about their particular activities in a very small world" (p. 280). Burke and Ornstein also remind us that our primeval ancestors had no need to consider the entire planet because it was "too big to have any meaningful impact" (p. 280).

Today, however, individuals in remote areas of the savannah are influenced by events in mega-cities around the globe. "Meanings, messages, and people" are circulating worldwide at unprecedented levels. Human beings are leaving indigenous places and spaces, searching for economic security, fleeing persecution, and being dispersed by ethnic conflict and war. Alkman Granitsas (2006) reports that "there are almost 200 million international immigrants, more than double the 84 million of 30 years ago" (p. 2). This great encounter with diversity contributed to the attack on September 11, 2001; the assassination of Theo van Gogh; the killing of Afghanistan's Northern Alliance leader, Ahmad Shah Massood; and terrorism in general. Four hundred years ago, the human species had not spread as rapidly, and conflict between what Freidman (1999) refers to as "lexus and olive tree worlds" was held in abeyance primarily because a multiethnic, multiracial society had not become a reality. But what happened?

To understand the interplay among immigrant loyalties, traditions, and empathy, let us examine, however briefly, the Treaty of Westphalia (1648) and other events that contributed to the present situation. I argue that the Treaty of Westphalia was a foundational event that sheds light on the ongoing frictions occurring between immigrants and nonimmigrants today. This perspective suggests that the transition from one historical moment to another should be understood as a continuum rather than as one marked event in time. The perspective suggests, furthermore, that even though the Westphalia system is not the only reason, it nevertheless sowed seeds for cross-border fragmentation in the 21st century, as we shall see.

The Treaty of Westphalia

The Treaty of Westphalia or the Congress of Westphalia is, as Jennifer Jackson Preece (1997) notes, "conventionally taken as the dividing line between the medieval and modern periods in the conduct of international affairs" (p. 75). Scholars maintain that the treaty was responsible for the creation of nation-states and that it provided a transition from the old world to the new. If we look especially at Europe prior to 1648, we find a world of sovereigns who are in turmoil and constant strife and embroiled in a Thirty Years War with the Holy Roman Empire. Prior to 1648, the Holy Roman Emperor reigned supreme, bounded by the Catholic Church. Westphalia marked the end of the Holy Roman Empire and the rise of such countries as France, the Netherlands, and Sweden, the latter more briefly than the former.

Although some of the politics involved in the establishment of nation-states was evident in England, Spain, France, and Sweden earlier, the creation of sovereign states diminished the influence and reach of the Catholic Church. Prior to 1648, all roads literally led to Rome, and the papacy held sway over many peoples, who, at that time, did not distinguish in theory and practice between church and state.

The tightly knit Catholic Church grounded identity in a structure that both favored and manipulated kings, potentates, and empires, thus ensuring that a great deal of empathy would be attached to the Church and those who were a part of it. The Church, in conjunction with Saint Augustine, who firmly believed that people were divided into those who were favored and those who were not, "defined the attitude that would direct Western society through the centuries of confusion that lay ahead" (Burke & Ornstein, 1995, p. 96).

As we know, a vexing issue in the 17th century was a competing doctrine between Catholicism and Protestantism. Prior to the 1517 epoch-making Protestant Reformation, the Catholic Church's ideology functioned as a tool for manipulating and controlling the secular rulers of Western Europe and, by extension, their subjects (Burke & Ornstein, 1995, p. 97). This tool helped to ensure that empathy's blessings would accrue to those who could read and write, most notably the clergy. Thus, there was a symbiotic relationship between church and state—between the clergy who could read and write and the kings and princes who relied on the former to assist them with executive matters. As Burke and Ornstein (1995) argue, "It was easy for the church, primarily through its monastic communities and bishops, to control an illiterate world" (p. 98).

The Westphalian system undermined the Catholic Church, "weakened papal authority," and "solidified national sovereignty" (Farr, 2005, p. 1). A huge consequence of the Westphalian system is that it altered the power dimensions of human relationships invested in Catholicism and encouraged cooperation between aristocrats and monarchs, fostering "mutual cooperation" (Farr, 2005, p. 2). Although financial incentives clearly played a role in generating synergy between the latter two wealthy groups, this transfer of loyalty away from the Catholic Church facilitated a human empathetic mission because after Westphalia, people were free to be French, English, Austro-Hungarian, and the like. Furthermore, the transference subverted some of the loyalty that had been imposed by the Pope, especially in the domains of language and nation-states.

But most significant is the patriotic-producing aspect of this newly formed system, especially its coupling of empathy and passion. Particularly revealing is how words, slogans, flags, and other symbols that became a part of nation-states were used to galvanize publics around national symbols. The symbols, in turn, held many cultures together and broke others apart. As I noted in the introductory chapter, in the 1990s, when Yugoslavia disintegrated over ethnicity and culture, Milosevic appealed to ancestry, myths, and memory to sustain Serbians during their conflict with other cultural groups. Later, in the 20th and 21st centuries, the universal human propensity to turn symbols into intense modes of loyalty would jeopardize one's fellow-feeling, one to another. As recently as October 23, 2007, Ambassador James Bissett (2007) claimed that the origins of the global framework for dealing with ethnic turmoil in Kosovo date "back to the peace of Westphalia in 1648 which ended the horrors of the religious wars that devastated Germany and other parts of Europe for more almost half a century."

Westphalia: Revolutions, Politics, and Immigration

The changes that occurred as a result of Westphalia should concern us for two other significant reasons. First, it paved the way for both the American and the French Revolutions that aligned the rights of the state with the rights of man. Locke's 1689 *Essay Concerning Human Understanding* and his essay "On Liberty," with their compelling support of human toleration, set in motion cataclysmic revolutionary human events and gave to the world concepts of natural rights as opposed to the rights of princes. Locke sensibly maintained that since God was the creator and maker of us all, no human being had a right to govern the will of another based on ancestry. Of course, Locke left open a door for governing based on collective political rights. However, by decoupling state rights from human rights, Locke ushered in a notion of the "consent of the governed" that animated Thomas Jefferson, George Washington, and the band of revolutionary men who fomented a successful rebellion in North America in 1776 against the tyrannical rule of Great Britain—a rule based on natural rights and not rights peculiar to kings, queens, and potentates.

As I will note later in this chapter, the same rights that inhered in the French Revolution of 1789, with its rallying cry of "liberty," "equality," and "fraternity," would haunt France in the 21st century when Muslim youths rioted in the suburbs of Paris in 2005.

The Treaty of Westphalia concerns us for another reason: how more mature nation-states, once organized and formed into more stable "imagined communities," dealt with the presence of the other in their midst, that is, with immigrants. Following divisions into nation-states, the issue of what to do with and how to manage minorities and immigrants came to the foreground, that is, how to welcome strangers. After World War I, nation-states had to grapple with nationalities that emerged out of the "defeated Ottoman, Habsburg and Hohenzolelrn Empires in the East-Central Europe after 1919" (Preece, 1997, p. 81).

The political impact of these population changes was significant. Political leaders charged with rearranging geopolitical borders populated by complex and various humans soon discovered that the job of homogenously reconstructing the post-1919 boundaries of East-Central Europe was "virtually impossible" for many reasons. A major reason is the fact that the former ruling elites—Hungarians and Germans—remained in their original places sowing seeds of resentment and hostility over their loss of power and influence.

This paralyzing attitudinal frame of mind, in turn, bred ethnic tensions among people in Poland, Romania, Czechoslovakia, and other places dependent on newly constructed nationalistic discourses. Again, the Treaty of Westphalia is implicated because in 1919, issues of what constituted nationhood reemerged and tampered with empathy's powers. Questions also arose, such as should a nation-state be defined on the basis of language, ethnicity, culture, or all of these factors, and how could the task of empathizing with others along such lines be maintained.

History further records that World War II also played a vital role in ushering in discourses and feelings surrounding immigration and immigrants. Although the sociocultural factors following the defeat of Germany and other Axis powers in 1945 are nuanced, a push for a fresh start among peoples in Europe has affected empathy and immigration. Poverty; deflation; price supports; a power struggle in Russia following Joseph Stalin's death in 1953; the granting of independence to India, Pakistan, and Burma in 1947; oil interests in the Middle East; and the exodus of Jews from Europe to Israel all figured prominently in the spatial and cultural rearrangement of Europe between 1945 and 1948.

Although it is important not to overstate the importance of such factors and events, they contributed to empathy's flickering flames. As immigrants from Palestine, Pakistan, Africa, and other places rushed into Europe in search of work, and as Europeans "opened wide freedom's gates," the sociocultural outcomes proved to be daunting. But not in all cases, however. The single market of the European Union encouraged a movement of people across borders, encouraging individuals to immigrate from poorer to wealthy regions. A major consequence of this migration, as Judt (2005, p. 732) notes, has been a transfer of resources to poorer countries, which helped to eliminate the "aggregate gap" between rich and poor. Not surprisingly, other intercultural benefits of such global flows include travel, exchange of ideas, and increased study at universities throughout Europe.

Immigration: The Changing Environment

If we detour to the United States in 1789, the year that witnessed the ratification of the Constitution following vehement debates over the principal arguments for and against its adoption by Patrick Henry, James Madison, Benjamin Franklin, and other "founding brothers," one can understand how American leaders skillfully managed newly arriving individuals. In 1789, the young country was eager to define its core cultural and political self, and for this reason, but not exclusively, American leaders insisted that the beliefs, attitudes, behaviors, values, religion, and ethnic makeup of immigrants entering the country most resemble the people who were already there. One reason for this insistence, as Huntington (2004) observes, is that leaders had to "define America ideologically to justify their independence from their home countrymen," that is, from Britain (p. 38).

This helps to explain why the ethnic makeup of America stayed so close to the European model from 1789 to 1960 and why Americans more easily welcomed individuals from Ireland and Scandinavian countries but were not as eager to welcome people from Eastern Europe (Buchanan, 2006, p. 91).

One should not, of course, overlook America's generosity of feelings toward Indians at the beginning of the Plymouth and Massachusetts Bay settlements in the 1620s. Boyer et al. (1996) remind us that in the spring of 1621, Pilgrims and English-speaking Indians, including Squanto, a Pawtuxet Indian, were friendly and civil toward one another. This was indeed a memorable moment in the history of North American empathy. But the era of good feeling was short-lived because "the colonists became the dominant partner, forcing the Indians to acknowledge English sovereignty" (Boyer et al., 1996, p. 48). This occurred despite the fact that Indians "taught the newcomers how to grow corn" (Boyer et al., 1996, p. 48).

Boyer et al. (1996) question whether Indians were as keenly interested in acts of kindness or had come up with a technique to prevent Plymouth settlers from stealing corn from Indians. Although these human impulses might have been present and partly expressed through practical motives, moral sentiments were in the right place and at the right moment. Later, however, the settlers drew even sharper land boundaries between themselves and Indians, "hasten[ing] the colony's militarization under the leadership of a professional soldier, Miles Standish, who threatened Plymouth's Indian 'allies' with its monopoly of fire power" (Boyer et al., 1996, p. 48). In the final analysis, Indians were given a choice of a public policy based on expulsion or one based on extermination, and President Andrew Jackson worked vigorously on behalf of extermination and Indian removal (Takaki, 1990).

Of course, Indians were not immigrants because they were in America long before the first settlers arrived. The confrontation between the two groups is mentioned here because of the curious connections and treatment of a group already occupying a spot of ground and the group's demise as a result of the coming of another clan, whether that group (Pilgrims) is viewed as "settlers" or as immigrants. Notwithstanding the "metaphysics of civilization" and "the red race on our (United States') borders" (Takaki, 1990, p. 80), the implications of the era of cooperation between Indians and Plymouth settlers are apparent: "the possibility of a multicultural society in America," even though that possibility "was not to be revived for three hundred years" (Huntington, 2004, p. 53).

Confidence in American empathy also manifested itself again in 1900, with immigration reaching a peak in 1914. But at the time, the wave of immigration was met with more restrictions and limitations from Congress in the form of literacy tests and an ideology of "Anglo-Saxonism" that found uncompromising expression in the writings of such scientists as Josiah Strong and Lothrop Stoddard. Fearing that the United States was in great peril from "hordes" of immigrants coming from Southern Europe with their "strange" habits, ignorance, immorality, and Roman Catholicism, Strong elevated the clash between "the dangerously poor" and the "dangerously rich" (Takaki, 1990, p. 260). Strong's high-intensity, empathy-undermining discourse highlighted the blight and bruises that were occurring among immigrants, including their residence in congested cities. Strong believed that the wretched conditions under which such immigrants lived fueled the ambers of socialism and "threatened the republican society of individual liberty" (Takaki, 1990, p. 260).

It did not take long for Strong's discourse to reflect virulent prejudices and for the discourse to reach back to John Winthrop's "city upon a hill" shipboard sermon in which the latter proclaimed that America "shall be as a city upon a hill, the eyes of all people are upon us" (Bercovitch, 1978; Takaki, 1990). Winthrop's shipboard sermon meshed well with Strong's announcement that "we (Americans) deem ourselves a chosen people" and "incline to the belief that the Almighty stands pledged to our prosperity. Probably not one in a hundred of our population has ever questioned the security of our future. Such optimism is as senseless as pessimism is faithless" (qtd. in Takaki, 1990, p. 261). Thus, aspects of immigration discourse during the 1900s continued to reflect exclusionary ones and sentiments of Anglo-Saxon culture and society. And if the United States followed a line of reasoning based on Strong and Stoddard, it was clear that American culture should adhere to narratives and ideology rooted in legal and normative principles that privileged English civilization with its exclusionary tenets.

Social and Legal Impact on Immigration

An aftermath of Strong's and Stoddard's ideology is also reflected in the course of action that Congress took to limit immigration from Eastern Europe in 1921. According to Huntington (2004), as a result of "a permanent ceiling of 150,000 immigrants a year and country quotas based on the national origins of the U.S. population in 1920," "82 percent of the slots were assigned to northern and western European countries and 16 percent to southern and eastern Europe" (p. 57). As a result of a deliberate policy, the United States effectively shut off a huge flow of immigrants from Southern and Eastern Europe, raising serious questions about America's ability to "cross over and experience, in the most profound way, the very being of another—especially the other's struggle to endure and prevail in his or her own life journey," to use a quote from Jeremy Rifkin (2004, p. 271).

By 1924, North American attitudes regarding who should come to its shores began to change somewhat, despite the fact that many Americans did not hold favorable views of immigrants. U.S. President Franklin D. Roosevelt is credited with inaugurating a symbolic change in attitudes toward American immigrants when he declared in 1938, "Remember, remember always, that all of us, and you and I especially, are descended from immigrants and revolutionists" (Huntington, 2004, p. 38). Thirty years later, President John F. Kennedy repeated the memorable line in his book, *A Nation of Immigrants,* published posthumously (Huntington, 2004, pp. 38–39). Even today we hear echoes of Roosevelt's comments in the hard-edged debate over immigration issues. The most constant refrain given for the opening of the U.S. borders to Mexicans and other immigrants is that "America is a nation of immigrants," an inclusive and humanity-affirming statement that fosters goodwill among humans.

A beautiful feature of Roosevelt's provocative discourse is its signaling of empathetic potential. Endowed with a favorable attitude toward immigrants, many Americans were given new reasons to pay attention to strangers in their midst, despite the "Charter group" emphasis on "the effective possessor" of the land having "the most to say" about societal values and structure and despite Huntington's (2004) argument that "in its origins America was not a nation of immigrants" and that it "was a society, or societies, of settlers who came to the New World in the seventeenth and eighteenth centuries" (p. 39). Notwithstanding Huntington's strict interpretation of historical events, President Roosevelt's rhetoric effectively contributed to a turning away from the "settler" mind-set to an embracing and a more spacious orientation toward immigrants, as manifested in President Kennedy's comment.

It is the case, however, that from 1820 to 2000, about 66 million immigrants found their way to America, creating a highly heterogeneous society in terms of religion, ethnicity, and ancestry, as Peter D. Salins (1997) notes in his work, *Assimilation, American Style.* The early decades of the 19th century witnessed a decline in immigration to the United States to about 8% of the country's population in 1800. The year 1870 marked a spurt in the number of immigrants coming to the United States and was accompanied by a shift from immigrants coming largely from Western Europe to immigrants originating in Southern and Eastern Europe (Starr, 2004, p. 233).

A significant change occurred in America as a consequence of "the effective shutting off of significant immigration from eastern and southern Europe," and it "paradoxically contributed to the virtual elimination of ethnicity as a defining component of American identity" (Huntington, 2004, p. 57). Although Huntington's (2004) language suggests that there is something less than desirable about "the virtual elimination of ethnicity as a defining component of American identity," the rupture underlines a crucial point: "In the long sweep of human history, what becomes clear is that the human journey is, at its core, about the extension of empathy to broader and more inclusive domains" (Rifkin, 2004, p. 271). But a significant question arises from the apparent death knell of "ethnicity as a defining component of American identity": Did emphasis on Anglo-Saxon ethnicity have to die so that the march of empathy could continue?

Public Space and New Immigrants

I am uncertain as to whether many scholars and laypersons alike would answer the question in the affirmative, but it is clear that mainstream Anglo-Protestant culture has created public space for other cultures and groups, including Indians, Asians, African Americans, and a host of other ethnic people from the 220 nations that comprise the global community, if we accept Harold "Bud" Hodginson's statistical rendition. In a lecture at Walden University, Hodginson argued that America has a representative from each of the 220 nations living within its borders. Using such numbers, one can argue that this movement represents a new form—at least a new level—of empathy in the United States. The crucible of the issue is, of course, another matter all together because the alchemy of ethnicity and race is still being melded in the 21st century. The reality of immigration is here, however, and it is changing the political and cultural environment in America and elsewhere.

No set of numbers better exemplify the shift in empathy's cultural direction than in the wave of immigrants coming to the United States from south of the border. And some North Americans are pretty exercised by the coming, including author and journalist Patrick Buchanan (2006). To make his oppositional case against illegal immigrants, Buchanan offers the following stunning statistics: "In 1960, America was a nation of 180 millions, 89 percent of whom were of European ancestry, 10 percent blacks, with a few million Hispanics and Asians sprinkled among us. Ninety-seven percent of us spoke English" (p. 36). Lamenting the numerical and ethnic shifts occurring in the United States, Buchanan worries about movement away from America's Anglo-Saxon-dominant culture. He writes, "Though of two races, we were of one nationality. We worshipped the same God, studied the same literature and history, honored the same heroes, celebrated the same holidays, went to the same movies, read the same newspapers and magazines" (p. 36).

But Buchanan (2006) leaves out of his cultural weeping the fact that during the 1960s, many Blacks were also marginalized—pushed to the corners of culture and voiceless. His constant refrain of the "same God," "same heroes," "same holidays," and "same newspapers and magazines," effectively works against inclusion because by definition and implicitly, diversity sanctions inclusion writ large. Is Buchanan surrounded by echoes of his own voice?

Immigration in Europe

On the contrary, Buchanan (2006) is not alone in his outcry against immigration. Across the pond in Europe, the cultural environment is also changing in favor of inclusion and consideration of the other, although there clearly are some bumpy roads ahead. Such writers as Rifkin (2004) embrace the change, while journalists Claire Berlinski (2006) and Mark Steyn (2006) are very concerned about immigrants and immigration. "Menace in Europe," cries Berlinski, and "America Alone, The End of the World as We Know It," thunders Mark Steyn (2006). Berlinski finds Europe in the "grip of . . . [a] strange passivity" that finds expression in

> the new ordering principle of European society—a form of weak rationality, a kind of utilitarianism. Europeans now obey their authorities not because they rule by divine right, nor because those authorities promise a utopian future, but because law and order are preferable to chaos and anarchy. . . . Social and moral structures in Europe are now, essentially, bureaucratic structures. (p. 31)

Steyn (2006), in calling attention to the shrinking fertility rates in Europe and other places such as in Canada and Russia, which are "running out of babies" (p. xvi) as a result of fertile immigrants coming from North Africa, the Caribbean, and the Middle East, warns that

> by 2050, 60 percent of Italians will have no brothers, no sisters, no cousins, no aunts, no uncles. The big Italian family, with papa pouring the vino and mama spooning out the pasta down an endless table of grandparents and nieces and nephews, will be gone, no more, dead as the dinosaurs. (p. xvii)

Such statistics undoubtedly give new meaning to and test the West's tolerance, as the end of this chapter makes clear. Why the dire predictions? And why has immigration led to this state of affairs? To give a fair answer to this question, let us consider the empathy of elites and the road that they have traveled in the long narrative of global immigration. The story here is one of preaching openness and inclusion, and it demonstrates that well-intentioned motives can have opposite and sometimes unintended consequences.

Empathy of Elites and Global Immigration

"White guilt—the need to win enough moral authority around race to prove that one is not a racist—is the price whites today pay for this history. Political correctness is a language that enables whites to show by wildly exaggerated courtesy that they are not racist," Shelby Steele (2003) writes in *The Wall Street Journal*. Implicit in Steele's comment is the idea that Westerners are indeed atoning for their many years of sinful ethnic oppression in such former colonial places as Algeria, Nigeria, Congo, and Zimbabwe and that this atonement has put Europeans, as well as North Americans, in a cultural cage, which makes it exceedingly difficult for them to escape culturally, economically, psychologically, linguistically, and socially.

Steele's (2003) comment also speaks piercingly to the dilemma that Westerners confront as a result of their postcolonial, post–civil rights sensitivity and period of openness and inclusion—all generously advocated by elites. On one hand, Westerners want and have extended a measure of sympathy to their former colonists, many of whom have left their former countries to settle in Europe. On the other hand, Westerners' fellow-feeling for immigrants escaping oppression, poverty, and disease from such places as Morocco, Algeria, Sudan, and other environs has put them in a terrible bind, one worthy of Prometheus unbound, thus complicating nets of empathy worldwide.

Claims of equal recognition by ethnic groups to the public square have their ideological and intellectual roots in the politics of universal dignity spawned by "the rapid growth of nationalist sentiment among a coming generation of activists throughout the empires except perhaps but in India, but even there citizens underestimated its scale and determination" (Judt, 2005, p. 279).

Judt (2005) also argues that "neither the British, nor any of the other remaining European colonial powers, anticipated the imminent collapse of their holdings or influence overseas" (p. 79). "Other remaining European colonial powers" include France, Germany, and Belgium. By the early 1960s, French colonies of Tunisia and Morocco; English colonies of Kenya, Nigeria, and Gambia; and Belgian colonies of Congo and Rwanda had secured their freedom. The newly freed countries added fresh meaning to principles of justice and equality. Former colonial people "changed the understanding of second-class citizenship" (Taylor, 1992, p. 39) such that by 1955, African Americans had taken some inspiration from their kindred spirits in Ghana and Kenya and had begun the civil rights movement of the 1960s in a push for human dignity and equality. Grassroots movements in Europe and the United States shared one central thing in common: a gargantuan need for equal respect and human dignity.

Elites on College Campuses

Although the nation-states in Europe and the United States felt a bit uneasy "with the idea of accommodating distinct cultures" (Rifkin, 2004, p. 247), elites entered the fray and began a sustained campaign to both recognize and include the dispossessed. Much of the activity occurred in the form of opposition to Western intellectual canons on university campuses. Writer and critic Roger Kimball (1990) dubbed this movement toward canonical inclusion "the assault on the canon" (p. 1). The term *canon,* as Kimball (1990) observes, "comes to us from the Roman Catholic Church, where it refers to an official rule or decree, a particular section of the Mass, or the list of canonized saints" (p. 1). Canonical application today refers to "the unofficial, shifting, yet generally recognized body of great works that have stood the test of time and are acknowledged to be central to a complete liberal arts education" (Kimball, 1990, p. 1).

A shift toward canonical inclusion simultaneously paved the way for academics, politicians, policy makers, and other elites to see real value in examining the robust relationship between canon and empire. Thus, students at such prestigious institutions as Brown, Berkeley, Harvard, Yale, Columbia, Princeton, and Stanford took notice; students at the latter school echoed the sentiments of their cohorts on other campuses across the United States as they chanted "Hey, hey, ho, ho, Western culture got to go" (Kimball, 1990, p. 28). Students at Stanford, for example, insisted that some Western courses be replaced by a series of courses called "Culture, Ideas, Values (CIV)." The action effectively eliminated the teaching of exclusive core courses with major excerpts from Socrates, Plato, Aristotle, Augustine, and other accomplished Western writers.

Professor Robert Scholes echoed the pregnant and historical role that hegemony had played previously when he said, "Where the Empire went, the canon and the Canon went too" (qtd. in Kimball, 1990, p. 5). Where Scholes saw in tandem a symbiotic relationship between empire and canon, even earlier, Allan Bloom (1987), using French Enlightenment and Catholic thought as streams of intellectual argument, saw chaos and destruction in the path that inclusive-thinking, empathy-promoting intellectual elites were taking. "The unity, grandeur and attendant folklore of the founding heritage was attacked from so many directions in the last half-century that it gradually disappeared from daily life and from textbooks," Bloom (1987) claims. "Openness to closedness is what we teach," according to Bloom (1987), creating "cultural relativism" that "succeeds in destroying the West's universal or intellectually imperialistic claims, leaving it to be just another culture" (p. 39). By implication, I am arguing that a substantive focus on canonical openness and interrogation of Westerners' hegemonic role in subjugating darker and black-skinned peoples coupled with public policy worldwide spilled over into issues of immigration and encouraged the United States, France, England, Belgium, Germany, and the Netherlands to become more attentive to the downtrodden and dispossessed among us.

Hegemony and Immigration

Speaking and writing in the rubric of postmodernism, with its emphasis on "grand meta-narratives, nation-state hegemony, and monolithic ideologies," scholars and public intellectuals began to argue that the "emphasis on single-perspective and unified visions only supports a colonial agenda that breeds intolerance of other views and spawns repression and violence against minorities at home and subject peoples abroad" (Rifkin, 2004, pp. 247–248). In light of such postmodern reasoning, Western countries began to change their behavior and social attitudes toward immigrants, but the change was not to be long-lived, given the appearance of terrorism in 2001, Al-Qaeda, Hezbollah, and train and subway bombings in Madrid in Spain and in England.

At the historical juncture of the 1980s and 1990s, however, elites played a crucial role in extending empathy into new domains of meaning and experience. Terry Eagleton (2003) implicitly pays tribute to that august group of academics and intellectuals when he opines that they aimed to "create space in which the dumped and disregarded can find a tongue" (p. 13). In 2000, according to Huntington (2004), "The British government's Immigration and Nationality Directorate estimated that about 30 million people were smuggled into countries worldwide each year" (p. 179). As Huntington observes, "Both poverty and economic development promote immigration, and the plethora and relative cheapness of transportation modes make it feasible for more and more people both to migrate and to maintain ties with their country of origin" (p. 170).

One should not, however, miss the complicating variables surrounding the issue of immigration; it is sanguine to point out that even though immigrants flowed into Western countries for a variety of reasons, the story here is that Westerners were more welcoming in contradistinction to what is occurring today. This is a meaningful distinction to make because in 2000, empathy's flame was burning more brightly, and immigration numbers attest to the fact: "In 1998, foreign-born people were 19 percent of the population in Switzerland, 9 percent in Germany, 10 percent in France, 4 percent in Britain, 17 percent in Canada, 23 percent in Australia, and 10 percent in the United States" (Huntington, 2004, p. 179).

Three Troubling Incidents

Liberal policies toward immigrants and emigration would, of course, come to trouble Westerners in a post-9/11 world, as I will demonstrate later. But for now, it is important to stress that countries in Europe were open and welcoming to immigrants. In commenting on the rise and death of conservative Dutch politician Pim Fortuyn in 2002, Harm de Blij (2005) records that "the Netherlands had by some measures been the most liberal and accommodating among those countries receiving Muslim (and other) immigrants, its social policies, including those relating to drugs that are illegal elsewhere, creating an atmosphere of freedom and comfort" (p. 172). By 2004, about 1 million immigrants had arrived in the Netherlands in an overall population of 16 million (de Blij, 2005, p. 172). Dutch openness is but one remarkable manifestation of elites' warmest regards for the sufferings of others.

Historical impetus of this phase of empathy was begun after World War II when Germany, Belgium, Switzerland, and other countries lost so many young boys to war. To help promote labor shortages, the countries began to import labor from Southern Europe in the late 1950s and 1960s. Although cheap labor came from Turkey and North Africa, and this change was propelled along by economic interests, a level of ethnic and cultural tolerance was also evident.

According to the European Commission, by 1999, fully 19 million people, about 5.1% of the total population of European Union (EU) countries, came from non-European countries (Rifkin, 2004, p. 251). By 1994, however, tolerance of immigrants in Europe had begun to show signs of diminishing. "Only 21 percent of Europeans polled in 2000 considered themselves to be 'actively tolerant' of immigrants" (Rifkin, 2004, p. 250). Great Britain, which had long been tolerant of outsiders, had also become somewhat less tolerant of immigrants.

One event in particular cast a troubling shadow over the prospects for a sustained era of good feeling in parts of Europe—the murder of Theo van Gogh.

Amsterdam: Murder of Theo van Gogh

"Theo and I never actually met again, but we used to call each other from time to time. He ignored my pleas that he get protection, and even joked bout it. He told me, 'Ayaan, you have no idea. I've been threatened for fifteen years. Everyone has threatened me: the Jews, the Christians, the Social Democrats, the Muslims—they've done it the most—and nothing has ever happened to me. Nothing is going to happen'" (Ali, 2007, p. 317).

So commented Theo van Gogh to Ayaan Hirsi Ali, the controversial Dutch politician who, with van Gogh, made the movie *Submission,* which disturbed the very fiber of radical Islamic values. But something terrible, almost unimaginable, happened to Theo van Gogh, the great-great-grandnephew of artist Vincent van Gogh, on Tuesday, November 2, 2004. van Gogh was "shot, stabbed and slashed across the throat by a suspected Islamic radical" (Higgins, 2004, p. A1; see also Ali, 2007). A note "tacked onto Mr. van Gogh's chest with a knife included citations from the Quran in Arabic, but was written mostly in Dutch. It fulminated against 'infidels,' vowing death to Ayaan Hirsi Ali, a Somali-born Dutch legislator" (Higgins, 2004, p. A11).

When Ali (2007) learned that van Gogh had been murdered, she "started to cry . . . ran back to Iris's room, closed the door and tried to breathe." She "felt so helpless and shocked, so horrified" (pp. 318–319). Ali barely had time to collect her thoughts because she was also in grave danger. Her security detail appeared and warned her, "We have to leave, now" (Ali, 2007, p. 319). In many places, political, economic, and cultural leaders on both sides of the Atlantic have put the issue of immigration on the front burner in a serious way, especially in light of post-9/11 fears of radical Islam and terrorism.

Empathy was being tested. Would newly arriving immigrants to the Netherlands and other parts of Europe also "have to leave now"? Did van Gogh's death weaken empathy's already fragile and flickering flame? Clearly, the murder of Dutch filmmaker van Gogh by a 26-year-old Dutch Moroccan, Mohammed Bouyeri, who found the film *Submission* offensive, exacerbated issues over immigration and caused some citizens to see the plight of the dispossessed in a different light. Steyn (2006) writes that "radicalized Islamic compatriots" were "expert at exploiting the 'tolerance' of pluralist societies" and that the murder of van Gogh and the bombings in Madrid and London "were the opening shots of . . . a European civil war" (p. 38).

Reactions to van Gogh's Murder

Stef Blok, a member of parliament and chairman of a committee that reviewed policies toward immigrants in the Netherlands, called the brutal killing of van Gogh "a rude awakening" (*The Wall Street Journal,* 2004, p. 1), and Berlinski (2006) warned that Dutch response to the killing was faithful to their tradition of "bargaining with depravity," "perversions of the noble Dutch tradition of accommodation and tolerance, one that dates from the Dutch Golden Age of the seventy century—the age of Erasmus and the birth of humanism—when Dutch art, trade, and science were among the world's most acclaimed" (p. 21). Implicitly, Berlinski blames Netherlands' elites for part of the "permissive" climate that gave birth to Bouyeri, who was born and educated in Holland but who often "in writings and speeches" made "crude jokes about Jews and riled Muslims with scatological insults" (*The Wall Street Journal*, November 22, 2004).

Most critically, the killing of van Gogh opened "Dutch eyes to threat of terror" (*The Wall Street Journal*, 2004, p. 1). It was an intercultural moment that the Netherlands had not quite counted on. As *The Wall Street Journal* notes,

> Like other former colonial powers in Europe, the Netherlands first drew immigrants mostly from former possessions. As the demand for cheap labor grew, a new wave of immigrants arrived from Turkey and North Africa. Initially, governments assumed they would one day leave. They didn't, and starting in the 1980s, the country switched towards a policy of assimilation. (Higgins, 2004, p. A11)

After the killing of van Gogh, a diminution in empathy occurred, and human consciousness took a different route. Western countries were forced to grapple keenly with their application of universal principles of brotherhood and sisterhood to unassimilated immigrants from North Africa, Turkey, and other places.

The Dutch government took some pretty drastic measures in response to the murder of van Gogh, including "deporting terrorist suspects, closing extremist mosques, and shutting down Islamist websites" (Berlinski, 2006, p. 29). Berlinski (2006) claims that despite police intervention and a few arrests, "Dutch politicians and civic officials displayed a public and almost parodic inability to recognize the significance of the murder or respond to it appropriately" (p. 29). By "respond to it appropriately," Berlinski is referring to the belief that a harder line should have been taken against Bouyeri. Berlinski is very clear regarding her stance on immigrants, symbolism, culture, and empathy: "In the aftermath of the murder, the stories of perverted tolerance multiplied," Berlinski regrets. To prove her case regarding an over-sympathetic Dutch response, Berlinski offers the following "now famous incident" as proof (p. 30).

Apparently, a Rotterdam artist, moved by anguish of the moment, created a mural inscribed with the following words: "Thou shalt not kill." Outraged by the words, according to Berlinski (2006), Moroccan youths "gathered around the mural and spat on it" (p. 30). When a local leader of a mosque complained to the police that the words on the mural were "offensive and racist," the mayor of Rotterdam "ordered the mural, not the Moroccan youths, removed by the police" (p. 30). Berlinski is most concerned about what she considers to be injuries to free speech in the land of Spinoza. According to her reckoning, this is proof positive of the damaging effects of an overwrought empathy surrounding issues of immigration and culture. Thus, the notion of tolerance in Europe is changing conceptual frontiers in significant ways. And the murder of van Gogh is symptomatic of what can be construed as a trend away from immigration and deep empathy for immigrants.

De Blij (2005), also in most discouraging antiempathetic tones, writes that van Gogh's murder "had a major impact on Dutch opinion and was a reminder of the consequences a single act of terrorism can have on the dynamics of society—a point undoubtedly not lost on those returning to Europe with the experience gained in Iraq and elsewhere" (p. 172).

One critical thing stands out considerably in de Blij's (2005) comments: the fact that van Gogh's murder was defined and treated not as a crime but as an act of terror. In this regard, the murder of van Gogh not only underlined issues of free expression and individual liberties inside Western borders but also contributed to the shaping of cultural discourse about difference and empathy. The discourse, in turn, placed upon Western cultures an enormous immigration dilemma. This would not be the last time within a period of 3 years that something like the murder of van Gogh would galvanize Europeans and cause them to reassess their empathetic stances. And the connections would, once again, be linked to immigrants and immigration, especially to Muslims. Thus, another incident contributed to the redistribution of empathy—one borne of Paris burning. Would the consequences be too grave for empathy?

Paris Burning: Rioting by Muslim Youths

In 2005, France was struggling to live up to its democratic principles and fully integrate its Muslims into all sections of national life. At least that was an ideological view prior to a wave of rioting that occurred in France in November 2005 following an October 27, 2005, incident involving teenagers Zyed Benna and Bouna Traore, who were electrocuted after climbing into an electrical substation in the Paris suburb of Clichy-sous-Bois. The youths were allegedly trying to hide from police, who were engaged in racial profiling, although policemen deny that that was the case. Following the incident, a wave of disturbances swept across France for about 3 months, challenging the social, political, cultural, and empathetic landscape of the country. By November 8, 2007, youths had burned more than 1,400 cars, authorities had brought into custody nearly 400 people, and at least 36 police officers had been wounded in Paris and other French cities, according to Edward M. Gomez (*World Views,* an international news and culture virtual magazine [http://www.sfgate.com/cgi-bin/blogs/worldviews/author?blogid=15 &auth=48]). Two days before the electrocution of Benna and Traore, French Interior Prime Minister and later president of France, Nicolas Sarkozy, visited the Paris suburb of Argenteuil to determine how measures were working against urban violence.

In assessing the social situation, Sarkozy said that "crime-ridden" neighborhoods (suburban areas typically referred to as *banlieues*) should be "cleaned with a power hose" and then described violent elements in Argenteuil as "gangrene" and "rabble." Straight away, Sarkozy employed disease metaphors to characterize the demonstrators, and his language manifested a fissure in French attitudes toward Muslim youths. His language also shed light on a serious problem in France and called into question the limits of empathy. As I noted in Chapter 1, during much of human history, human beings have identified most with those who are near and close. As a consequence, sometimes self-interest and threats to the well-being of others can strain the limits of moral resources. Such was the case with some French men and women following the riots of 2005.

The French newspaper *Le Figaro* reported asymmetry between the escalation of violence and the limits of tolerance for French youths, as evidenced by the discourse of conservative politicians who called for the French Republic to "unite" in the face of unrest by Muslim youths. *The Wall Street Journal* ("French Sissies," 2005) summed up the collective concern: "The riots have shaken France . . . and the unrest was of such magnitude that it has become a moment of illumination for French and Americans equally" (p. A10).

Included in the linguistic nets were immigrant youths of African, Arab, and/or Muslim background—all singled out because they not only looked the same but also were perceived as a threat to the civic and political order. The work of linguistic compression suggests that the sensibilities of the French were being sorely tested. Undoubtedly, the French were more than embarrassed because the unrest had called into question the distance between creed and deed regarding their attitudes toward immigrants and immigration.

The Wall Street Journal ("French Sissies," 2005) read into the rioting "some longstanding conceits about the superiority of the French social model" that had "gone up in flames" (p. A10). Alec G. Hargreaves (2007) claims that "the long and tortuous route through which anti-discrimination policy (in France) has gradually developed illustrates all too clearly weaknesses of French discourse of integration. For years, many politicians on both the left and the right denied that discrimination was a serious problem in French society" (p. 3).

Although the French Revolution of 1789 "improved the lives of the peasants," and soon after the revolution, "real freedom had begun to look

illusory" (Horne, 2005, p. 202), over the centuries, employing such symbolically potent and emotionally laded words as *liberté, égalité,* and *fraternité,*
France profited greatly from this compelling empathetic symbolism. Some
politicians "blamed the French 'integration' policies on the alleged unwilling-
ness of minority ethnic groups to be integrated into French society"
(Hargreaves, 2007, p. 1). This causal bifurcation of the failure of French integration and rioting by youths also carries an equally potent message about
immigrants and immigration—"a landscape littered with . . . failed policy initiatives and social models," according to Patrice de Beer (2005, p. 1).

"Failed policies" promoted a view of the world as rosier than statistics
and facts attest. At the time of the rioting, for example, unemployment
among immigrant youths in some areas was as high as 50%. This is a significant statistic when one considers the fact that the Muslim population in
France in 2005 was "five million out of a total of about 60 million" ("French
Sissies," 2005, p. A10). When the rioting occurred, I could hear strong and
resonant echoes of a friend's voice enveloping the event. Whenever a French
friend and I talked about race matters in the United States, she would quickly
and forcefully say in her beautiful accent, "We don't think in terms of race,
we don't talk about race. We are all French." My friend's fidelity to the ideology of France is testament to how well the ideology of France worked until
November 2005, when the veneer began to smudge. In fairness to the French,
one should bear in mind that France, in some ways, had tried, however,
abstractly, to adopt universal principles that could give support for empathetic practices. The question was whether other events in Europe added
more fuel to the flames of empathy. The historical dimension of discourse surrounding depictions of Prophet Mohammad brought other troubles and
placed them on empathy's shoulders.

Cartoons, Prophet Mohammad, and Empathy

In Chapter 1, I argued that myths—religious and otherwise—can be used to
justify our communicative behaviors. These may be Westerners' employment
of Christ's injunction to "Go ye therefore into all the world" and preach the
gospel in such far-flung places as Nigeria and the Philippines, or it may be a
Hindu's belief in a caste system that "has come to be the symbol of India's
own brand of human injustice, victims of a system that kept people alive in
squalor" (Gannon, 2003, p. 73).

Regardless of our fidelity to religious systems, however different, religion has a strong pull on human beings worldwide, primarily because a lot
of our identity is stored in religious symbols. And when fidelity to the expectations and tenets of a culture's religion is broken, and when dignity or

"standing in community" is broken or perceived to be broken, there can be damage to reputation, a diminution of harmony, an intensification of emotions, and a general feeling of not being understood.

On September 17, 2005, such emotions surfaced as a result of the publication of inflammatory cartoons depicting Prophet Mohammad in the Danish newspaper *Jyllands-Posten*. And it was the beginning of one of the most unpalatable and disturbing episodes between Islam and the West. Muslims generally expressed horror and outrage over the cartoons while Westerners saw violations of freedom of speech in the row over the cartoons.

Things did not bode well for empathy. However, before discussing some of the scorching rhetoric that surfaced after the publication of the cartoons, it is important to explain how and why the events unfolded as they did. In marked contrast to the Paris riots that were spontaneous for the most part, the cartoons were accompanied by willfulness and by implication, a "clash of civilizations." First, animating reasons for the event occurred innocently enough on September 17, 2005, when a writer could not find an illustrator for a book about the Prophet Muhammad. Taking up the perceptual cause of what was, to some Westerners' way of thinking, an utter disregard for freedom of speech—a principle of Western culture that dates back to the time of Socrates, who drank hemlock in defense of his right to freedom of speech—in response, *Jyllands-Posten* published 12 cartoon drawings of Prophet Muhammad (Fattah, 2006, p. A13).

Reactions to Cartoons

Jyllands-Posten's rhetorical act galvanized the Muslim community. Once communities across the Middle East learned of the "satirizing" of the Prophet, meetings took place among the world's 57 Muslim nations. In Mecca, the holiest of places in Islamic culture, leaders of the Organization of the Islamic Conference met and issued a joint communiqué that spoke to the abuse Muslims felt over the publication of the cartoons. Muslim leaders expressed "concern at rising hatred against Islam and Muslims and condemned the recent incident of desecration of the image of the Holy Prophet Muhammad in the media of certain countries" (p. 1).

In moral and cultural terms, it is important to note how Muslim leaders interpreted the incident as well as how they framed the language used to articulate their injury. Although the cartoons were most in contention, leaders employed spacious rhetorical framing that might have provided Muslims in the Middle East with just the reason they needed to present the case of the cartoons to the larger public. However, had Danish political leaders met earlier with representatives of Muslim groups, the outrage might have been confined to Denmark. Lebanese-born Ahmed Akkari, of Denmark, invited the Danish government to take action, but such action was not forthcoming (Fattah, 2006). In fact, for more than 2 months, Akkari and other Muslims worked to secure an audience with Danish officials; in the process, they collected 17,000 signatures and delivered them to the office of the prime minister. But still Danish political leaders did not grant Muslims a hearing.

Changing venue, in early December 2005, Akkari and others "decided then that to be heard, it must come from influential people in the Muslim world" (*The New York Times,* February 2, 2006, p. A13). At that stage, the group flew to Egypt and met with grand mufti Muhammad Sayid Tantawy; Foreign Minister Ahmed Aboul Gheit; and Amr Moussa, the head of the Arab League. Encounters with this heady group finally got the attention of the Danish ambassador, who was summoned to Cairo in Egypt for a discussion of the cartoons. Thus, for 2 months, grassroots Muslims worldwide remained unaware of the molten lava that was about to spread, and that would bring the "intolerableness of things" to the foreground and challenge empathy's heated impulse. To make matters worse, on January 10, 2006, *Magazinet,* a Christian newspaper in Norway, published the cartoons, using freedom of press as an ideological reason for doing so, causing Saudi Arabia to withdraw its ambassador from Denmark and initiate a boycott of Danish goods.

By late January to early February 2006, Western journalists and newspapers vied for the opportunity to demonstrate the primacy of freedom of the press. *The New York Times* (Fattah, 2006) reports that by early 2006, at least 14 countries had reprinted the cartoons, creating a smoky road for empathy. Here is where matters became very complicated. It was difficult for Westerners to accept the proposition that one could not, at a time when reason reigned, reprint cartoons in the interest of freedom of the press. Many Westerners believed that not doing so was an assault on reason itself. *The Wall Street Journal* (February 11–12, 2006) wrote that *Jyllands-Posten* and other Western dailies published the cartoons as "a way of addressing the Islamist threat to civil liberties in Europe" even though this was "hardly ideal" (p. A8).

Despite *The Wall Street Journal*'s seemingly empathetic portrayal of the events surrounding the publication of the cartoons in the *Journal,* the newspaper soon raised an argument of immense importance: the radicalization of two seemingly antagonistic cultural stances on the presentation of information: when, where, and under what circumstances. I am referring to the language of empathetic struggle borne of ideology that threw the event into sharper relief. That is, a stance on the role of church and state in furthering political ends and civic discourse and behavior. This is a second serious outcome of the publishing of the cartoons, coupled with a clash between premodern and postmodern cultural and political tenets and beliefs.

Bernard Lewis (2002) queries whether "Islam is an obstacle to freedom, to science, to economic development?" (p. 156). Furthermore, Lewis argues that the "inflexibility and ubiquity of the Islamic clergy" has a deleterious effect on not only postmodern progress but also on cultural perceptions of Muslims. In a sense, by implication, the problem with Westerners not empathizing fully with the aftermath of the publishing of the cartoons had a great deal to do with what Lewis terms "the place of religion and of its professional exponents in the political order" (p. 157).

And this is precisely where clergical rights and premodernism versus postmodernism enter the proverbial symbolic warfare between Islam and Western ideology. How could elites in the West empathize with an "obsolete, incompatible, weary and worn system" at odds with progress and everything that the West stands for? Did not a denial of the publishing of the cartoons and Muslims' resentment over the tampering with Western propositions about the nature of such precious virtues as democracy, equality, approaches to technology and information, and a myriad of other factors invite jeopardy?

Armed with beliefs in Western values of free expression, newspapers throughout Europe led with such headlines as "The Muslim Fury," "The Rage of Islam Sweeps Europe," and "The Clash of Civilizations" is coming (*The Wall Street Journal,* February 8, 2006, p. A16). Amir Taheri (2006) noted in *The Wall Street Journal* that the "rage machine" rumbled when the Muslim Brotherhood—a political organization that is virtually outlawed in Egypt—told sympathizers to "take the field"; translation: issue a fatwa against Denmark and Scandinavian consulates and shops.

Within days, Syrian Baathist, the Islamic Liberation Party, the Movement of the Exiles, and other Muslims with and without strict organizational ties made it excruciatingly clear that Prophet Muhammad could not be insulted and disrespected with visual depictions by the Christian West. Thus, notions of brotherhood and sisterhood were sacrificed to make Muslims conform to the commands of moral law. Some writers and scholars questioned the theological basis on which such injunctions were based. Taheri (2006) recited a long list of depictions of the Prophet from "a miniature by Sultan Muhammad-Nur Bokhari, showing Muhammad riding Buraq, a horse with the face of a beautiful woman," to "a painting showing Archangel Gabriel guiding Muhammad into Medina" (p. A16). Taheri, of course, omitted one important fact from his recitation: the power of geopolitical and cultural events to rearrange the furniture of the mind—creating, elevating, and intensifying issues that had lain dormant for years.

A Clash of Civilizations?

When one adds memory, history, ethnicity, and Muslims' perceptions of Western disdain and attempts to impose values of liberalism and freedom upon the Middle East, it is understandable why the narrative of Muhammad became more sociological and overlain with ecclesiastical and psychic tension. Furthermore, one can understand why empathy could not gingerly be inserted into the cultural climate and made manifest to those who saw ghosts of the Ottoman Empire, Suez Canal, and invasions of Afghanistan and Iraq assaults on Islam at every turn. Depictions of the Prophet Muhammad were rightly or wrongly seen as being of powerful Western instrumentation.

As I noted previously, the discourse of the West clearly reflected Muslims' intolerance of modern ideas of human, civil, and political rights. Muslims' reactions to the cartoons offered the best example of their disdain for Western notions of inclusion, mutual respect, and civility. Despite "Islam's Golden Age" and the fact that "Islam presided over a burst of exuberant scientific and philosophical inquiry" "for a few centuries at the turn of the first millennium," attentiveness to reasoning and such heady intellectual activities as "free-flowing inquiry and debate" had long since disappeared and served as a source of irritation between the West and Islam" (Murray, 2003, p. 400). Murray (2003) adds that "the burst of accomplishment in the golden age was aberrational, not characteristic, of Islamic culture" (p. 401).

Lewis (2002) writes that "in most tests of tolerance, Islam, both in theory and in practice, compares unfavorably with the Western democracies as they have developed during the last two or three centuries" (p. 114). In the eyes of some Westerners, including Murray and Lewis, both implicitly and explicitly, there is not a goodness of fit between an Islamic culture that devalues "free-flowing inquiry and debate" and Western culture that values it. Following this line of reasoning, a first requirement, and perhaps a harsh rule for the West to empathize significantly with Islam, is for the latter to push, however reluctantly, toward the West's and North America's "golden age." According to this line of thought, this is what the march of progress both invites and demands. This argument systematically and urgently pushes the outer limits of moral worth in the area of immigration. But what would this portend?

Western Culture and the Immigration Dilemma

Increasingly, immigration and immigrants are viewed as sounding the death knell for Western civilization. And something is straining empathy, as evidenced by the growing worrying titles of books coming out of the United States and Europe. Immigrants present "challenges to America's national identity" (Huntington, 2004), are "a menace in Europe" (Berlinski, 2006), are creating a "state of emergency" (Buchanan, 2006) and a "day of reckoning" (Buchanan, 2007), and are signaling "the end of the world as we know it" (Steyn, 2006). As these titles suggest, the intellectual tone of such writings is not especially calming. The rise of immigrants is particularly threatening to North America and Europe.

In his book *Who Are We?* Huntington (2004) argues pointedly that the "subnational, dual-national, and transnational identities" of the 1960s witnessed an erosion of "the preeminence of national identity" (p. xv) that September 11 "dramatically" helped to restore. But September 11 is symptomatic of a larger concern that confronts the United States. In particular, the primacy of "Anglo-Protestant culture, not the importance of Anglo-Protestant people," gradually is falling from view, and this should be considered dangerous, some argue.

Huntington (2004) laments the fact that a once-proud nation that was ever so faithful to "the Anglo-Protestant culture and the Creed of the founding settlers" (p. xvii) is being whittled away and is becoming marginal to the concerns of a great nation. The presence of immigrants coming from Mexico is changing America "into a culturally bifurcated Anglo-Hispanic society with two national languages" (p. 221) and toward "the demographic *reconquista* of areas that Americans took from Mexico by force in the 1830s and 1840s" (p. 221). In a word, Huntington, like Buchanan (2006), fears the "Hispanization" of American culture (Buchanan, 2007; Berlinski, 2006; Steyn, 2006).

Lessons Learned

Thus, the importance of demography as destiny is brought home in dramatic form in the numbers that both Huntington (2004) and Buchanan (2006) cite. Huntington notes, for example, that "about 640,000 Mexicans legally migrated to the United States in the 1970s, 1,656,000 in the 1980s, and 2,249,000 in the 1990s" (p. 223). The potency of these numbers drives home some crucial considerations and lessons about the relationship that obtains among "geography matters," culture, identity, and empathy. But what are some inflicted consequences?

The first one is the "not business-as-usual" lesson. During normal, business-as-usual cultural times, empathy can help to absolve differences. However, when numerical balance and such dynamic events as rioting in France, September 11, debate over Prophet Muhammad's cartoon, and other activities pose a threat to a culture, people hew very close to the center of Hume's concentric circles, toward the near and away from the intellectually and culturally distant. We saw such dynamics occur following the breakup of the Soviet Union and the demise of Yugoslavia in 1991. When Marshal Tito ruled Yugoslavia, Serbs, Croats, Slovenes, and Bosnians lived together in relative peace and harmony, not only because Tito ruled with an iron fist but also because matters of identity and memory were suppressed. However, after Tito died, people who had lived together peaceably returned to a fidelity of memory. Issues of nationality, identity, and culture reappeared. When elevated, such events present empathy with perhaps its greatest challenge and raise a bottom-line question about the causes, circumstances, and cultural imprinting of empathy. Does true empathy ever really exist across cultures, or does it merely lie dormant, waiting for an evocative opportune moment to become resonant again and act at will?

I raise this trenchant question because history is strewn with examples of nations and people living harmoniously with one another until issues of threat to the civic order or to cultural identity reemerge, creating havoc and exclusion at best and brutality at worst. The message that culturally the United States and Europe are not what they used to be is repeated with keen new intensity and interest daily by conservative writers and pundits. Identity, myths, and memory matter deeply and are implicated in the consequences that one little act can have on the stability of empathy. Empathy's mission, whether it can accept it or not, is to make people thrive more robustly during moments of heightened threats to the moral side.

The second lesson that immigration, Hispanization, and Islamization teach is that the arrival of new ideas, customs, and traditions in an original venue can undermine traditional ways of thinking, feeling, and being in another. Nowhere is this orientation more sharply felt than in what is going on in Europe and North America today. Once upon a time, in the 1960s, before the migration of peoples from Mexico to the United States and before the migration of peoples from North Africa, Asia, the Middle East, and the Caribbean to Europe, threats to Western ideas were rarely commented upon. One reason for this, of course, was that multiculturalism, the politics of recognition, and a quest for people to simply "be" had not found clear expression in the world because North Americans and Europeans, to a large extent, imposed their culture upon subject peoples—that is, the culture of colonial masters and original "settlers," to use Huntington's (2004) phrase.

The third lesson, demography matters—that is, the effect of birth rates on feelings of empathy—is dramatically exemplified in Berlinksi's (2006) dirge at the beginning of her book, *Menace in Europe*, titled "No Past, No Future, No Worries" (p. 129). She paints a vivid and moving description of what it was like for one to grow up proud and Italian in the city of Perugia. While wandering the streets of Perugia, Berlinksi recalled prideful moments of stopping in the "Pasticceria Sandri, a ravishing, high-ceilinged pastry shop built in 1871" (p. 129). As she continued her delectable tour of the sweets shop, she "took in the pyramids of chocolates on filigreed silver platters, wrapped in sparkling blue-and-silver foil," the trademark of Perugia chocolates worldwide (p. 129). Soon, a sensorium of memories enveloped her, evoking not only gustatory pleasures but also visual, tactile, and auditory ones. She saw "exuberantly frescoed walls" and witnessed dolls, marionettes, music boxes, and other things that evoked in her and other Italians "nostalgic memories of that shop" (p. 129).

As Berlinksi (2006) came to the end of her nostalgic journey, she observed, "The place was, clearly, designed to delight children" (p. 129). The problem, of course, was "there were no children in the Pasticceria Sandri. Not one. Nor were there any on the streets of Perugia" (p. 129). Adding a measure of quasi-scientific scrutiny worthy of those who delight in the power of numbers, Berlinski offered that there were no children; she had "looked carefully" (p. 129).

Other scholars and pundits have also drawn similar parallels to demography where they anticipate a new Europe filled with Islam and Muslims that may ultimately end Europe and Europeans as we know it and them. A central reason for this view is that Europe is not reproducing itself. In *State of Emergency,* Buchanan (2006) dubs the continent of Europe "Eurabia" and writes,

> Welcome to Eurabia. Twenty million Muslims reside there and are the fastest growing minority on the smallest continent where the native-born are failing to reproduce themselves. Europe is facing the crisis of post-Christian civilization [through] birth control, abortion, and sterilization, the suicide potions of modernity; its population is aging, shrinking, and dying, as its need for workers to sustain its generous health and pensions programs and take care of its retired and elderly forces European governments to bring in millions of Muslims. (p. 206)

Tensions, Population, and Assimilation

While it is the case, again, using Hume's concentric circles as a model, that Europeans and North Americans should be concerned about dwindling population rates, the most compelling thing about the discourse surrounding the alarm is its bellicosity and its pitting of Muslim and Mexican immigrants against "indigenous" groups. As such, discourse of immigration, by implication, is marked by religiosity and anti-Muslim expressive oppositional framing, centering the problem on immigrants and immigration rather than on failed public policy. Of course, it must be noted that some oppositional writers tilt in this direction.

Buchanan (2006), for example, writes that "behind the radicalism of these Arabs is a failure to assimilate them" (p. 206). Of course, by "radicalism of these Arabs," Buchanan is referring to the March 11 Madrid bombers, September 11 attacks, and other incidents that speak to the failure of Western culture to see the coming cultural crisis. In this regard, however, the underlining tenor is this: Had the "radicals" been more like us, such things would not have happened. And empathy's flames would not be flickering.

These caveats notwithstanding, the enemy is defined sometimes as Muslim, sometimes as Turkish, and sometimes as North African. But the primary attack is on archenemy "radical Islam," because September 11, bombings in London and Madrid, and the war in Iraq offer striking emotional undergirding for public understanding of the "menace" to Western civilization. Wilson's (1993) notion that "tolerance and intolerance are two sides of the same coin, each growing out of the attachment we develop to family and kin" (p. 50), has a special importance to the way empathy is framed regarding demographics as a threat to Western culture and identity. Fukuyama asks whether the seriousness of demography and other threats to Western values and identity "may constitute a Rubicon that will be very hard to re-cross" (qtd. in Buchanan, 2006, p. 208). Will the aftermath of population shifts jolt the West beyond recovery?

Whether this occurs or not, it is certainly the case that present-day discourse, with increasing frequency, collides over such issues as immigrant and immigration danger to the West, greatly facilitated by demography that has altered humans' level of empathy toward one another. Just consider some recent evidence. In Teviso, in the northern part of Italy, a city councilman, clearly exercised over the immigrant situation there, resorted to the discourse of the Third Reich to reveal his level of disdain, disgust, and fear of immigrants. Said Giorigo Bettio, at a public council meeting, "With immigrants, we should use the same system the SS used, punish 10 of them for every slight against one of our citizens" (Pullella, 2007, p. 1).

Although Bettio spoke freely and unlovingly, Pullella (2007) reports that he was "roundly condemned by politicians and editorialists" (p. 1). Rhetorically, it is fascinating to observe how Bettio frames his discourse. Despite the fact that many immigrants to Italy are indeed citizens, it is important to observe that they are framed as being "outsiders" instead of "insiders" and privileged to all that empathy bears. The matter is further exacerbated by rising crime rates against "Italian citizens" by Roma; in fact, as *The Week* ("Italy," 2007) reports, "Italians have finally lost patience with the half-million migrants from Romania who now live among them" (p. 15).

Italians "don't like the ragged Romanians who pounce on drivers at traffic lights, wielding buckets and sponges. They're enraged by statistics showing that Romanians are responsible for two-thirds of all car thefts, burglaries, and muggings" ("Italy," 2007, p. 15). This passage is instructive. In such places as Germany, England, and France, statistics about crime and immigrants are congruent. However, the thing that really riled the Italians and caused dormant attitudes toward Roma to reach a crisis point centers on the arrest in November 2007 of a young Roma for the murder of a 47-year-old indigenous woman.

The indigenous woman's murder became emblematic of pent-up frustrations regarding what Buchanan (2006) calls an "invasion." Clearly, the discourse of the period is filled with the intensity of statements befitting an invasion. For empathy, this issue has existential resonance because when people feel as if they have no way out of a sociocultural situation that they themselves have spun, it is easier to appeal to cultural differences rather than to sameness. In northern Italy, people "are worried by rises in crime rates and unemployment" and have "called for crackdowns on immigrants" (Pullella, 2007, p. 1). The *Economist* ("Demographic Tear," 2007) notes "that immigration accounts for so much of the predicted rise in Britain's population that makes discussing the problem of overcrowding politically difficult, for migration frequently tops the list of voters' concerns these days" (p. 66).

In still another instance, to add fuel to the fire, in November 2007, French suburbs exploded again, although these disturbances did not match the intensity and scale of the 2005 riots (Sciolino, 2007, p. 1). Such incidents did much to accelerate and underscore the distance between Western values and non-Western values, highlighting the fact that Europe and the West are no longer teacher and everyone else pupils. It is sometimes very difficult for Westerners to accept these new habits of mind. This is one unexpected result of the contact between immigrants and nonimmigrant populations in such places as France, Germany, Amsterdam, and London. This new approach to host countries is then a key factor in the relations between former colonialists and former subject peoples from North Africa, the Middle East, Asia, and other places. At the height of Western dominance, before the advent of globalization, a push toward multiculturalism, and a prideful reduction in learning and speaking the colonizer's language, it was easier for empires to enforce their folkways, norms, and standards of and for behavior upon indigenous people.

David Brooks (2006) put his finger on the whole notion of embracing the worldview of dominant cultures when he wrote in response to events surrounding the Danish cartoons, "We in the West were born into a world that reflects the legacy of Socrates and the agora. In our world, images, statistics and arguments swarm around from all directions. There are movies and blogs, books and sermons. There's the profound and the vulgar, the high and the low" (p. A27). By implication, it is clear which cultures are designated as high and which cultures are designated as low. But where is space for the incorporation of other cultures' ways of doing and being? Of some semblance of empathy? Must the dominant cultural legacy always remain supreme? Or is there space for negotiation and celebration of difference? Can there be modes of harmonization? Must one culture monopolize others regardless of their advanced technology, intellectual accomplishments, and nobility of purpose?

A lessening of Western cultural identity markers and impact is also a rapier-like reason for conflict between former colonizers and immigrants. Undoubtedly, it is troubling for those who believe in Western triumphalism and for those who perceive of their culture as vibrant and forward looking to be snubbed by a "pernicious and corrupting culture" (Lewis, 2002, p. 135). The Middle East, as Lewis (2002) gleefully points out, in the area of music, "with the exception of some Westernized enclaves—remains a blank on the itinerary of the great international virtuosos as they go on their world tours" (p. 136).

Similarly, in the areas of such expressive creations as the visual arts, painting, clothing, uniforms, shoes and hats, literature, dramatists, and historians—all these were "of no interest" and yet "clearly a cultural rejection" in Middle Easterners' scheme of social and cultural change. Lewis's (2002) point is that Middle Easterners translated things from the West that were useful, such as "primarily medicine, astronomy, chemistry, physics, mathematics, and also philosophy" (p. 139), and rejected cultural artifacts such as drama and literature.

Lewis's (2002) commentary applies to pre-21st-century happenings, but it is interesting and instructive for how we view the confrontation between Westerners and immigrants. Why the rejection of the West given that "modern Western civilization is the first to embrace the whole planet" (p. 150)? "The dominant civilization is Western, and Western standards therefore define modernity" (p. 150). But not necessarily in the eyes of everyone. It is this crucial intersection of culture that is most concerning for empathy's sake. Westerners, seen through the eyes of such scholars as Lewis, have difficulty understanding how "Western freedom . . . freedom of the mind from constraint and indoctrination, to question and inquire and speak; freedom of the economy from corrupt and pervasive mismanagement; freedom of women from male oppression; freedom of citizens from tyranny—that underlies so many of the troubles of the Muslim world" (p. 159) cannot be embraced *by* the Muslim world.

Even Muslims educated in the West have "retreated in disgust from the inconclusiveness and chaos of our [Westerners'] conversation" (Brooks,

5

Crafting Images

Media and Empathy

Framing: Imaging the Cultural Other

When author and activist Randall Robinson (2007), in his book, *An Unbroken Agony: Haiti, From Revolution to the Kidnapping of a President,* describes the way that the Central African Republic is portrayed in the media, he identifies a strong connection between how we imagine the cultural "other" and the production of empathy. Robinson writes,

> Almost never were there accounts of Africans doing the kinds of constructive but mundane life-building things—couples holding hands, children playing happily, students talking at school, parents coming home, preparing dinner—that people do all over the world, day in and day out. (p. 231)

Before arriving in the Central African Republic to rescue Jean-Bertrand Aristide, a former president of Haiti, who had been exiled to Africa by the U.S. government, Robinson (2007) admitted that he had "heard much about the elaborate palace in Bangui," where he would be staying, but none of which "had been commendatory." Robinson says, "Virtually all of the stories written about Africa in the American press were unflattering" (p. 213). In this telling way, Robinson's commentaries underline mainstream media's ability to place some people "outside the normal frame" of human existence and, by extension, convey the message that some individuals are virtually insignificant in the scale of things.

According to social scientists, framing is the process of selectively influencing the way others organize and interpret messages. The process shapes ways of perceiving people, objects, and events and involves a complex means of responding to data in our environment and choosing what data we see, hear, feel, smell, taste, and process. Although the process of framing is complex and far-reaching, for our purposes, media framing consists of components that we rely on to craft images of the cultural other, including expectations and behaviors. George Lakoff, a cognitive science and linguistics professor at the University of California at Berkeley, is more specific about the nature and function of framing, and his view comes closest to what I mean by the word *framing*. Lakoff (2008) says that "a frame is a conceptual structure used in thinking." To flesh out what he means by a frame, Lakoff invites readers to carry out the following directive: "Don't think of an elephant!" Lakoff's point is that is impossible to not think of an elephant because the very word *elephant* "evokes a frame with an image of an elephant and certain knowledge: an elephant is a large animal (a mammal with large floppy ears, a trunk that functions like both a nose and a hand, large stump-like legs and so on)" (pp. 22–23). If we take Lakoff's notion of framing and apply it to media, it is easy to understand how and why selective framing shapes such human domains as emotions, fear, pleasure, and an ability to persuade a person to feel for or against others.

Through selective framing, media create in readers and viewers a "not there" phenomenon for those outside the frame. In this way, media shape how we both define and imagine the cultural other. Charles Taylor (1992), in writing about how we define human beings, says, "A person or group of people can suffer real damage, real distortion, if the people or society around them mirror back to them a confining or demeaning or contemptible picture of themselves" (p. 25). Although Taylor's work centers primarily on recognition and its absence, implicitly, his research is valuable for what it reveals about the nature of media framing and the crafting of human images, and it is a fact that media promote both depreciatory and elevating images of the other through filmic, televisual, and other modes of framing. Casting some people in a demeaning light can undermine their dignity and render them morally insignificant. As Taylor observes, the idea of equal dignity is "underpinned by a notion of what in human beings commands respect, however, we may try to shy away from the 'metaphysical background'" (p. 41).

As I noted in Chapter 1, Kant uses the words *human dignity* to locate all people in time and space. In Kant's philosophical and moral estimation, all humans count, are rational, and are owed "standing in a community."

This idea is linked to media because of their ability to choose and define who is considered significant or insignificant by virtue of placement inside or outside a frame—with positive or negative consequences.

Crafting the Cultural Other

Three factors are most critical to understanding the crafting of the cultural other. First, framing is imbued with an ability to secure the attention of recipients of media. This power to attract is revealed in Lakoff's (2008) dictum for us not to think of an elephant. Because of the inherent way that language and images lock humans into frames, it is impossible for us not to think of an elephant.

Second, framing directs and redirects the crafting of images in terms of who is present and who is absent from public media messages and public memory. An absence of being also amputates one from the "public sphere"— the sphere that is of public discussion, public knowledge, and public opinion (Starr, 2004, p. 5). In this regard, unlike Adam Smith's invisible economic hand that rules over the marketplace, rendering the cultural other invisible, if left unattended, it can, in both subtle and nonsubtle ways, place someone outside the orbit or narrative meaning-making scripts of what it means to be human. Keeping with the main theme of this book, how can one be considered or talked about if one is marginalized or perhaps treated as nonexistent? We know that who is present or absent from human consideration can also shape attitudes toward the "other" hugely with both instrumental and symbolic consequences. So, in terms of empathy, it matters a great deal whether one is inside or outside the boundaries of human consciousness.

The third factor that is crucial to framing is the language of bifurcation, which is, in many instances, how framing does some of its most sinister work as regards empathy: rich against poor, tall against short, and good against evil. We are concerned about how humans are framed because pushing cultural otherness to extremes can create hostility, confusion, conflict, and even genocide. Take the case of Rwanda. According to Philip Gourevitch (1998), the elevation of separateness as opposed to sameness was instrumental in the Rwandan genocide of 1995 in which more than 900,000 people were killed. Using new-fangled periodicals, radio, songs, newspapers, and other forms of media designed primarily to dehumanize Tutsis, Hutus depicted Tutsis as "cockroaches" and those who empathized with Tutsis as "accomplices" of the "cockroaches" (pp. 96–97).

Thus, Hutu newspapers framed Tutsis as a dramatically different species than Hutus. Grief, misery, and much wretchedness emanated from something seemingly so basic as the construction of language—rearranging of 26 letters of the alphabet in such combinations as to wreak havoc upon the lives of others. Such brutal and nasty things happen when people are framed in evil, bifurcated ways and when "organized ways of thinking" about the cultural other transcend altruistic feelings.

Intense bifurcation in the case of Rwanda was most striking. Consider the following oppositional words and descriptors regarding Hutus and Tutsis:

> Tutsis tend to be tall and Hutus tend to be short. The Tutsis owned cattle and the Hutus farmed the land. In pre-colonial times, the Tutsis were the ruling tribe and sometimes exploited the Hutus ruthlessly. (Glover, 2001, p. 120)

"The extremist paper" *Kangura* circulated the idea that Tutsis had "infiltrated positions of power like 'snakes,'" reviving in the minds of Hutus the belief that Tutsis would once again occupy positions of power akin to the pre-1959 feudal regime (Mitchell, 2007, p. 9). Furthermore, *Kangura* aptly used compelling questions to cement its audience base and wreak terror on Tutsis: "What weapons shall we use to conquer the *Inyenzii* (cockroaches) once and for all?" The newspaper answered with a picture of a machete on the front page. Moreover, the newspaper also characterized Tutsis as being outside of God's race and merely a collection of ill-sorted types: "thieves, hypocrites, liars and killers" (Mitchell, 2007, p. 10). In this way, the condensation of symbols ensured that Tutsis would meet their ultimate fate—genocide.

This is one example of many twisted abuses of humanity. In other instances, of course, elites can facilitate empathy's mission by virtue of who both constructs and disseminates images of the cultural other. "Because the elite media is dominated by cosmopolitans who inhabit the wider world beyond the nation-state," Kaplan (2002) argues, "it has a tendency to emphasize universal principles over national interest" (pp. 124–125). Former news anchorman Walter Cronkite says that "most newsmen feel very little allegiance to the established order. I think they are inclined to side with humanity rather than with authority and institutions" (qtd. in Kaplan, 2002, p. 125).

Even though this may generally be the case, media elites also push a limiting view of the cultural other and stay well within the framework of customary ways of thinking and being, as we shall see later. At the heart of the matter, however, is the notion that how media frame the cultural other has a serious influence on humans' understanding of the world and how they behave in it.

Media and Ideology

Media and ideology also provide a useful prism through which to view empathy. Hegemony is "a process of convergence, consent, and subordination"

(Lull, 2000, p. 54). The process of hegemony works in this manner. Ways of living, social institutions, owners of the means of production, and industries are compressed into a mosaic or format that preserves the folkways and "cultural advantage of the already powerful" (Lull, 2000, p. 55). Lull (2000) argues that hegemony is most powerful when it has in place a "system of ideas that has persuasive force" and can be both "represented and communicated" (p. 14). Media do this with astonishing speed and sometimes to the detriment of those whose wishes, aspirations, and points of view are slighted or ignored altogether because, as Lull notes, "systems of ideas are used in ways that favor the interests of some people over others" (p. 15). For this reason, we must never underestimate the meaning and force of ideology.

It is also in this linguistic rendering that empathy's vitality can be found because ideology can also act with "persuasive force" on behalf of empathy and its subjects. It may, of course, also act oppositionally. I argue, by extension, that because together media and ideology promote "a system of ideas," we must never "underestimate" the relationship between ideology and empathy. Whether media construct a positive image of the highborn or lowborn or an image of one with mobility or locality, the influence may be found in science, art, ecology, literature, drama, economics, and, most of all, values.

In discussing the complex nature of media effects, we must heed Lull's (2000) observation that although a great deal of ideology is spread via television, there are other forms, ranging from "postage stamps, store windows, breakfast cereal boxes, automobile bumper stickers, tee-shirts, grocery receipts, golf tees, matchbook covers, [and] restaurant menus" (p. 16). All these forms do the bidding of ideology by carrying some messages and omitting others. These change over time, of course. And how!

Mini-Case: Ethiopia

We are no longer living in the simple world of Herodotus—a world in which "cruelty was routine and usually went unremarked upon," as Kaplan (2002, p. 28) observes. Today, because of the ubiquitous nature of global media, most forms of human behavior can be remarked upon, from the cruel assassination of former president of Pakistan, Benazir Bhutto, in 2007 to the beheading of *Wall Street Journal* reporter Daniel Pearl in 2001.

Today, we live in a world in which media tell us what to be for and what to be against, whom to praise and whom to blame, and what to value or disvalue. For this reason, media are rarely neutral and quiescent. Let us briefly consider the country of Ethiopia. Most of the images of Ethiopians on television are of starving, fly-smitten, emaciated people, leading many people to believe that *all* Ethiopians are woe-smitten people. The example of Ethiopia also illustrates the fact that images selected by media, if repeated often enough, ultimately function holistically; that is, they function such that a part stands for the whole or a whole for a part, moving us into the realm of the heady trope, *synecdoche*.

Such images of Ethiopians, through quantification over time, also function "as if" they are facts. Media, with the cooperation of ideology, place Ethiopians in an empathetic double bind. On one hand, such images invite viewers and readers to empathize with the plight of starving children. On the other hand, such images place cultural curtains around Ethiopians, inviting viewers to think of them in special and peculiar ways and within a narrower human lens. Such images further encourage such hard-nosed and unfriendly questions as, "Why can't Ethiopians feed themselves?" and "What manner of people are they?" As a consequence, empathetic distancing can occur.

My point is that empathy for Ethiopians can start out in a very positive way and then tumble downhill into a pejorative world, making Ethiopians synonymous with poverty and disease and even inviting haughty but well-intentioned attitudes toward the objects of empathy. Potentially, these kinds of media-sponsored, empathy-generating images can diminish the very humanity they wittingly or unwittingly promote. The story of Ethiopia also parallels the work of media during apartheid's reign in South Africa. Although North American media provided abundant images of Black South Africans that were very instrumental in dismantling the horrific practices of dehumanization (through the evocation of a liberal, democratic ideology), it is also the case that simultaneously, Americans saw on their television screens images of tarpaulin-covered "shacks."

When I visited South Africa for the first time in 1999, I witnessed the inherent ability of media to sculpt some images at the expense of others through the promotion of a system of ideas about the way things in sheer actuality are and are supposed to be. I noted, for example, that not all of South West Townships (SOWETO) contained dilapidated houses. Later, however, my mind grasped the awe-inspiring reality that perhaps it was *because* of media's universalist moral ideological tones in promoting the plight of Black South Africans, and not *in spite* of it, that the darker skinned people ultimately prevailed.

Images of starving children in Ethiopia also illustrate how intersections between empathy and ideology complicate and problematize, raising the question of whether some people can and do become superfluous in our highly globalized world by virtue of continuous and sustaining circulation of unflattering images of them. How long, for example, can images of starving children from Africa persist without forsaking humanity's sustaining love and attention? Can the very fact of media repetition of such images and ideological drive reinforce the idea that such people are hopeless? And invite a cessation of caring?

Media Amplification

Subsumed in these questions is the concept of media amplification. That is, who has the capability of magnifying and circulating empathy worldwide and with what effect? Clearly, empathy can be hobbled by media monopoly borne of ideological resonance. Because media circulate specific images and not others, they have the ability to amplify certain problems and de-emphasize others. Kaplan (2002) maintains that the intimate relationship between media and ideology played a pivotal role in the way that the world viewed Somalia—a troubled country of civil war and tribal violence.

In making the point that "a statesman's primary responsibility is to his country, while the media thinks in universal terms," Kaplan (2002) concluded that "emotional coverage of Somalia by a world media foreshadowed an American intervention . . . [and] because it [media coverage of Somalia] was ill-defined, led to the worst disaster for U.S. troops since Vietnam—a disaster that helped influence policymakers against intervention in Rwanda" (p. 129). Kaplan's keen observation is important for what it reveals of the complicated nature of media-sponsored productions of empathy. By implication, Kaplan advances the claim that North American and Western ideologies worked so well in the case of Somalia that they produced the possibility of empathy's tilt in Rwanda.

Kaplan's (2002) astute observation also calls attention to another dimension of the intertwining of media, ideology and empathy. And it is the fact that the killing of American soldiers in Somalia heightened the risk that they faced and also refocused attention on self-interest. Put another way, because media covered Somalia astutely, they focused attention on the relationship between public policy and empathy. In the case of Somalia, as Kaplan points out, Western media have a robust and dramatic capacity to affect publics "while bearing no responsibility for the outcome" (p. 129). Kaplan's insights further interrogate the role between ideological intent and outcomes that beset empathy and heighten Kant's notion of a "morality of intention rather than of consequences, a morality of abstract justice rather than of actual result" (qtd. in Kaplan, 2002, p. 129). Both Kaplan and Kant brilliantly imply a heady dilemma for empathy. Can one ever disentangle this relationship? And where does such a relationship place the objects of empathy, driven, however intentionally and ideologically, by media?

Although Kaplan (2002) does not provide a facile answer, perhaps because the situation is so pregnant with meaning and consequences, he roils waters even further by claiming, "The world media shows little sympathy for the challenges and awful ironies facing those who will power; it upholds the safer virtue of sympathizing only with the powerless" (p. 115). Even though Kaplan's conclusion regarding media's empathy for the poor is open to debate, it nevertheless raises a question of great importance: How far can and should media and ideology go in furthering the ends of the dispossessed and the downtrodden? We will not attempt to answer such a complicated, sensitive, and vexing question. Rather, we leave such a query for our dear, gentle reader to ponder.

Despite the constraints that are embedded in such questions regarding Ethiopia and Black South Africa, the questions point out something very crucial to our understanding of the link between media, ideology, and empathy. It is a fact that North Americans' and Europeans' focus on Ethiopians, Black South Africans, and others occurs as a consequence of such virtues as charity, goodwill, morality, and decency that sprang from Christian and other forms of ethics. Such virtues in turn help to promote a kind of loyalism and a sense of benefaction between North Americans and Europeans. The point of North American and European benefaction will be elaborated upon in Chapter 6—on global practices of empathy. However, even if Westerners are, as some people might claim, self-congratulatory in the special realm of empathy, to their credit, some Whites have long thundered against enslavement and human abuse, as we learned in Chapter 1 in the story of Thomas Clarkson. As Schama (2006) says, print images of African slaves were very instrumental in publicizing "live cargo" and crammed bodies during the Middle Passage: "It was this image that brought the campaign [against slavery] out from its secure base among Quakers and Evangelicals to a much larger public" (p. 209).

Amplification of Blacks

Let us consider other noteworthy examples of media amplification and their relationship to empathy. For starters, media and ideology have an impact on the way in which Blacks, especially Black men, are viewed. To see "the other" in clearest light, we need to be mindful of media's ability to distribute information, paint vivid pictures, and regulate the dominant ideas of a culture. The presentation of Black men in media has painted a less than empathetic picture of them in the domains of crime and hip-hop music. The presumed link between Black men and White crime has a long history rooted in such things as enslavement, beliefs in Blacks' predispositions toward criminality, presence of advertisements, and regular appearances on the evening television news (especially local news). As Welch (2007) notes, "Aside from the actual involvement of Blacks in crime and the criminal justice system, other potential contributors to the profiling of criminals as young Black males may be various media sources" (p. 281).

Researcher Barlow (1998) says that the association of crime in the minds of many North Americans with Black is so prevalent that "it is unnecessary to speak directly of race because talking about crime *is* talking about race" (p. 151). Knowing how people perceive Black men is a meaningful way of grasping how human beings understand their world and whether Black men are a part of it. The implications of the ideological linkage between crime and Black men are especially important for empathy because the linkage sets up *relational* qualities that move people away from Black men, thus helping explain why some people end up being treated like strangers. This is precisely what Cicero warned against in first century B.C.E. when he said, "'The whole foundation of the human community' is threatened by treating foreigners worse than fellow Romans" (Kaplan, 2002, p. 29).

Although Cicero's foundational remarks are from another era, in the sense that he provided a basis for international society during his time, they strengthen our understanding of what happens when some people are placed in the stranger category and others in the familiar or friendly citizen category. Chiricos and Eschholz (2002) point out several ramifications of the link between crime and race and race and ideology that are well documented in literature. These range from "the refusal of pizza delivery in Black neighborhoods and the 'unavailability' of taxicabs to Black travelers to hair-trigger responses that result in shootings of unarmed suspects by police in some urban neighborhoods" (p. 401).

Data indicate that differences in penalties for crack and powder cocaine are "often attributed to the fact that about 90 percent of federal prosecutions for crack involve Black defendants, as compared to about 30 percent for powder cocaine" (Chiricos & Eschholz, 2002, p. 401). Roberts (1993) maintains that the imbalance between penalties for Blacks and crime and for Whites resides in "a belief system that constructs crime in terms of race and race in terms of crime" (p. 1947). As a result of this symbiotic relationship, Miller argues that "when we talk about locking up more and more people, what we are really talking about is locking up more and more black men" (qtd. in Chircios & Eschholz, 2002, p. 401).

Former senator Bill Bradley once remarked that "the fear of black crime covers the streets like a sheet of ice" (qtd. in Chircios & Eschholz, 2002, p. 401). The most pressing result of such media coverage is the associative vector that operates: Black men become associated with crime, and crime becomes associated with Black men. This causal association led Entman to conclude that such repetitive dispersals can create an "anti-black effect—a general hostility towards blacks" (Chircios & Eschholz, 2002, p. 401). This dispersal can and sometimes does weaken humanity's response to the dilemmas of Black men not only in America but also in such global places as England and France.

In calling attention to the impact of media circulation of images on human behavior, I am not unmindful of the crimes that Black men commit. Even Jesse Jackson once admitted that he felt a bit of "relief" when approaching strangers (Black men) in dark and dimly lit urban streets. Allen (2004) devotes an entire book to the importance of political friendship in civic culture, and her rhetorical message has a bearing on the way Black men are perceived in society as a result of negative circulation of images in media. She argues, for example, that conversations with strangers can go a long way in developing sensitivity to the other. And she provides a humanitarian strategy for dealing with confronting strangers "on a street late at night, when there aren't other watchful eyes around" (p. 167).

To manage the approach of the stranger in a decent and dignified manner, Allen (2004) advises, "It's better to cross sooner, rather than scurrying away at the last minute, it's better, if possible, to change one's route, instead of simply crossing to the other side" (p. 167). "To cross early," Allen says,

> is to leave open the possibility that one has crossed for reasons unrelated to the stranger's approach; that possibility gives the stranger a chance not to take personally the fact that one has crossed the street. Democratic trust depends on public displays of an egalitarian, well-intentioned spirit. (p. 167)

Allen's (2004) example teaches that we should be concerned with the moral tone of our behavior and the effect that it can have on human relations.

Associative Circulations

But consider how associative relationships between unfavorable things, whether crime and Black men or other events, impinge on humans' ability to perceive Black men clearly and objectively.

First, some people do not have direct experiences with people whose images are often circulated on television, in film, or in newspapers and magazines; images are unidirectional. They tell listeners and viewers—explicitly and implicitly—that they *ought* to think negative or positive or pleasant or unpleasant things about the cultural other when meeting, greeting, hearing about, or seeing the object of attention on television or in film. Such is the power of "organized thought" or ideology. Typically, however, the symbiotic relationship between ideology and media is so strong that it places many subjects in the negative category. We have already noted that "business-as-usual" thoughts and behavior rarely disturb our sensibilities because of the expectations that govern so much of what we do and how we think about cultural others.

During French riots in 2005, for example, international newspapers used the following characterizers and descriptors to refer to Muslim youth: "thugs," "scum," "rabble rouser," "fire-starters," "a gang of criminals," "gangster," "extremist," "insurgents," "troublemakers," "riff-raff," "extremist," and "nihilist," all of which specify a diseased, nonrational genesis for the disturbances that occurred in France (Calloway-Thomas, 2007). Such descriptors served as veiled threats about the relationship that should obtain between Muslim youths and others within French civic order. As a consequence, language used to characterized Muslim youth potentially distanced them from the human family.

In still another example, according to Fenton (2005), North American media "demonized the Serbs during the civil wars in former Yugoslavia" and "left out the context that the ethnic Albanians, who were the victims in the 1990s, had themselves routinely slaughtered Serbs in World War II" (p. 58). Fenton concludes, "Now that America has come to the Albanians' rescue, the Albanians are busy trying to ethnically cleanse Kosovo of all Serbs" (p. 38). Kaplan (2002) argues that avoiding face-to-face encounters "makes cruelty easier to accomplish, as we enter an abstract realm of pure strategy and deception carrying few psychological risks" (p. 12).

Consider another power dimension of Fenton's (2005) comments and its bearing on empathy's struggles. His words suggest that empathy for other human beings can be compromised if one does not understand the role and resonance of historical context. Because of the ideological nature of media, temporal constraints on television news broadcasts, dominant ideological structures, and a lack of historical knowledge on the part of listeners and viewers, we ally our emotions with one group instead of with another. And media often fail to give listeners and viewers enough information to make informed and proper links between morality and fairness and between dignity and rival narratives.

Largely as a result of media circulations, listeners/viewers are too often held hostage to negative thoughts, encouraging and, in many instances, forcing people to think ill of others. As a consequence, emotionally charged hostage-generating images tell us that we should care about some people and not about others, that some people have noble souls, and that trust is a virtue that is virtually absent in the lives of particular groups.

Finally, the cumulative effect of negative media circulations is that negative images diminish the likelihood that empathy for those portrayed negatively will grow precisely because they are viewed as lacking humanity.

Media and ideology then play a role in conditioning humans to move their energy and resources in particular directions. How does it matter which views, ideology, customs, traditions, and attitudes are promoted and which ones are not? Is it possible for humans to ever live in a world where media outlets truly push the idea of "fair and balanced" that has become the linguistic trademark of North America's FOX News channel? Media should bear some responsibility for the way in which they rearrange human motives globally. But what are the limits of bias, and how do inputs skew the "mechanics of meaning" and shape the distribution of empathy? We turn now to a discussion of inputs and outputs, ever mindful of the close relationship between ideology and such cultural variables as input and output.

Inputs and Outputs

An elite group of individuals and corporations influence what we read and especially what we watch on television. Holtzman (2000) says that "television is the most pervasive form of contemporary media" and that "a popular television show can reach 15–20 million households" (p. 34). According to Park and Wilkins (2005), "It is the job of media to construct images of people, events, and settings; it is the industry of media to do so in ways that reflect the political interests and economic parameters of the governing class" (p. 1). The result? Consistently narrow and sometimes misleading portrayals of social and cultural others. Part of the reason for this is the asymmetry (imbalance) of scale in terms of production, content and information (inputs), and consumption/audience listener reception (outputs).

In many instances, production is in one place and consumption is in another. By exploiting imbalances of meanings, information, content, settings, and circumstances, those in control of media production and distribution manipulate the way acceptance or rejection of the other is rendered. This does not necessarily mean, of course, that strong distribution processes have a total and tyrannical control over human agency. But issues of input and control do raise serious questions concerning the codification of empathy. For example, who will decide what content and information will be distributed? And whose agenda will be promoted or not promoted?

Since the world relies less on such traditional human expressive forms as drumming, smoke signals, and face-to-face communication today, it stands to reason that in the management of meanings, some humans have the capacity to shape events in more expansive and compelling ways than others. The truth is that some people dictate outcomes more powerfully than others. As Hannerz (1992) observes, "By way of its superior power over the entertainment industry, news bureaus, the advertising industry, and the media through which we operate, the West strongly influences cultures in other parts of the world" (p. 29).

Although researchers, psychologists, political scientists, and historians tout the role of "cultural imperialism" in shaping what people see and how they respond, we are most interested in how dominant flows of meanings can both monopolize and shape human beings' ability for empathizing with others. For example, the fact that media mogul Rupert Murdoch's News Corporation owns the FOX Group in the United States, several British and Australian media outlets, along with television stations and newspapers, including the *Daily Telegraph,* the *Herald Sun,* the *Sunday Telegraph,* and *The Wall Street Journal,* raises critical questions about the flow of meanings. Given this hegemonic power, it is possible for Murdoch to reach at least 5 billion humans worldwide, circulating his story about how viewers ought to interpret their world (Kirkpatric, 2003). Holtzman (2000, p. 37) also gives us a sense of the extraordinary impact that corporations have over the content and information that shape how people think.

> As media consumers, we are often unaware that the many different pro-
> duction companies whose programs we might enjoy in a given week are
> actually all owned by a single conglomerate. If in one week you see a film
> from Miramax and a film from Buena Vista, rent videos from Blockbuster
> that were produced by Touchstone and Hollywood Pictures, watch ABC-
> TV, and turn to cable for ESPN and specials on Arts and Lifetime, you have
> actually spent a week watching programs from just one source: Disney.
> (Holtzman, 2000, p. 37)

Media consolidation, behavior of what's termed agenda-setting elites, hegemonic power, and a symbiotic relationship between corporations and media are key reasons why Herman and Chomsky (1988; Chomsky, 2003) have called for media reform and for a return of the airwaves to the public.

Afghanistan

Of course, input distributions can work for or against empathy, depending on media organizations, topics, content, context, and geopolitics. In 2001, for example, at the height of America's war in Afghanistan, *The New York Times* carried many stories that were accompanied by pictures detailing the war, from photographs of "stars and stripes" (December 19, 2001) to pictures of devastated families to gleeful pictures of "children at work in Kabul" (December 12, 2001). To dramatize bombs that America was dropping in

Afghanistan, on December 11, 2001, *The New York Times*, in the section titled "A Nation Challenged," depicted a mud-like bunker covered with a sheet of white plastic that was overlaid with a brown and green cloth (p. B1). To the right of the photograph was a picture of a mother wearing a red and green scarf with her head turned. The caption under the picture reads, "A mother and her 10-day-old girl in a refugee camp in Aliabad, Afghanistan. An American aid drop missed the camp by a few miles showering food on Northern Alliance troops" (p. B1).

It took me several studied glimpses to find the cradled baby because of the prominence of the mother's head-wrap and the stark environment evident in the picture; the caption conveyed much empathy for mother and child, even though the child was not readily visible. The point is that the emotional and iconic nature of the picture (input) and the bare earthen shape of the surroundings fostered empathy for mother and child (output/ consumption), even though the picture of the baby is not highly visible.

Potentially, it was possible for the average *New York Times* reader to miss the baby altogether because the caption had already strategically and emotionally choreographed the presentation of the image. In this way, the photograph promoted good, warm, and fuzzy feelings for mother and child. My argument is not there was willful intent on the part of *The New York Times,* but rather that there was keen and dynamic interaction between media input and empathy.

In many cases, input variables can be bifurcated and complex in terms of the distribution of meanings, human subjects, and empathy. On December 12, 2001, for example, a huge picture of "Afghan tribal fighters" appeared in *The New York Times*. Representations in the foreground included a picture of a fighter dressed in an olive to brown long-flowing garment disarming the ammunition of a tank—"what appeared to be remains of Al Qaeda's camp"—according to *The New York Times* (p. B1). The man in the foreground, who is disarming the ammunition of a tank, has an anguished expression on his face that suggests both sadness and fierce determination.

Because of the evocation of strong blended emotions, and depending on the reader's ideological stance, the photograph could be read very empathetically in support of Al-Qaeda, although it is highly unlikely that *The New York Times* intended this at all. But how was the reader to process the bold caption under the picture, which said "Spoils of War"?—no question mark was included in *The New York Times* piece, of course.

We know, for example, that outcomes are also greatly influenced by perceptions and socialization and that the latter, in turn, helps to shape human responses to incoming stimuli. We are all taught ways of perceiving people, objects, and events. As the song from the musical *South Pacific* so aptly states, "You have to be carefully taught."

Other examples of strong input capacity in *The New York Times* at the height of the war against terror in Afghanistan included an emotionally wrenching picture of turbaned Muslim men huddled together in a refugee camp with grief-stricken faces. One man has what appears to be a registration card in his hands because, as *The New York Times* (December 12, 2001) notes, "The aid was available only to families that had registered previously" (p. B3). The same piece also included representations of "two young children" carrying a 110-pound bag of wheat. Clearly, the picture contained a complex layering of values, beliefs, and ideas that were heavily laden with connotative meanings.

Regardless of whether images of the "other" are positive or negative, the point is that powerful people and media sources largely control symbolic input. And as a result, asymmetry of meanings can occur.

A clear monopoly of input helps to explain why so many news stories about people in Third World countries focus on poverty, disease, violence, misery, AIDS, scarcity of resources, and other ills. The problem for the objects of such images is that media sources can produce demeaning discourses and depictions of Africans, South Americans, and others and, as a consequence, violate the equal dignity rule that Kant promotes. Some newspapers, for example, typically reserve special spots for the presentation of such images. In *The New York Times,* such images are normally featured on the front page in bold headlines (with photographs) or on the second through fourth pages. Although *The New York Times* is considered to be a more liberal newspaper than *The Wall Street Journal,* the former, in some cases, offers far more disease-ridden stories regarding the cultural "other" than the latter.

Asymmetry of Images

To the extent that topical and feature placement in newspapers matters, presentation of the other can, in unconscious ways, promote an alien view of people. As Hannerz (1992) notes, "A flooding of perspectives, either through a massive redundancy of messages in sheer quantitative terms, or through a use of cultural forms of peculiar qualitative potency" (p. 105), can have strong effects.

Asymmetrical presentation of less than flattering images of Africans and others also fosters concepts of dependency and visibility mainly in terms of what is wrong, even though the intent might be to generate empathy.

Through technologically enhanced inputs, media can make such stories as "a poor dusty village of 500 people," where "four babies died of malaria" (*The New York Times,* December 23, 2006, p. 1), strikingly visible to a global audience, inviting empathy, or it can promote the opposite.

Clearly, "sheer quantitative" rendering of subjects as objects of pity has moral significance. Such images communicate such notions as "for Africans, this is what it means to be human." A crucial implicit offshoot of this mode of output thinking is that too often, Third World people are not allowed to be themselves—that is, have control or human agency—in media representations. Furthermore, well-intentioned, disease-oriented images of Africans seriously underestimate the place of Third World people in human dialogue. These images come close to what Taylor (1992) calls the existence of "first-class" and "second-class citizens," promoting a politics of difference rather than a politics of sameness (p. 37).

Of course, as Taylor (1992) suggests, another outcome of such human conditions is the creation of "redistributive programs and special opportunities offered to certain populations" (p. 39), commonly referred to as affirmative action or millennial projects, as in the case of the United Nations program to aid Africa and other countries. Such placement further complicates universal dignity and brings to the foreground questions of distinctions that obtain between pity and empathy. I will not stop here to parse the difference but rather to observe that consistent with empathy's content, it relies very heavily on pity to direct human affairs.

Consider as well that affirmative action comparisons of objects of pity relative to others can lead to "depreciatory judgments as rendered in the oft-quoted comment" attributed to author Saul Bellow: "When the Zulus produce a Tolstoy we will read him." This statement of input is not only "a (possibly insensitive) particular mistake in evaluation" but also a "denial of a fundamental principle" of human equality. Such is a consequence of the "commoditized flow of meanings" and how human perceptions are shaped by such flows (Hannerz, 1992, p. 107).

Clawson and Trice's (2000) research on media portrayals of the poor, for example, reveals that "poverty was disproportionately portrayed as a 'black' problem, even though blacks make up less than one-third of the poor" (p. 53). However, because of input mechanisms, as Clawson and Trice note, "Black elderly poor and black working poor were rarely portrayed" (p. 54). By extension, the virtual absence of input variables regarding these groups promotes a diminution of generally positive attitudes that Whites hold concerning the portrayals of Blacks in media and a lessening of empathy for the latter in such vital areas as economics and education.

Clawson and Trice (2000) further report that stereotypes shape majority Americans' views "that most people who receive welfare benefits are taking advantage of the system," "lack effort," and have "loose morals and drunkenness" (p. 54). These stereotypical (input) representations of Blacks foster the view that some people count and others do not.

In contrast to Clawson and Trice's (2000) studies, Gerbner's (1997) research on representation (inputs) of the other reveals that televisual images create a general effect, what he calls "mainstreaming" (Holtzman, 2000, p. 39). In 1997, Gerbner looked at 1,755 prime-time characters on ABC, CBS, NBC, FOX, WB, and UPN. Among some of his major findings are the following: Poor people are almost invisible on television, and African American men are usually depicted as wealthier than their White counterparts. Gerbner's findings contrast sharply with Clawson and Trice's work, further demonstrating the complexity of media image inputs.

Gerbner's findings regarding the marginalization of the poor in terms of major and minor character representations on television are rather disturbing because they suggest that the poor occupy a "not there" status in North American society. This "not there" assignment implies not only that the poor are less worthy of respect than others but also that they lack some capacities that all humans share—most critically, self-worth and agency. To what extent do attitudes and treatment of poor people grow organically out of the absence of specific media inputs? At bottom, the matter of inputs extends intricately to who's attentive to whom? And in what way?

Centers and Peripheries: Attentive to Whom?

"Look, there's Angelina Jolie! Angelina, how is the world faring on the health and human rights fronts? Oh, my gosh! It's Bono. What needs to be done about African poverty? Hey, Richard Gere and Sharon Stone, how can we tackle the AIDS crisis?" (*The New York Times,* January 31, 2008). In these half-serious and half-breezy questions, one finds embedded the significance of centers and peripheries (Cs & Ps), the relationship between "star power and social change," and the relationship between Cs & Ps and empathy. As we turn to the issue of who's attentive to whom, we must aim for an understanding of how the *distribution of credibility* helps to galvanize empathy on behalf of the world's poor and dispossessed.

Under the auspices of such organizations as the World Economic Forum (WEF), Angelina Jolie, Bono, and Sharon Stone (stars who occupy the very center of the world stage) clearly are able to influence the course of human events precisely because of their centered existences. By centers and peripheries, I mean an ability of certain individuals to make huge differences in human affairs because of their credible and charismatic powers of persuasion. Typically, individuals who are relegated (for whatever reason) to the periphery often depend on the largess of difference- and impact-making agents of goodwill and empathy. The former are *empathy makers and shakers* because they serve as key symbolic instruments for the transfer of meanings and goodwill to others. Of course, any discussion of the relationship that obtains between centers and peripheries and empathy is more complex than space will permit here.

Nowhere, however, is "the ability to shape events in human brains" more noticeable than in a general recognition that empathy also relies on star power to "great effect." There are two central reasons for this. First, as Bhagwati (2004) argues, and as I noted in Chapter 1, there has been an inversion of Hume's concentric circles of "reducing loyalty and empathy" primarily because of the powers of media, especially television and film. Bhagwati offers because of Internet and CNN, "no longer can we snore while the other half of humanity suffers plague and pestilence and the continuing misery of extreme poverty" (p. 19).

Media Effects: Sharon Stone

Enter *empathy makers and shapers*. Let us consider a few case studies of these centered humans and their dramatic and compelling effects. In 2005, by knowing "when and where to enter," actress Sharon Stone, using her star power, interrupted a speech that was being given by Tanzania president Benjamin Mkapa and challenged the august audience of less than 2,300 participants at the World Economic Forum in Davos, Switzerland, to raise $1 million for malaria-stricken Tanzania. And she did so in 5 minutes! (*The New York Times,* January 31, 2008, and *Telegraph,* January 15, 2008, p. 1).

When Stone interrupted Mkapa's speech, she simply said, "I am Sharon Stone. I would like to offer you $10,000 to help you buy some mosquito nets today. Would anyone else like to be on a team with me and stand up and offer some money?" Three things are immediately apparent from Stone's persuasive performance. First, her sheer audacity—although one could argue that centered power itself carries with it sheer audacity, in Davos, Stone, a centered individual with gall and determination, interrupted the speech of the president of a country! Second, the simplicity of her language is also important for what was absent. Because of star power, she did not have to offer other introductory statements such as "I was in A or B film," or "I am from the United States of America." Instead, her position at the hub of meanings spoke for her and on behalf of poor Tanzanians.

Third, the specific temporally driven interrogative but very direct nature of Stone's discourse: "I would like to offer you $10,000 to help you buy some mosquito nets today," followed by "Would anyone else like to be on a team with me and stand and offer some money?" Implicit in the latter words is the singular belief that Stone's offer would indeed be matched, not only because of who she was but also because of who was present at the World Economic Forum (WEF). *The New York Times* reported that 72 cabinet-level ministers and about 500 global business leaders were at the 2008 "Rolls Royce of business conferences." In 2005, at least 400 global decision makers were in attendance at the World Economic Forum.

Case Study of Effects: Bono

In 2006, Bono, another person with star power, also moved among the august group of CEOs, journalists, politicians, and nongovernmental organizations (NGOs) and academics at the WEF to stir up empathy and support for millions of human beings worldwide who were stricken with AIDS (Kaisernetwork.org). Taking a page from advertising industry with its infinite capacity to rearrange human motives, Bono came up with not only a mechanism for fighting AIDS but also a way for audience members to gratify their consumer needs. Bono created a brand product called *Product Red* that earmarked some of the proceeds for the Global Fund to Fight AIDS, Tuberculosis and Malaria.

Such globally important partner organizations as American Express, Converse, Giorgio Armani, and Gap immediately signed on. The timeline for giving is 5 years, according to Kaisernetwork.org. Bono's comment regarding the initiative speaks to the role of the center in mobilizing empathy for those on the periphery of human existence. Said Bono, "Philanthropy is like hippy music, holding hands. RED is more like punk rock, hip hop. This should feel like hard commerce" ("Kaiser Daily," 2006, p. 22).

In Chapter 6, I will discuss the interplay between charity and justice. Here, I underscore how centers and peripheries operate. Furthermore, Bono had thought about "hunger, disease, the waste of lives that is extreme poverty" prior to his appearance at the WEF, as he reveals in the foreword to Sachs's (2005) book, *The End of Poverty*. Sachs is director of the Earth Institute at Columbia University and heads the United Nations Millennium Project to fight world poverty. I mention Bono's foreword to Sachs's book because it reveals a network of centered individuals in the poverty business. For example, in the foreword, Bono, the "singer with an ear for a melody," makes it clear that he is not only a friend of Sachs but also a friend of Bobby Shriver, a member of the influential Kennedy family of Massachusetts.

Bono also wrote of Sachs's (2005) book,

> It's about the alternative—taking the next step in the journey of equality. Equality is a very big idea, connected to freedom, but an idea that doesn't come for free. If we're serious, we have to be prepared to pay the price. Some people will say we can't afford to do it . . . I disagree. I think we can't afford not to do it. . . . The destinies of the "haves" are intrinsically linked to the fates of the "have-nothing-at alls." (pp. xvi–xvii)

Bono's moving comments go straight to the heart of why the empathetic concerns of people at the center matter a great deal. The ability of people to be heard is even more critical when one considers the proliferation of messages that the average individual receives today. With all the competing voices and messages, it is a good thing for master narratives to circulate on behalf of people at the peripheries of the human exchange system.

One can see as well the intricate relationship among empathy, the distribution of meaning, and what Hannerz (1992) calls a "flooding of perspectives" (p. 105). Bhagwati's (2004) words regarding the power of media and empathy movers and shakers and the ability of the innermost circles of empathy to become the outermost ones are insightful: "So the young see and are anguished by the poverty and the civil wars and the famines in remote areas of the world but often have no intellectual training to cope with their anguish and follow it through rationally in terms of appropriate action" (p. 19). Of course, not all would agree with Bhagwati's assessment of young people's capacity for seeing things from the other's perspective. In fairness to Bhagwati, he was also referring to 1999 student protests against the World Trade Organization and the decision that protesters made concerning shrimpers on the high seas in the debate over dumping and the environment. Bhagwati argues that the protesters were unmindful that the environmentalists had won "the fight against shrimpers"—hence, his utterances about the intellectual training of young people.

But does one need to be trained to feel an appropriate measure of empathy for other people? As I noted in Chapter 3, World Trade Center bombings on 9/11 influenced American discourse in far-reaching ways. In an effort to understand the role of mediated messages in solidifying empathy, in the next section, I examine how the media covered terrorism and the extent to which empathy was troubled as a result of 9/11. This next section should reveal a great deal about stresses and strains on empathy in light of such a huge, catastrophic event as 9/11. For example, to what extent did the creators, producers, news correspondents, editors, and other individuals charged with the presentation of news deftly manage mourning, and what bearings did coverage have on empathetic judgments? And what specific content did audience members depend on during the presentation of news surrounding 9/11?

Covering Terrorism and Insurgencies

9/11

Hanson (2001) tells a gripping story of how Greeks "smashed through the royal Persian line at the battle of Cunaxa, north of Babylon" in the war between Greeks and Persians. He recounts that Greek soldiers were "caught in snowdrifts," "traversed high mountain passes," and suffered "frostbite, malnutrition and frequent sickness" in their efforts to reach the safety of the Black Sea, where they finally triumphed (p. 2). Such was the nature of battle during the 27-year Peloponnesian War (431–404 B.C.E.). Then, killing was pretty much reciprocal and confined to bloody battlefields—at huge cost to soldiers, of course. When terrorists struck on September 11, 2001, and killed 3,000 innocent human beings, a new mode of warfare was introduced to modern society. In commenting on 9/11, Brown and Waltzer (2004) remark that "such events, in modern times, are the grist of pervasive and extensive news coverage and commentary" (p. 25).

The events of 9/11 were traumatic and far-reaching. Terrorists struck not only the Twin Towers in New York City but also the Pentagon in Washington, D.C., and a calm field in western Pennsylvania. The dramatic and surprising event had immense and compelling signaling power. It signaled to newspapers, magazines, television, film, ABC, CBS, NBC, FOX News, *The Economist, The New York Times, The Wall Street Journal,* and other news sources that the event had to be covered repeatedly. For several weeks, the event dominated the news and attention of the American people as well as people in global villages worldwide.

Mourning and 9/11

For our purposes, several things are important to note regarding the link between terrorism, empathy, and media circulation of images.

First, an attack on the World Trade Center was a mind-altering event. In their analysis of "organized interest advertorials," Brown and Waltzer (2004) capture the effects of collapsing buildings, conflagration, black smoke, and casualities to civilians on the American psyche: "It dominated the news media and the attention, minds, and emotions of people, whether or not they had personal ties to the victims, and it dramatically altered their behavior and lives. It shattered—ended—the historic sense of security and invulnerability within their borders of the American people and their leaders" (p. 26).

Second, in the aftermath of 9/11, one could see beautiful manifestations of Hume's concentric circles of empathy radiating out from center to periphery. Third, the shattering of America's sense of impregnability ultimately caused most North American media outlets to specialize in mourning the lives of the 3,000 victims who died on that fateful day. The latter statement leads to the fourth overarching point that I wish to examine in this section— the role of the media in managing mourning. Later, I will raise a question regarding the relationship between media's mourning for victims and America's decision to go to war with little or no opposition from congressional representatives. But first, some case studies of the role media played in Americans' mourning the loss of 3,000 victims at the hands of Al-Qaeda.

In Chapter 3, I also detailed the outpouring of sympathy for Americans following the violence of Al-Qaeda and its "Islamic Jihad" ideology and how sympathy for Americans eventually waned because America's moral standing in the world was compromised. Moral compromise occurred largely because the Bush administration found no weapons of mass destruction in Iraq. For my purposes here, however, I underline not only the sheer power and elegance of empathy but also its generative and potential power to numb critical faculties of media producers—setting the stage for America's entry into Iraq and media coverage of same.

Immediately after 9/11, thousands of letters, e-mail messages, missives to President Bush from international leaders, support for the victims and their families, and overall expressions of sympathy for Americans flooded the airwaves. Some have reported that outpourings of sympathy for the unspeakable act of cruelty helped Americans to redefine their national identity and promote patriotism in a manner not seen since World War II. If we take identity to mean "who we are" and "where we are coming from," (Taylor, 1992, p. 33), it is easy to understand media's role in cementing empathy and identity after 9/11. The comment that 9/11 had "special news value" because of "its magnitude, consequence, pathos, proximity, or drama" (Brown & Waltzer, 2004, p. 29) is significant for what it signifies about the behavior of the media thereafter. The north tower of the World Trade Center (WTC) fell at 8:45 a.m., and by 8:49:50 a.m., CNN was on the air with live pictures with "unconfirmed reports" that a plane had struck the WTC. Eighteen minutes later, when the south tower fell, ABC, CBS, NBC, FOX News, and other media outlets had joined CNN with stories of what was happening that day and why.

Media reporting led to extensive coverage of the event and dominated headlines for months. On September 24, 2001, *Newsweek* magazine led with a cover story titled "After the Terror: God Bless America," and *Time* focused on "One Nation Indivisible: America Digs Out and Digs In." The September 12, 2001, issue of *The New York Times* led with a front-page, well-developed banner headline that read "US ATTACKED: Hijacked Jets Destroy Twin Towers and Hit Pentagon in Day of Terror." *The New York Times* also featured a special section titled "A Nation Challenged." The *Times* coverage extended from features on "Portraits in Grief" to "Vanquished Taliban, Fear of Chaos Lingers as New Leaders Arrive" (*The New York Times*, December 12, 2001, p. B5) to "Al Qaeda is Beaten in Afghanistan, but Its Leader is Elusive" (*The New York Times*, December 12, 2001).

The "Portraits in Grief" section in *The New York Times* consisted of brief profiles of victims known or dead and interviews with family members. *Newsweek*'s "After the Terror: God Bless America" story placed attention on the enormity of the situation and implicitly signaled allusions to God's special grace for America, extending back to the Pilgrims at Plymouth Rock in 1620 to spiritual leader Jonathan Winthrop's sermon in 1630 on board the ship *Arbella*, prayers and hymns, and thanksgiving and remembrances that characterized America's cultural affirmation and unswerving faith at that time. The words "US ATTACKED" not only carry a message of incredulity but also emphasize implicitly that the harmony that had been America's was being sorely disturbed.

Furthermore, such emotionally charged words as "US ATTACKED" underscore the numerous casualties that Americans already knew existed after the first tower fell. Hence, the "Day of Terror" language. Contained within the words is also the disheartening idea that the strongest country on earth could be psychologically traumatized by "hijacked jets" from a Muslim group named Al-Qaeda. Also embedded within the words *hijacked jets* are incalculable notions of Al-Qaeda's gall and America's surprise regarding the gall.

Chinks in Memory

The idea that America could be both challenged and surprised by a band of men from the Middle East does indeed signify a huge disturbance to America's cultural armor, reviving memories of the ideology of "the chosen people" and the "city upon a hill" rhetoric and action. The banner headlines also symbolize the beginnings of a profound perceptual shift in America's cultural consciousness facilitated by, but not singly of course, enmeshment between displays of empathy and media reporting of same.

Together, implicitly, North Americans' lineage and remembrances of things past threw in sharp relief distinctions that German historian and philosopher Reinhart Koselleck (2004) makes between "space of experience" and "horizons of expectation." Koselleck argues that temporally, before/later concepts are created through the intersection of "space of experience" (events that "have been incorporated and can be remembered") against spaces of experience (things that take "place in the today; it is the future made present") (Koselleck, 2004, p. 259). In this way, there is accord between the space of experience and the horizon of expectations—between before and later—as modes of understanding events. So, in terms of empathy, it matters a great deal whether one is inside or outside the boundaries of temporal human consciousness, "out there" or "in here," or between previous and later.

Furthermore, to return to media headlines, such banner headings as "Remains of the Day" explained the import of what it means to mourn for a country by superimposing such symbols as the American flag, patriotism, visible love of country, and community upon the landscape of the United States. Later accounts indicate that symbols of empathy fortified Americans' attachment to their country and paved the way for the Iraq War and fear to be used as instruments of social control. These, in turn, became very visible expressions of "Remains of the Day" empathetic discourse.

Fear-Arousing Appeals

Nowhere is the import of the association between the generation of empathy and 9/11 clearer than in appeals to fear. Media reactions to the tie-in between 9/11 and the war in Iraq seemed inescapable. I have already discussed the war in Iraq, but here I specify the role of the media in promoting it. Even if pundits, editors and reporters, and general owners of the media doubted the tie-in, by March 2003, empathy for 9/11 victims ensured that stories would be heavily scripted given the scarred souls and troubled mood of the country.

Everyone "wanted to be part of the battle against 'them,' the terrorists, to express their sympathies to the victims, and to display themselves in a patriotic and favorable light," according to Brown and Waltzer (2004, p. 32). Bill Moyers of the Public Broadcasting System (PBS) acknowledges that American forces were instructed not to cover civilian casualties in Afghanistan. In this regard, Walter Isaacson of *The Washington Post* reports that although there was "not direct pressure from advertisers," "big people in corporations were calling up and saying, 'You're being anti-American here'" ("Buying the War," 2007, p. 4).

Media strategist Roger Ailes of FOX News "had privately urged the White House to use the harshest measures possible after 9/11" ("Buying the War," 2007, p. 4). Newspapers were also implicated in the move toward a patriotic coverage of the war on terror in Afghanistan. In this context, to ensure that sympathy for the victims and their families was not overshadowed, Isaacson recalls that the media were "caught between the patriotic fervor and a competition (Fox News) who was using that to their advantage; they were pushing the fact that CNN was too liberal, that they were sort of vaguely anti-American" ("Buying the War," 2007, p. 4).

Media coverage was particularly suited to an ideological tug of war between "meanings, messages, and people." Empathy for 9/11 victims and their families and the war on Al-Qaeda opened up new discourse opportunities for those who were considered to be favorable toward the war to have a platform from which to speak on television. On November 11, 2001, Richard Perle, a source very close to the Bush White House, declared on ABC *This Week* that "weapons of mass destruction in the hands of Saddam Hussein, plus his known contact with terrorists, including Al Qaeda terrorists, is simply a threat too large to continue to tolerate" ("Buying the War," 2007, p. 4). Bill Kristol, editor of *The Weekly Standard,* and Fred Barnes also added their voices to the "let us topple Saddam" chorus that was gathering high decibels. And William Safire of *The New York Times* wrote at least 27 opinion pieces in favor of the war against Hussein ("Buying the War," 2007, p. 4).

Major newspapers and magazines allocated "prime space" for Bush supporters "to make their case, including the possibility that 9/11 had been" sponsored, supported, and perhaps even ordered by Saddam Hussein ("Buying the War," 2007, p. 5). Howard Kurtz of *The Washington Post* argues that he had gone back and figured mathematically, "From August 2002 until the war was launched in March of 2003 there were about 140 front page pieces in *The Washington Post* making the administration's case for war" ("Buying the War," 2007, p. 174).

Kurtz observes, of course, that the media should have given administrative officials a chance to speak to the American people under the rubric of "The President said yesterday," "The Vice president said yesterday," and "The Pentagon said yesterday," but the harsh reality was that only a handful of stories ran in *The Washington Post* during the same period that made the opposite case ("Buying the War," 2007, p. 17). Although clearly texts and contexts surrounding the coming war in Iraq complicate matters, it is also apparent that American beliefs, values, and a wounding of spirit plus great injury to the soul of the country could not help but foster generous amounts of empathy and, as a consequence, constrain what media could and could not report or say during and following the crisis of 9/11.

It also seems safe to say that the anti-Hussein rhetoric was also designed to keep at bay the possibility of encouraging North Americans to have huge empathy for Afghans. Isaacson said that the phrase, "Don't even show what's happening in Afghanistan," became part of media norms and expectations. One newspaper in Florida advised its editors, "Do not use photos on page 1a showing civilian casualties . . . our sister paper A . . . has done so and received hundreds and hundreds of threatening e-mails" ("Buying the War," 2007, p. 17). These comments vividly contrast empathy for Americans with empathy for Afghans. When the possibility of feelings for Americans killed on 9/11 is contrasted with empathy for Afghans, contrast for whom sympathy should have been directed could not have been sharper and more vivid.

As such, the media not reporting extensively on the unbearable grief that Afghans suffered in the early stages of the war raises a question of weighty proportion: Can human emotions simultaneously sustain bifurcated notions of empathy when patriotism, nationalism, flags, days of reckoning rhetoric, and other forms of mine versus thine thinking are highlighted? In the eyes of true believers, however, complexities of empathetic responses were nearly muted because of the unprecedented level of devastation and loss in America after 9/11.

The Arrival of Insurgents

Soon after the fall of Hussein and the toppling of his giant statue in central Baghdad, Iraqi insurgents began fierce efforts to free Iraqis from American occupation and mobilize empathy—for the hearts and minds of the Arab world. Insurgents' use of the media provides an opportunity for us to understand how mobilization of empathy can be played out against what Appiah (2008, p. 125) calls a conceptual background. By conceptual background, I mean the ability of people to use concepts that are available to them; this is a central aspect of culture. "It's only because of an institutional and conceptual background that one can say, a Republican or a Democrat, a Catholic or a Muslim," according to Appiah (2008). Absent such conceptual background, being both a Baptist and an artist and "acting as one" would be literally inconceivable. I argue in this section that although American media and Iraqi insurgents produced highly divergent images, it is instructive to see how each group sold its empathy-bearing ideas to its respective publics. Seeking to make a persuasive case for their cause based on their values and beliefs, each group constructed and disseminated narratives that extolled the virtues of its culture, creating similar appeals in the process.

Categories of Insurgents

Iraqi insurgents may be placed into three broad evolutionary categories, according to Ahmed Hashim of the U.S. Naval War College: regime loyalists,

Iraqi nationalists, and Islamist groups. The regime loyalist group surfaced after the demise of Saddam Hussein and emerged not to restore the *ancient regime* back to power but rather to fight for the return of Saddam (Al-Marashi, 2004). The second group that emerged directed its energies toward the removal of American forces from Iraq. Comprising Iraqi nationalists from such towns and cities as Fallujah, Ramada, and Samarra (commonly referred to as the "Sunni Arab Triangle"), this group limited itself to "guerilla-type" warfare and used kidnapping of foreigners as an instrument of empathy.

The third group, "Islamist insurgents," added to its repertoire of killing such grisly things as beheadings, creating in the minds of the public actions that became synonymous with "global terror." The last faction will serve as the focal point of this section to demonstrate how it used culturally embedded features of empathy in its struggle for recognition and possible political ascendancy.

Framing Insurgents

Despite categorization of insurgents, it is simply the case that the forces arrayed against America from 2003 to the present writing comprise a diverse and shadowy group of individuals. However they are viewed, the American media soon used the lexical, umbrella term "The Guerrilla War" to situate the new form of warfare in the minds of Americans and others worldwide, employing such descriptors as "Jihadist terrorists," "Islamic insurgents, " "Cyber Jihad," and "Islamic extremists" to refer to insurgents.

Once such descriptors began circulating, they forcefully locked themselves into the psychic of America and helped to usher in an Amerio-centric response to the war—virtually concealing what was happening to everyday ordinary Iraqis. With such images and practices in place, it was easier for President Bush discursively to shift from framing the war in Iraq as one aimed at weapons of mass destruction to a war of liberation. And a good number of the American press went along with the new moral credo. For example, Katrina vanden Heuvel, editor of the *Nation,* a journalist who opposed the war in Iraq, said, "It quickly became a war of liberation in the coverage. Only late in the war was more attention paid to the professed reason we went to war, weapons of mass destruction" (Kurtz, 2003, p. A01).

As Americans struggled to make sense of the war, the Pentagon invited the media to become embedded in the war so that, in the words of Pentagon spokeswoman, Victoria Clarke, "reporters would be welcomed into the front lines and given the freedom to do their jobs" (Kurtz, 2003, p. A01). Defense Secretary Donald Rumsfeld and Joint Chiefs Chairman Richard Myers also sent a special "P-4" memo to American soldiers urging them to cooperate with the media. Strategically, "embeds," as the press who covered the war were called, served two important functions (Kurtz, 2003).

First, Pentagon officials ensured that they would have access to and some control over the diffusion of sympathetic images and narratives emanating from Iraq. Second, the embeds worked to humanize American soldiers and present a concrete, visible, and friendly face on war. In 2004, Ted Koppel, then anchor of ABC's *Nightline,* with fluid drama, read the names of the then 721 dead soldiers in Iraq with great effect—heightening emotional intensity and feelings for American soldiers (*Los Angeles Times,* December 1, 2008). Howard Kurtz (2003) noted, "Even some journalists conceded it would be hard to write critically about their units" (p. A01). And Kurtz quoted ABC's John Donvan as saying, "They're [American soldiers] are my protectors" (p. A01).

An *Atlanta Constitution* (Kurtz, 2003) photographer demonstrated the visual power of the embedding empathetic process when he "held an intravenous drip bag over a wounded civilian's stretcher," and CNN correspondent and doctor Sanjay Gupta "operated on a 2-year-old Iraqi boy." Gupta's noble and emblematic act spoke volumes about the humanitarian mission of America in Iraq. "Embeds" not only covered the war but also managed to perform acts of generosity toward Iraqi people. Such acts were emblematic affirmations of human dignity and demonstrated that American values of kindness and magnanimity worked even in the throes of fierce battle.

War: Iraqi Style

Clearly, such images went a long way toward encouraging American empathy for American soldiers. But such wonderful acts as Gupta operating on a young Iraqi boy notwithstanding, did such empathy extend equally to Iraqi civilians? A study of the images flowing out of Iraq suggests that media efforts to report what it was like for the average soldier to be in Iraq helped limit imagistic space for ordinary Iraqis, creating a credibility gap between moral commitment toward one group as opposed to another. And this is a huge complication for the nature, structure, and promotion of empathy during times of war. What is one's moral obligation to others in times of war?

Vanden Heuvel claims that "we haven't seen the other side of the war that the Arab world saw—the anger and humiliation that millions of Americans won't understand emanating from the Arab world" (qtd. in Kurtz, 2003, p. A01). Insufficient attention to Iraqi citizens was further compromised by who actually did the hard work of reporting the war from battle fields. To a great extent, American media relied very heavily on local Iraqi citizens to do the reporting from Baghdad, Falugi, and other places.

The New York Times correspondent Richard Pérez-Peña (2007) reported that about two thirds of the street correspondents comprised local citizens, raising the issue of whether the press had indeed done a good job covering the war. Furthermore, of the 124 journalists killed in Iraq by 2007, and since the beginning of the war in 2003, 102 were Iraqis. Iraqis "went to the most dangerous places" and died "in the greatest numbers" (Pérez-Peña, 2007). Dangerous constraints upon world journalists understood, statistics are striking for what they tell about moral imbalances during the Iraqi war. For our purposes, the question is to what extent did such limitations prevent the narratives of Iraqis from circulating more widely? And whether a fuller coverage of the suffering of Iraqi women and children might have added humanistic force to the gravity of the war and contested the incongruity and incompatibility of America's discourse of freedom and democracy as against Iraqi casualties. Consider the following statistics.

Project for Excellence in Journalism's first quarterly report of 2007 ("Iraq Dominates," 2007, p. 1) revealed in chilling statistics that of the war coverage, "55% had been about the political debate in Washington," "31% on events in Iraq itself and about one half on American soldiers," and yet "in all, just one in five stories about the war had been focused on Iraqis, Iraqi casualties, or the internal political affairs of their country" (p. 1). Whether Al-Qaeda and insurgents in Iraq were aware of such big discrepancies will not be argued here. Rather, I argue that the third insurgency group that I covered earlier set loose—both on process and image making—a way to counter American images and a way to galvanize the Middle East. The latter was designed to present sympathetic views of what insurgents were doing in Fuluga, Baghdad, and other places in Iraq. I will not take time here to discuss the roster of characters involved in insurgency work. Instead, I note that Osama bin Laden and other major leaders' tactics are emblematic of the overall mission they tried to accomplish.

Insurgents' Use of Media

Using Al Jazeera as a vehicle for amplifying the distinction between American-led and insurgent-sponsored empathy, insurgents exploited some of the most complicated forms of media, including satellite television, the Internet, and cell phones, to reach Arab audiences. These powerful means of technology were also used to disseminate information and train potential recruits. Lukaszewski (1987), a public relations counsel and a former adviser to the U.S. military, argues that "media coverage and terrorism are soul mates—virtually inseparable. They feed off each other. They together create a dance of death—the one for political or ideological motives, the other for commercial success." Secretary Rumsfeld also recognized the dexterity of insurgents. He said that they "had skillfully adapted" to the media age (*BBC News,* February 17, 2006, p. 1).

In elevating the level of empathy for their cause and in trying to secure a favorable hearing from Middle Eastern audiences, insurgents exploited and are exploiting the media. They use media in two important ways. First, in a perverse way and in a nonspiritual sense, insurgents have used mayhem, torture, kidnappings, and other gross acts of violence to rally the moral resources of a narrow Middle Eastern audience to their cause. In the war against terror, especially in the early phases of the Iraq War, pictures of decapitation, in the eyes of radical insurgents, served as tools of awakening and public announcements about events. The sheer magnitude of such acts of violence, insurgents believed, warned those inclined to support America and the Iraqi government that their sympathies should lie with insurgents and not with the occupiers and their supporters. In October 2004, for example, a group associated with al–Zarqawi posted on its Web sites the beheading of two Iraqis, Fadhil Ibrahim and Firas Imayyil, who were believed to be members of the Iraqi secret service.

By selecting two local officials tied to the Iraqi government for beheading, insurgents telescoped how empathy can be used for cruel purposes. Demonstratively, the group aimed to socialize converts into disassociating with those who collaborated with Americans. Furthermore, from time to time, lapses of moral conscience could be seen in the beheadings of American contractors in Iraq. In 2004, for example, 48-year-old blindfolded Jack Hensley and American hostage Eugene Armstrong were also beheaded. Nick Berg, 26, a freelance telecommunications contractor from West Chester in Pennsylvania, was beheaded on a video posted by Al-Qaeda.

Since the latter's beheading followed U.S. abuse of Iraqi captives at Baghdad's Abu Ghraib prison, there is reason to believe that Berg's killing was a *rebuttal killing.* By rebuttal killing, I mean that similar to rebuttals in collegiate debate, insurgents and the United States, through attack and defense, tried to uphold their moral positions. If true, this was an instance of mayhem feeding off mayhem. The violent acts show how modes of intensity, adaptation, and juxtaposition of one group's empathy-bearing behavior against another sometimes can almost be mirror images of the same.

Torture at Abu Gharib prison and grisly beheadings on the part of insurgents raise such vexing questions regarding why human beings resort to such spectacles of violence in the first place. Appiah (2008) claims that "faced with a suffering person . . . our natural response is an emotion—compassion, let's call it—that gives us a pro tanto reason to express sympathy and offer aid" (p. 130). And yet, the human capacity for compassion left the arenas of the places where Al-Qaeda and insurgents concocted their elixirs of fear and mayhem.

Properly and necessarily, must we place human beings—people who look like the rest of us in terms of biological equipment and faculties for reasoning—outside the theater of human compassion? At the level of depravity, are we to indict culturally specific concepts as reasons why people behave outside the limits of moral norms? And, if yes, what special inputs encapsulate the thinking of terrorists? Research on psychopaths provides some explanations for why conscience-lacking behavior occurs, and reasons range from an absence of soft conditioning to a greater tolerance for pain (Appiah, 2008, p. 129; Wilson, 1993, p. 107). In one study, for example, Robert Hare found that psychopaths' tolerance for tones that are followed by electric shocks is greater than their counterparts. Another way of stating this is that ordinary people only require a few electric shocks before they become apprehensive, while psychopaths are far less apprehensive (Wilson, 1993, p. 107).

While the research on why some people abide the suffering of others is both rigorous and persuasive, it still does not fully explain what sets of trigger mechanisms lead to low tolerance in the first place. In other words, what is there about being human beings that makes psychopaths less *inclined to be human?* But let us leave this discussion for another day. Instead, I note insurgents' efforts to create compassion for their cause as a tactic that they used and are continuing to use in the theater of war. Of course, the entire panoply of insurgent behavior also bothers what constitutes acceptable cultural killing. Are some forms better than others, for example? These sets of questions lead to the second way that insurgents use media.

Al Jazeera television network serves as perhaps an unwitting media accomplice to insurgents and Al-Qaeda. *National Interest Online* argues that the network amplified "the human suffering of Arabs and Muslims around the world" (Lynch, 2006). One reason for the amplification is that Al Jazeera exploits a rule of human suffering that is as old as human suffering itself, and it is this: If you want people to identify with their own folkways, paint very graphic and detailed horrific pictures of others' (enemies') behavior. Then underscore the painting with a powerful narrative that frames the acts of terror as bestial. In this regard, this is where modes of identification and Huntington's notion of a "clash of civilization" play a critical role. Al Jazeera is quite adept at producing and stabilizing Arab identity via mechanisms of empathy-bearing footage that reaches millions of Arabs and Muslims daily.

Furthermore, Al Jazeera is mindful that the television network must please its audiences, provide footage that resonates, and, by extension, both sustain and attract audiences. As such, the network has been influential in mobilizing empathy for Arabs and Muslims. On one hand, by broadcasting beheadings, Al Jazeera has fed into insurgents' conceptions of "them" (America and the West) against "us" (Muslims and Arabs). On the other hand, Al Jazeera highlights a striking contrast with regard to promoting differences in levels of empathy between Islam and Christianity.

Although President Bush, Secretary Condoleezza Rice, and other members of the Bush administration have been careful to use language of bifurcation in distinguishing between wayward, out-of-control adherents to Islam and faithful followers of the religion, Al Jazeera widens the very empathetic media fissures that the Bush administration is trying to close. In Chapter 3, I discussed why America's image abroad suffered even as Bush's public relations envoy, Karen Hughes, tried valiantly to dramatize the moral underpinnings of America to Middle Easterners. Although Al Jazeera does not explicitly support insurgents' and Al-Qaeda's violent tactics of kidnapping and beheading as ways of promoting empathy for Arab and Muslim people, the television station nevertheless circulates images and narratives that lend implicit support to terrorist groups. A key reason for this is the power and narrative-inducing amplification of the network itself that reaches Muslim and Arab audiences.

Clearly, the Bush administration sees Al Jazeera as an effective mechanism for bending the minds and wills of Arabs and Muslims. According to *The Nation* (December 19, 2005), Bush "ceaselessly" attacked Al Jazeera, "bombed its offices in Afghanistan in 2001," and "shelled the Basra hotel where Al Jazeera journalists were the only guests."

Apparently, Bush felt the sting that came from Al Jazeera's symbolically close relationship and identification with Arabs and Muslims. On December 5, 2002, in a speech at Eid-al-Fitr, the Islamic Center in Washington, D.C., Bush said, "America treasures the relationship we have with our many Muslim friends." Furthermore, an examination of Bush's discourses on Islam reveals that he framed his language as one of goodwill for Muslims in general and ill will toward specific individuals who were/are committing acts of terror. Bush employs positive and uplifting phrases, such as "Islam brings hope," "a war not against a religion," "the face of terror is not the true faith—face of Islam," and "we fight not a religion . . . ours is a campaign against evil," to remove any ambiguity or doubt that might exist in the minds of Arabs and Muslims about his strategic, moral mission in Iraq—one on the side of right (www.whitehouse.gov). Bush likes to remind Arabs and Islamic audiences both explicitly and implicitly that there is no way that there could be a link between an ideological war against Al-Qaeda and insurgents and the good people of the Middle East. In effect, Bush invokes a rhetoric of moral high ground.

So perceived, Bush's discourse is designed to give Arabs and Muslims a different perspective on empathy and America's mission in Iraq. Consequently, Bush tried to weave narratives of empathetic continuity between his stated goals of bringing freedom and democracy to Iraq and his feelings for Muslims and Arabs worldwide. Intercultural discourses, of course, can have other far-reaching consequences. For example, what relationship obtains between moral imperatives and political structures as regards such crises as tsunamis and Katrinas? What can be done to avert such changes in the future?

6

Catastrophes, Tsunamis, and Katrinas

The Moral Imperative

Thirty million people devastated by floods in Bangladesh in 1998, 20,000 people killed in an earthquake in Pakistan in 2005, 1,464 victims perished in New Orleans in Louisiana in 2006, 150,000 individuals killed by tsunamis in 2004, and 3 million people displaced by war in Iraq. This partial listing of natural and manmade catastrophes speaks achingly to and illustrates a need for what Hume (1751) called "a tender sympathy with others and a generous concern for our kind and species" perhaps at no other time in recent history. The tsunami especially called to mind events of enormous, biblical proportions as people tried to make sense of a world beset by misery and disasters.

Trying to cope with the severity of the tsunami compelled former *The New York Times* columnist, William Safire (2005), to ask, "Where was God?" The "Leviathanic force of nature," as Safire aptly called it, evoked discussions about the Book of Job written over 2,500 years ago. Job, a resident of Uz, as the biblical story goes, wrestled with the question of whether he had done something horribly wrong to deserve his unbearable suffering.

The Old Testament records that the Lord "brought evil upon Job" and that he lost his vast fortune: 3,000 sheep, 3,000 camels, and 500 oxen. His seven sons and three daughters were taken away by the Sabeans, but through it all, Job refused to curse God and die. In the end, in an act of restorative justice, God gave Job "twice as much as before," a sign that Job was not alone in his misery (Book of Job).

Questions about good and evil and why good people suffer clearly are terrorizing ones that humans grapple. Like Job's wife, we wonder how to keep human integrity amid such catastrophes as tsunamis and Katrinas. And yet, we still practice empathy.

Today, there is a moral imperative to help the poor and save the planet in multiple ways in an almost unimaginable way. North American tycoons in the Gilded Age (1870s–1890s) were among the first members of a super-class to elevate the pursuit of wealth to the status of a social philosophy. Archetypal giving man, Andrew Carnegie, who had "risen from bobbin boy to modern Croesus" (Wrage & Baskerville, 1960, p. 256); oil baron John D. Rockefeller; and automobile entrepreneur Henry Ford, as well as others, for various reasons, gave away hundreds of millions in the 20th century. Carnegie's philanthropic impulse encouraged him to remark, "The man who dies thus rich, dies disgraced." He urged the wealthy to practice a beautiful art of giving for civic purposes. He understood that North America was about more than the accumulation of material goods; it was also about pro-tecting the interests of the poor.

Historian Paul Johnson (1997, p. 555) argues that Carnegie was one of the most important persons in America, including presidents from Lincoln to Theodore Roosevelt. Carnegie died in his sleep at the age of 84, but not before he had disposed of a massive fortune—virtually everything he had. Free public libraries, Carnegie Hall of the performing arts, the Carnegie Endowment for International Peace, church organs, and programs in the humanities and sciences are among the projects that his $50,695,653.40 largess funded (Johnson, 1997). Carnegie still remains the quintessential man of gift giving, although he just might be surpassed by Warren Buffett and Bill Gates in the 21st century.

Climate, Empathy, and Charity

Clearly, we are in an empathetic era of gift giving, creating what contribut-ing writer to *The New York Times Magazine* James Traub (2008) refers to as the "celebrity-philanthropy complex" and the "giving age" (p. 37). David Rothkopf (2008, p. 17) uses a clinical metaphor, "charity craze," to capture the enormous scale of what is happening in today's "do good" social change movements. In the final chapter, I will interrogate whether giving still is inadequate to meet the economic and social needs of the poor.

As of this writing, Warren Buffet has donated $31 billion to the Melinda and Bill Gates Foundation to alleviate suffering, uplift the poor, and provide health care for hundreds of people worldwide. In 1971, following the devastating floods in Bangladesh, powerful and influential George Harrison and Ravi Shankar focused worldwide emphasis on the poor with their Concert for Bangladesh. In 1985, Irish rocker Bob Geldof organized a Live Aid concert to benefit starving Ethiopians. Employing a compelling, defiant directive, "Not on Our Watch" fundraising organization, a galaxy of stars, including George Clooney, Matt Damon, Don Cheadle, and Jerry Weintraub, raised $9.3 million for refugees fleeing war-torn Darfur, Sudan (*The New York Times Magazine,* March 9, 2008).

Singer Alicia Keyes also uses her special charity, "Keep a Child Alive," to fight poverty. In 2006, North Americans gave $295 billion to charity, a handsome sum that equals 2.2% of America's gross domestic product, according to the Center on Philanthropy at Indiana University (Leonhardt, 2008). These are all wonderful, uplifting improvements, signs of one human being caring deeply for another.

Polar ice cap melts, the spread of HIV/AIDS, the struggle against terrorism, the human resources crisis inside poor countries, population shifts, movement of immigrants from emerging countries to industrial countries, the oil crisis, and a host of other "ills" are causes that require constant, vigilant attention from donors. A "charity craze" is upon us. But what is driving this movement toward gift giving? As we have seen, it is difficult to miss the recent explosions of problems confronting the planet as animating forces. Reasons for the healthy impulse can be grouped in the following categories.

Huge Global Inequalities

The question of human inequalities is central to any discussion of empathy not only because imbalances between rich and poor are glaringly visible today but also because of scale. Consider this fact: Approximately 6,000 people constitute the world governing class; this means that the superclass comprises one in a million of the 6 billion people on planet Earth. Furthermore, this means that the average American CEO makes 350 to 400 times what the average American makes. These huge disparities in income are not confined to the United States, however. In Chile, "the top 20 percent earn almost 67 percent of the country's income while the bottom 20 percent earn just over 3 percent" (Rothkopf, 2008, p. 54). And the second richest man in the world, Carlos Slim Helu, controls more than 90% of electronic power lines in

Mexico (Rothkopf, 2008, p. 288). Sociologists and other scholars (Aronowitz, 2003) who study the interpretive schemes that make up social reality suggest that inequalities between classes can exist side by side as long as perceptions of fairness and justice are evident. Later, we will contrast concepts of charity and concepts of justice.

Age of Vulnerability

A postmodern world characterized by interconnectivity, international financial systems, financial instability, threat to the world's environment, and intertwined global markets poses growing problems for the planet in the long haul. In such a climate, compassion for others is a sure way of preserving one's own livelihood. This notion is consistent with Darwinian thought, the work of Richard Dawkins, and the writings of Wilson (1993, p. 43), who argue that affectionate behavior toward others extends beyond kinship into the areas of nonrelatives and caring for the cultural other. This is called "reciprocal altruism," a form of "You scratch my back and I'll scratch yours" philosophy. Reciprocal altruism is a utilitarian system of exchange and encourages humans to give to others. Whether we give to impress others or not, our beneficence increases the likelihood that we will also have future profitable exchanges, if need be. In this way, empathy conspires with cultural and social capital to provide assistance to the weak and exploited among us.

Finally, at the level of cultural imprinting, giving helps individuals become reproductively successful, not only by guaranteeing one's own offspring but also by helping to ensure that enough other humans will be around to sustain the well-being of the "saved." This is part and parcel of a "together, let us all save humanity" philosophy. Not giving generously guarantees all of us an unsure future—one not worth living.

These acts of solidarity with the poor echoes Shakespeare's King Lear's discourse of commitment:

> Poor naked wretches, wheresoe'er you are,
> That bide the pelting of this pitiless storm,
> How shall your houseless heads and unfed sides,
> Your loop'd and window'd raggedness, defend you
> From seasons such as these? O, I have ta'en
> Too little care of this! Take physic, pomp;
> Expose thyself to feel what wretches feel,
> That thou mayst shake the superflux to them,
> And show the heavens more just. (Act 3, Scene 4)

Celebrity-Corporate Nexus Competition

Without impugning the personal motives of such stars as Angelina Jolie and Bono, as well as corporate executives such as Warren Buffet, Bill Gates, and others, who give liberally, it is the case that there is an implied, positive strain of reputation-enhancing symbolism—both expressed and implied—operating in the "do-gooding" philosophy of charitable givers. In Chapter 5, I described how Sharon Stone interrupted the speech of a president of an African country and forcefully challenged the World Economic Forum (WEF) members to match her charitable contributions.

In 1997, Ted Turner dared other billionaires to match his $1 billion donation to the United Nations over a 10-year span—and this was at a time when giving had not quite reached a fever pitch. Recognizing how much money earmarked for poor people often pays salaries of professionals, Turner said of his giving, "This is not going to go for administration. This is only going to go for programs, programs like refugees, cleaning up land mines, peacekeeping, UNICEF for the children, for diseases, and we're going to have a committee that will work with a committee of the U.N. The money can only go to U.N. causes" (http://edition.cnn.com).

Former president of the United States Bill Clinton uses the Clinton Global Initiative (CGI) to facilitate universal giving among the governing class. The purpose of CGI is to "help turn good intentions into real action and results" (www.ClintonGlobalInitative.org). CGI brings together "global leaders to devise and implement innovative solutions to some of the world's most pressing challenges" (www.ClintonGlobalInitative.org). At CGI meetings, Clinton's persuasive tactics testify powerfully to his ability to garner commitments from comrades and world leaders.

Using a compelling storytelling mode that displays the classic DNA of empathy, the CGI Web site features a virtuous video clip of actress Angelina Jolie. Echoing the Good Samaritan of biblical times, in plaintive tones, she recites a heartrending story of a Syrian refugee who had been "set on fire," "tortured," "badly burned and infected." An 8-year-old boy selling tissue happens upon the badly burned Syrian refugee. The boy gives money to the badly wounded and maggot-infected man. Upon seeing the dreadful condition of the old man, the boy runs away only to return later to bind the wounds of the victim. Moved by his sympathetic efforts, Jolie encourages the young boy to become a doctor so that he can help the weary and wounded in the world.

CGI's mantra, "Help Improve the World—One Action at a Time," dramatically illustrates the role of words in changing human behavior. To further implement his goal of turning "good intentions into real action and results," at CGI meetings, Clinton literally gives potential donors a diploma-like document, "like a government declaration," and then he invites them to sign it (Rothkopf, 2008, p. 282).

In 2006, by elevating the celebrity-corporate nexus and by juxtaposing rhetoric against concrete reality, 215 participants pledged a total of $7.5 million toward Clinton's charity. Most of the money is earmarked for a complex set of problems—poverty, global warming, education, energy and climate change, global health, and neglected disease programs. Clinton's philanthropic prowess is significant because he demonstrates goodwill for noble causes and has an amazing ability to promote needful action on behalf of the world's poor countries and citizens instead of engaging in "talkfests," which seem to be most typical of the WEF.

The Common-Good Angle

But is enough being done? Increasingly, scholars, social activists, politicians, world leaders, environmentalists, and critics of globalization are questioning laws governing intellectual property that protect U.S. and other Western drug companies. We know, for example, that most of the world's drugs are manufactured in North America. This presents a problem for emerging countries that need to have access to AIDS drugs that are patented by Squibb, Pfizer, the Roche Group, and Abbott Laboratories (Stiglitz, 2005, pp. 103–117). Fierce competition, then, has and is ensuing between the common good—"the good we share in common"—and rights to private property. At the level of profit making, this also presents a big ethical dilemma for drug companies. In the interest of empathy and concern for the well-being of others, should pharmaceutical companies sustain an economic loss? After all, in the tradition of hard-nosed Milton Friedman economics, if companies do not make a profit, they will lose business, and if they lose business, people will be laid off—thereby affecting a larger number of people.

To try to remedy such messy complications, on April 15, 1994, under the Uruguay Round agreements, world leaders pushed through an agreement on Trade-Related Aspects of Intellectual Property Rights (TRIPs; Stiglitz, 2005, p. 105). TRIPs effectively implemented the following things: (a) ensured that customers would pay higher prices for drugs, (b) sustained the law that gives inventor and innovators control over their intellectual property, and (c) ensured that only very wealthy individuals would be able to buy medicines. Enter demonstrators!

In January 2004, activists in Rabat in Morocco and in Paris, France, protested the new trade agreements between the Moroccan government and the United States. Activists believed that the agreement would damage a portion of humanity that sorely needed access to generic drugs. Activists also protested at the Fifteenth International AIDS conference in Thailand. The citizen activists pushed onto the world agenda an issue of great human significance: Who is entitled to the commons? And should intellectual property rights be unfettered? Who and what will be privileged? "Everyday," Burkhalter (2004) argues, "AIDS kills 8,000 people and infects 13,700 more" (p. 8).

A struggle today under the "public good" paradigm is how to align a capitalist market place with a genre of human caring. If, as is the case of African countries, HIV/AID drugs cost at least $10 to $1,200 per patient per year, how will people even in the richest countries on the continent—South Africa or Botswana—let alone the poorest afford health care (Chang, 2008, p. 123)? The issues of justice and fair play that are implicated here will be discussed later.

Stiglitz (2006) maintains that "when there is a common resource that can be used freely by all, each user fails to think about how his actions might harm others; each loses sight of the common good" (p. 162). Furthermore, Stiglitz argues that there are two approaches that might resolve the issue. First, one could follow the tradition that operated in Scotland in the 16th and 17th centuries; this entailed "privatizing the commons." As Stiglitz notes, "The Scottish lords simply took the commons for themselves" (p. 163). This arrangement ensured that each owner was invested in ensuring that the land was sufficiently grazed.

Negatively, this approach caused a sizable number of people to suffer because they were thrown off the commons. The second approach to resolving the common grounds issue is allowing governments to manage the common resources. It assumes that citizens will exercise their social and legal rights to ensure that common resources are used both efficiently and justly. The Slaughter House Cases of 1873, which granted the business of slaughtering cattle to specific businesses in New Orleans in Louisiana a monopoly, is an example of what is meant by protecting common rights. Of course, the cases were later used to deny Black Americans their civil rights on the grounds that the court ruling also gave states control over citizens, however unfairly (Foner & Branham, 1998).

To achieve the ends of community and the primacy of a free society, we must think of the consequences of not only the decision-making powers of the commons but also decisions of state. Lately, rich countries have begun to pass regulatory laws to limit pollution. At this writing, European Union countries are struggling with writing regulations to limit pollution for the social benefit of all. States recognize that carbon dioxide gases privilege no state or person. True to their ability to travel over time and space, molecules in France are as likely to travel to London as they are to travel from Paris to Lyon.

But can poor countries afford to pass and abide by strict regulatory emission laws when so many of their citizens have not even moved beyond the status of merely eking out a basic living? Haiti comes to mind, a poor country that has the worst health statistics in the world. Many trees in Haiti have been felled so that people can have access to fuel to cook basic foods such as cassava and rice. Haiti is also losing "a great deal of its soil" (Kidder, 2003, p. 21). In light of constraints on poor countries and to benefit all, we must continue to think of collective solutions to our common problems. As soon as the world thinks that it is making some headway for the implicit benefit of all, unfortunately, warfare, famine, ethnic bickering, and natural disasters such as earthquakes beset humans.

The Tsunami Strikes

Nowhere was this natural intrusion felt more keenly than the tsunami of December 26, 2004. I was sitting in my family room when news of the catastrophic natural event reached my television. There, on the screen, unbelievable tidal waves formed massive walls of water, causing much death and destruction. An undersea tsunami in the Indian Ocean, the world's most devastating natural disaster in the past two centuries, had struck, killing over 150,000 collectively in India, Sri Lanka, Indonesia, and the Maldives.

Jan Egeland (2005), the United Nations Emergency Relief Coordinator, said that "2004 had ended with a natural disaster at its very worst and 2005 had started with humanity at its very best." Indeed, the scale of the tsunami presented humankind with an opportunity to display empathy in unparalleled ways. Implicating relations between rich and poor citizens, given the magnitude of the tsunami, media vied for coverage of the event. Suketu Mehta (2004), author of *Maximum City,* called the tsunami a "pornography of images of disasters in the Third World" (p. A10). CNN, BBC, The Associated Press, Reuters, and Agence France Press all covered the victims of the tsunami. The tsunami did several things that relate specifically to the mission of this book; among them are the following.

First, donations from all over the world poured in. Rock stars, nations, businessmen, nongovernmental organizations (NGOs), Japan, Hong Kong, and Russia offered help almost immediately. Poor and rich countries donated aid; Mozambique, a very poor country, was moved to send $10,000 in pledges to tsunami survivors.

Second, media played a commanding role in focusing attention on the event, dominating the news worldwide from late December 2004 to early January 2005. In the process, dramatic stories of survival and heroism, lost relatives fleeing, footage of destroyed homes and villages, survivors revealed, and children with amputated limbs riveted world citizens (www.global journalist.org).

Of course, in the human drama that became tsunami, the situation was ideal for what it offered viewers in terms of empathy for international victims and survivors. Author Harm de Blij (2005, p. 12), in arguing why geography matters, tells a gripping story that had circulated widely in news media, of lives saved because one young girl, Tilly Smith, had paid attention to her geography lessons at Danes Hill Prep School in Oxshott, south of London. In Mr. Andrew Kearney's class, Tilly had learned that "the deep wave of a tsunami sucks the water off the beach before it returns in a massive wall that inundates the entire shoreline" (p. 12). Remembering her expert geography lesson, Tilly, who was on Maikhao Beach in Phuket, Thailand, when the tsunami struck, recounted the warning signs of a tsunami to her parents. More than 100 people heeded Tilly's advice and were saved.

Stories like Tilly's mattered because tearful survivors on holiday from Sweden and other industrialized countries helped keep focus on tsunami's aftermath before an attentive international audience. Scott (2005), in a piece on media reporting titled "Tsunami Coverage: Slow to Start, Left Us Wanting More," claims that within the first 24 hours, foreign correspondents "included very few personal accounts from the actual residents of the affected areas." Instead, "mostly European holiday-seekers told their stories from airports." In fairness to media, perhaps reporting on stories of European visitors mattered because many had video cameras and because of language barriers. Research suggests that television producers capitalize on nationalism, "culturally-based structures," and values to sell compelling stories (Lull, 2000, p. 19).

Author Mehta (2004) provides another take on whose empathy might have mattered most at the beginning of tsunami. Said he of local citizens in tsunami land, and of our short attention spans relating to global crises in general, "They all look so foreign—all these brown or black people, poor things. So it becomes easier to forget them, as our attention moves to a fresh disaster somewhere else, or to a celebrity trial right at home" (p. A10). Mehta's comments strike at the heart of how human beings deal with scale, degree, and kinds of disasters that occur. And his comments raise serious concerns about parceling out of resources, money, and capital—human, cultural, intellectual—in the future. In terms of the tsunami and other natural disasters, will we be able to lift struggling nations out of poverty and cope with natural disaster simultaneously? And will implications of whose lives matter most gain more salience?

Mehta (2004) also raises another haunting, significant question that bears on causes and consequences of empathy: Is it the case that huge natural disasters "reinforce our (the West's) sense of living in a blessed land. We may have our marriage troubles, honey, but at least we're not *those* people" (p. A10). Is having more equated with a repression of empathy borne of repetitive natural disasters? Does it diminish our capacity to see the other person's perspective in such tragic instances? People who are already on the margins? Terry Eagleton (2003) reminds us that "margins can be unspeakably painful places to be, and there are few more honorable tasks for students of culture than to help create a space in which the dumped and disregarded can find tongue" (p. 13).

Third, what I term *theories of disaster displacement* seeped in as a result of the tsunami. That is, given the magnitude of natural disasters over the past 5 years, the media, by highlighting one event over another, unwittingly increase the likelihood that disaster replacement will occur. As I noted, within several days after the tsunami occurred, donations poured in from around the world. In a zero-sum atmosphere, some critics began to question whether media coverage of the tsunami came at the expense of other equally important and sad causes.

At the time that the tsunami struck, hundreds of places worldwide were competing for human empathy. Wars or aftermath of wars in Somalia, Congo, Iraq, Liberia, and Darfu in Sudan are a few examples. Jefferson Morley (2005), writing in *The Washington Post,* said that the "South Asia tsunami not only wiped out more than 150,000 lives but also overwhelmed international media coverage of genocidal conflict in Sudan." "Before the tsunami struck, the U.N. described the conflict in the western Darfur region as the world's greatest humanitarian crisis," according to Australian *Age* (qtd. in Morley, 2005).

A fourth and final reason why the tsunami matters is because a disaster of such scale alters the moral calculus of human beings. K. Mahalingam, an Indian fisherman, whose life changed significantly after the tsunami hit, with much pathos, said, "We loved the sea. We lived by the sea. Now we hate seeing the sea" (Mehta, 2004, p. A10). A 9-year-old boy asked a reporter, "Where was God when this happened? God saved me, but why?"

These piercing existential questions go to the very heart of humans' relationship with their gods and with each other. In Indian Hindu culture, the Dance of Shiva has been described as the "clearest image of the activity of God which any art or religion can boast of" (Gannon, 2003, p. 65). In this regard, according to religious credo, every facet of nature—man, bird, beast, insect, trees, wind, waves, stars—all display a dance pattern; hence, we see the implicit interrelatedness of the tsunami and other aspects of life. "This is a part of the world where there are gods in the rocks, gods in the trees, gods in the sky and gods in the sea," writes Mehta (2004, p. A10). Stories about the link between religion, culture, and empathy abound, and I could offer more, but the point is made, I hope. I have shown that all the reasons cited helped to encourage a disposition of giving to tsunami victims, despite vexing questions of mixed motives on the part of givers. How could a grieving and giving world sustain another human catastrophe?

In Katrina's Waters

Less than a year after the tsunami hit Southeast Asia, in August 2005, people were in water again—this time, in Katrina's waters in New Orleans, Louisiana, and other cities and states in the South, including Mississippi and Alabama. Images of American women and children weeping and wailing for help, sick people mired in an overheated and oversized superdome, and scenes of poor Blacks fleeing devastation and despair told a story of who we are—magnifying the entire range of human temporality—time past, time present, and time future. Dan Barry (2006a, 2006b) noted that before Katrina, "30 percent of residents in Bayou La Batre, Alabama were living in poverty." "Poverty rate among New Orleans blacks stood at 35 percent," according to Juan Williams (2006, p. A19). Statistics on poverty among Blacks are even more devastating when one considers that, at the time, Blacks comprised 70% of New Orleans' population.

Because a majority of the victims in New Orleans were elderly and poor Blacks and Whites, stories and images evoked memories of the gross inequities that existed *before* the tragedy happened and *during* the tragedy, and they raised issues regarding the *future* of care in the United States. Before our eyes, television naturalized the experiences of thousands of unfortunate people—they became the embodiment of tragedy and suffering. In the process, a key argument emerged over whether the response time of the Federal Emergency Management Agency (FEMA), Red Cross, and other NGOs would have been quicker had the victims been rich and powerful.

In a presentation at Indiana University in September 2005, I pulled an empty picture frame from my more than ample handbag and encouraged the audience to do the following. I urged listeners, in their "mind's eye," to imagine the poor evacuees in New Orleans. Then, I challenged the audience to ponder how long it took FEMA to arrive and why. By then, members of the august audience knew a great deal about systems and logistics and predictions and procedures regarding the evacuation of victims from the Superdome.

Next, I asked my attentive listeners to clear their creative and caring minds, if they could, of pressing images of Katrina victims and put in the frame "Bush women" (Mrs. Laura Bush and her twin daughters)—they are now in the Superdome in New Orleans. How long would it have taken for the women to be rescued? Three days? Five days? A nanosecond? Finally, I invited the audience to put in the frame a convention composed of North American and global CEOs, including Bill Gates and the presidents of Halliburton, Exxon Mobil, Royal Dutch Shell, General Electric, Citigroup, and Wal-Mart. Then, as in the other imagined scenarios, I asked the final temporal question: "How long might it have taken FEMA to rescue this splendid, superclass group of people?"

The exercise served as an embodied snapshot of the relationship among such variables as time, animating forces, structures, who was present in Katrina's waters, and who was absent, who was valued, and who was disvalued. As the masses of poor Blacks, Whites, and elderly who were stranded in the New Orleans Superdome and convention center huddled, it became clear that bureaucratic organizational structures overshadowed concerns for human beings.

Anthropologist Edward T. Hall (1959, 1976) was one of the first scholars to study the priority that specific cultures give to organizational temporal functions. He posited two kinds of time: monochromic and polychromic. Monochronic time (M-time) people emphasize compartmentalization and are less likely to see their activities in context as part of the larger whole, whereas polychromic time (P-time) people tend to see organizational wholes. This difference does not mean, of course, that M-time people are unaware of wholes. Rather, it means that the goals of organizations are rarely seen holistically and can prevent cultural members from seeing the proverbial forest for the trees.

My point is that emphasis on compartmentalization and who was responsible for what job in rescuing those trapped in Katrina's waters undermined empathy. Thus seen, governmental officials' focus on efficiency and organizational flowcharts and roles and responsibilities undermined the central mission of FEMA and the Red Cross at a critical economic and cultural period. It is no wonder, then, that people suffered while micro-political negotiations were going on backstage.

Structures, Roles, and Functions

Scholars argue, for example, that by virtue of specific orientations, humans are "already predisposed to act in certain ways, pursue certain goals . . . and so on" (Bourdieu, 1999, p. 17). Such dispositions result in what is labeled *conscious calculation*. Conscious calculations in turn influence practice, loyalty, prioritizing, communitarian policies, fair game, and actions. In effect, under the National Response Plan, FEMA and the Red Cross are supposed to coordinate activities in emergency, domestic situations. But in Katrina's waters, the problem was one of *specific* coordination and maybe "unconscious" calculation.

Ambiguity between roles and functions further complicated matters because the two agencies "spent time during the response effort trying to establish operations and procedures rather than focusing solely on coordinating services," according to a report of the Government Accountability Office (Strom, 2006, p. A23). Few would dispute that such bureaucratic modes of decision making entailed much human misery on New Orleanians and people along the Gulf Coasts of Alabama and Mississippi. Think of it this way: Human beings suffered hugely while bureaucrats bickered over roles and responsibilities! The machinations and arguments between FEMA and the Red Cross are merely a microcosm of how, tyrannically, structures both curtail and derail human decision making. Much like decision making leading up to the Iraq War, as I noted in Chapter 3, groupthink and individual roles of human agents triumph over the collective good. Tightly woven structures appear to accelerate bad decision making. Meanwhile, professionals flourish while the poor suffer.

To make matters worse, while the poor suffered, the so-called North American "right" exploited images of looting, stealing, rapists, and criminals emanating from news media. Nightly, television showed scenes of Blacks taking food, chips, sodas, and other items from stores without contextualizing the issue. Although claims of willful looting turned out not to have been true, by then the die had been cast, and past negative images of poor people resurfaced—having been submerged, however temporarily, under the radar of concern and attention.

In the process, the shocking natural disaster also cast light on the great contrast between poor and rich in America—causing people to revisit conditionality what we thought had disappeared. Collectively, using repetition, the images and many photographs that circulated on television screens and in print medium mounted a strong argument about the distance between the rich and the poor in the United States. Who can forget the anguishing picture of victims waving homemade placards that read "HELP!" and uttering cries of desperation that echoed again and again, "Help," "Please help us!" One poignant person had left an "e" off the word *please,* making his cries all the more dramatic, piercing, and compelling.

One former resident of the Ninth Ward recalled images that filled her eyes one year after the waters had receded: "Everything was covered in brown crud," she remembered. "There was nothing living. No birds. No dogs. There was no sound. And none of the fragrance that's usually associated with New Orleans, like jasmine and gardenias and sweet olives. It was just a rain, all death and destruction" (Herbert, 2006, p. A23). In this moving and elegant testimony, the resident grieved not only for people who were displaced but also for sounds that had been silenced, lovely smells of flowers that had been removed from nostrils, and creatures such as birds and dogs, which had been stilled. In an area that is often associated with poverty and crime, the resident's words symbolically remind us that humanity was there—in the Ninth Ward—and that it deserves to return.

International Reactions to Katrina

Such sad scenes so effectively exposed the United States—a country that prides itself on abstract principles of democracy, freedom, and justice—to the world of public opinion. Despite having the civil rights movement to America's credit, past efforts to eliminate the war on poverty, and other governmental institutions that actively sought to change the economic calculus for the poor, especially during the 1960s, however momentarily, Katrina tinkered with such efforts. "Scenes of a devastated New Orleans," wrote Paul Krugman (2006), "reminded us that many of our fellow citizens remain poor, four decades after L. B. J. declared war on poverty" (p. A23).

At the time of Katrina's cruel waters, our soft, cultural underbelly found itself "out there" in international land for citizens worldwide to see, to gaze upon, to ponder. The message—implicit and explicit—amounted to this: "America had failed a large, vulnerable segment of her population." It is likely that the jarring message rearranged the cognitive and emotional frames of Americans. The exposure was comparable to a hidden relative in the attic suddenly being revealed, shamefully. International press had a field day. Using political allusions, Argentina's *Clarin* said that the wind and water "reveal the emptiness of an era, one that is represented by President George W. Bush" (www.worldpress.org).

Half optimistically, Spain's *La Razon* warned that the "country will probably be able to recuperate from the destruction, but its pride has already been profoundly wounded" (www.worldpress.org). In a devastating cut to America and an unflattering jab at Africa, Kenya's *Daily Nation* noted, "The images and even the disproportionately high number of visibly impoverished blacks among the refugees, could easily have been a reenactment of a scene from the pigeonholed African continent" (www.worldpress.org). And Paris's *Le Monde* wrote that "America is discovering, or rediscovering that it harbors the Third World in its own bosom" (www.worldpress.org).

Despite the harsh international criticism that America endured at the time, others recognized the humane capacity of America to respond generously during crises. Muhammad Yunus (2006), a caring man, spoke to moral options: "America's government and people," said Yunus, "brought charity to a new level last year (2005) in their responses to Hurricane Katrina" (p. A6). Despite the trauma that Bangladeshis encountered in severe floods, they gave the United States $1 million to help Katrina's victims.

Yunus (2006) advised Americans to give money directly to the poor, using microcredit loans similar to those offered in Bangladesh and other places, as a means of uplift. He gave good reasons why Katrina's victims should profit from microcredit systems, including a declarative, moral alert: "Sadly, it is also true that in catastrophic circumstances, very little of the cash so generously given ever gets all the way down to the very poor" (p. A6). Furthermore, Yunus advised, "There are too many 'professionals' ahead of them in line, highly skilled at diverting funds into their own pockets" (p. A6).

In the next section, I focus on the interplay between charity and justice, with an eye toward understanding whether poor people are exploited in the name of abstract principles. But Yunus's (2006) point is that we can build an egalitarian, empathetic society if we "lend money to disadvantaged people" because empowerment is involved: "It gives them a sense of pride, rather than the humiliation they may feel over a handout" (p. A6).

Mayor White and Other Responses

Giving also comes in forms other than money. In the wake of Katrina, one is hard-pressed to think of a person who answered the moral call to help more appealingly than Bill White, the mayor of Houston in Texas. White, a true practitioner, sweet and beautiful in his acts of kindness, witnessed the great suffering and realized that it would be impossible for victims in the lower Ninth Ward of New Orleans to find housing and rebuild community—even temporarily. Houston took in 150,000 evacuees, more than any other city. Mayor White acted with the full realization of the potential for crime. It appears that even after White's and other Houstonians' humanitarian, emergency efforts, they would not be repaid fully in kind. In less than one year, from August 2005 to July 2006, evacuees (as a suspect or a victim) were responsible for 21% of homicides in Houston—of the 232 homicides (http://www.breitbart.com).

Generous responses to and searing images of Katrina's victims also reveal other ways that human beings were damaged. Like displaced victims of Darfur and Iraq, Katrina's victims had another layer of suffering added on to their misery: harsh disruptions of "primordial kinship and rooted belonging," to use Gilroy's (2000, p. 23) language. The ancient word *diaspora* often is associated with the removal of Jews during the Holocaust and the Middle Passage that brought Africans to North America—in a word, nomadism, genocide, and slavery. But the term is also associated with disruptions that occur when people are uprooted from one geographic space and land in another within the same national boundaries.

In the case of Katrina, a form of exile and forced migration occurred. Gilroy (2000) suggests that disapora "is not just a word of movement" (p. 23) but rather a type of associative flight involving uncomfortable truths and disruptions that strike at the core of what it means to be human. In a real sense, existential anguish caused Katrina's victims to reevaluate their notions of identity and belonging, as the words of the resident of the Ninth Ward that I quoted previously indicate. Thankfully, there were people among us who were ready to lend a helping hand, although they were clearly stunned that something like Hurricane Katrina could occur in the United States of America.

It is noteworthy that North Americans, metaphysically, had redefined themselves away from the natural world of disaster to metaphorical safe harbor. Natural disasters are supposed to occur in such developing countries as Ethiopia, Bangladesh, Indonesia, and the Philippines—but not in the United States of America! In effect, Hurricane Katrina ruptured something that was fundamental to Americans' perceptions of themselves and their well-being. Hurricane Katrina surely caused Americans to entertain serious and troubling questions regarding their enduring technological capabilities. How and why could a dam in a gorgeous city like New Orleans not hold? Had Americans lost their technological edge? In perhaps an implicitly arrogant way, this day of reckoning was also part of the burden of shame that grabbed the consciousness of Americans. In a world of plenty, Americans realized that the margin of survival is extraordinarily small. Hence, undoubtedly, another reason for seasons of generosity among North Americans.

During spring breaks between 2006 and 2008, college students continued to lead crusades of generosity to New Orleans to help with restoration. And Hurricane Katrina Disaster Relief Fund of United Jewish Communities (UJC) and the Jewish Federations of North America raised several million dollars to aid victims (www.israelnewagency.com). The latter was in response to a request from Mayor Bill White of Houston to faith-based organizations to help victims there. United Jewish Community charities are emblematic of the millions of dollars that Americans and citizens of other countries raised for residents of the Gulf Coast.

On the first-year anniversary of Hurricane Katrina, President Bush traveled there to wish citizens and former residents well. Frank Rich (2006) of

The New York Times said that the president "brought the love to New Orleans" (p. 10). To demonstrate his solidarity with New Orleanians, Bush met the press, greeted citizens, and dramatized America's commitment to the unfinished work that remains in the city of New Orleans and other parts of the Gulf Coast. Despite the goodwill and contributions of well-meaning people, the aftermath of Hurricane Katrina is still apparent.

The Ninth Ward still is in ruins, trailers provided for citizens by the FEMA are contaminated with PCBs, and people remain exiled in Atlanta, Baton Rouge, Houston, and other cities and towns across the United States. Indeed, life has been very difficult for many former residents of the Gulf Coast. And many are still mired in wretched poverty. As I noted earlier, the percentage of Black Americans and Hispanics living in poverty is staggering: 24.7% of Black Americans and 21.9% of Hispanics were impoverished in 2004, according to the Census Bureau. If we are to understand why a huge gap exists between the rich and the poor in North America, we must interrogate notions of charity versus justice. Will diminishing resources ultimately undermine the distributive system of justice globally? In the next section, I discuss the extent to which people are working to change structural arrangements that encourage charitable giving.

Charity vs. Justice

In discussing the unequal distribution of wealth between the "superclass" and the non-"superclass," Rothkopf (2008, p. 31) provides compelling statistics. Of 6 billion people on the planet, 6,000 belong to the governing class (one in a million) and, through access and exclusivity, decide the fate of the rest of humanity. The average CEO of a North American corporation earns 300 to 400 times what the average person in the company earns (Rothkopf, 2008, p. 31).

There are basic assumptions underlying why some people have more and others less. One assumption derives from distinctions that Aristotle makes between "general" justice and "particular" injustice. Aristotle argues that "general" justice is a way of exercising virtue in relation to another human being; it consists of those virtues that concern the good or excellent person. "Particular" injustice is linked with *pleonexia* (Sherman, 1999, p. 235), which literally means "having more."

Pleonexia also concerns who has more of his or her share of common resources (wealth) in the community and the relationship between dispositions and having more things such as honor and money. In the competition between charity and justice, which one wins, or need there be an *either/or* dichotomy at the expense of a *both/and* model of cooperation? According to

Aristotle, it is possible to separate acts that are unjust from acts that are just, based on a principle of motivation. In other words, some actions bring about injustice even when the agent wills it otherwise; the corollary is also true: One can have a disposition to do injustice.

For example, in amassing huge fortunes, Bill Gates and Warren Buffet surely, as far as I can discern, in pursuit of wealth, were not motivated by injustice. However, a question can be raised regarding the consequences of the wealth: Is it fair for one person to earn and keep $20 billion when so many people in the world scrape by on less than a dollar or two a day? And does the fact that Warren Buffet donated $31 million to the Gates Foundation move him into the category of one who acts from pleonexia? Here, I am keenly interested in the extent to which political, economic, and social structures and policies contribute to an unjust global society. After all, even though I might consult the entrails of a rabbit, it is pretty difficult to judge the motives of humans successfully and accurately, and I will not even attempt to do so here. But it is possible to grapple with immense inequalities on such a global scale in such areas as charitable giving. Oxfam, Doctors Without Borders, CARE, CONCERN, International Monetary Fund, World Bank, and a host of NGOs in Sudan, Ethiopia, Guatemala, Bolivia, and other sites are names of organizations that do good work. But consider the following case studies of relations between ostensibly just societies, organizations, and charity.

Case Study 1: Africa and Justice

Chang (2008) argues that one of the reasons why African countries have difficulty coping with HIV/AIDS centers on a contest of ideas between pharmaceutical companies and intellectual property rights. To alleviate suffering in Africa, some countries such as Tanzania and South Africa began importing cheaper "copy" drugs from countries like India and Thailand. The drugs in the latter countries "cost $3–500, or 2–5% of the 'real' thing" (Chang, 2008, p. 123).

When 41 pharmaceutical companies found out what was happening, they cried foul, primarily because they believed that African countries were violating copyright laws. Pharmaceutical companies believed that the acts of African countries were tantamount to "stealing" ideas from Western innovators and creators of drugs. To prove a point and to make an example, in 2001, the 41 pharmaceutical companies brought what amounted to a class-action suit against the South African government. The companies argued that "the country's drug law allowing parallel imports and compulsory licensing were contrary to the Trade-Related Intellectual Property Rights (TRIPs) agreement" (Chang, 2008, p. 123). TRIPs was established by the

World Trade Organization (WTO) to protect the rights of creators and patent holders.

In the name of human justice and in the interest of the public good, people protested against the suit that the 41 pharmaceutical companies had brought against South Africa. Realizing the crippling effects of negative publicity, the companies withdrew their suit. Nestled inside this case study are not only questions about creativity, access to knowledge, patents, and ownership but also questions about what constitutes reasonableness and justice. Moreover, the difficult question of the relationship between constraining structures and the ability of some countries to break free of poverty is paramount.

Economic costs to poor countries can be enormous because developed countries monopolize patents. In Brazil, for example, Farmanguinhos, the state-run pharmaceutical company, claims that it can produce the AIDS medicine Kaletra for a lower cost than what Abbott Laboratories charges; in fact, by using generic Kaletra, Brazil could save at least $55 million (Stiglitz, 2006, p. 121).

The point is that savings from big payments to Western pharmaceutical companies could save Brazil millions of dollars—money that usefully could be spent building infrastructures, creating foundations of prosperity, and eliminating needs for increased charity in Brazil.

Supporters of TRIPs argue, however, that freely sharing ideas with others will dry up incentives for creativity. However sound this argument might be, one should remember, as Chang (2008) notes, "Material incentives, while important, are not the only things that motivate people to invest in producing new ideas" (p. 124). In an open letter to the *Financial Times,* 13 fellows at the Royal Society, the premier scientific group in United Kingdom, said, "Patents are only one means for promoting discovery and invention. Scientific curiosity coupled with the desire to benefit humanity, has been of far greater importance throughout history" (qtd. in Chang, 2008, p. 124). Stiglitz (2006), in anticipating the counterarguments of critics, remarks, "Critics might say: But then the developing countries are simply free-riding on the advanced industrial countries. To which the answer is: yes, and they should" (p. 120).

While developing countries actively pursue their common agenda of AIDS prevention and access to generic drugs, another emerging issue arises: competition between distributive justice and vaccines in the likelihood of a health pandemic. Garrett (2000) wonders whether there would be enough stockpiles of Tamiflu and other anti-influenza drugs in the event of a global outbreak of flu. She flat out says, "Resources are so scarce that both wealthy and poor countries would be foolish to count on the generosity of their neighbors during a global outbreak" (p. 17).

In a global scramble for medicines, some people would be advantaged (likely the rich worldwide) and some people would be disadvantaged (likely the poor worldwide). How can a division of resources be done justly in the event of a modern pandemic? And in the event of some other equally dreadful disease? What moral heuristics will guide humankind in the midst of such horrific possibilities? Is there a living discourse that would save us?

Case Study 2: Good Intentions

Our second case comes from Goma, Zaire (now Congo). We know that many NGOs and charitable organizations from USAID to Red Cross to CARE work throughout Africa distributing old clothes and plastic tarpaulin, working with AIDS patients, digging bore holes, and providing much needed mosquito nets and antimalarial medicines to citizens. While such organizations are to be applauded for their kindly acts, in some cases, the road becomes paved with good intentions that sometimes go haywire because charitable givers fail to do the necessary cultural work before arriving on site.

In the 1990s, CARE Germany sent 267 doctors and nurses to Goma to aid the refugees there. It turns out, however, that CARE did not consult with anyone in Goma about the culture of Zaireans before arriving in Zaire. When doctors and nurses landed in Goma, they learned to their surprise and amazement that doctors weren't really needed (Maren, 1997, p. 264). Moreover, because doctors and nurses "had no experience in places like Goma," they were "immediately beset with a kind of post-traumatic stress that incapacitated them" (Maren, 1997, p. 264). John Parker, a Red Cross official, remarked, "I need someone here [Goma] who has been selected for his attitude and his behavior. I do not need a bunch of do-gooders around" (Maren, 1997, p. 264).

Maren (1997) says the episode embodies a typical Western attitude—namely, that "anything that we (Westerners) send, anything we can do, is needed and useful. It is the same attitude that hammers home the message that for the price of a cup of coffee, we can alter the lives of poor children in the Third World. It is bargain-basement charity" (p. 264).

Of course, Maren's (1997) comment is not intended to signify that all Westerners who contribute to charities on behalf of poor people are flawed. Rather, it is to signify that we need to reconsider reasons why we give to charities, ways that we give, and the long-terms benefits of giving. Paul Farmer (Kidder, 2003, p. 40) also captures the sometimes flawed worldview that undermines the thinking of some "do-gooders." While working to cure infectious diseases in Haiti, Farmer had a fascinating conversation with an aid worker. "White liberals (WLs)," according to the aid worker, "some of whose most influential spokespersons were black and prosperous," are problematic. The problem is White liberals "think all the world's problems can be fixed without any cost to themselves," the aid worker said (Kidder, 2003, p. 40).

"We don't believe that," the aid worker noted. Mixing pathos with humane insight, the aid worker concluded, "There's a lot to be said for sacrifice, remorse, even pity. It's what separates us from roaches" (Kidder, 2003, p. 40). Some charities are also implicated in the "general" justice category because they do not take the time to adjust needs to people and people to needs.

Following are a few examples of mix-matched needs and deeds: (a) AmeriCares sent 10,000 cases of Gatorade to Goma to treat cholera patients; (b) AmeriCares sent 2 million Mars chocolate bars to St. Petersburg, Russia, and 17 tons of Pop-Tarts to Bosnia; (c) Bosnians received stocks of Prozac when they were in desperate need of vaccines and other drugs; (d) in Zaire, local farmers were forced out of business because of free food; and (e) foreigners infrequently hire local workers, especially Zairean doctors, engineers, and other skilled workers (Maren, 1997, pp. 264–266).

Case Study 3: Packets of Vestments

"Beyond mountains there are mountains" is a popular proverb that explains a whole lot of what happens to Haitians in the name of philanthropy. Take the case of the dam project (Peligre Dam) that was constructed in Haiti to stop waters in river Lac de Peligre. With funding from the United States and the U.S. Export-Import Bank, under the mantra "development project," the U.S. Army Corps of Engineers and Brown & Root of Texas built a monstrous concrete dam in Haiti—as a gift—to generate electricity and help stem severe drought (Kidder, 2003).

It turns out that no well-meaning elites associated with the project even bothered to consult Haitian farmers, whose livelihood depended on the land and "who lived in the valley upstream" (Kidder, 2003, p 37). As a consequence, the following wretched things happened: (a) Most Haitian farmers were not paid a cent as a result of physical displacement and disturbance to their land; (b) electricity from the dam benefited Haiti's tiny elite class in Port-au-Prince; (c) flooding of the valley created "water refugees," a term Farmer uses to describe the terrible price poor Haitians paid and are paying for munificence gone haywire; and (d) the "water refugees" in turn flocked to Haitian cities in search of livable wages and ended up stitching "Mickey Mouse dolls and baseballs!" (Kidder, 2003, pp. 36–38). Farmer reasons that there is a tie-in between displaced farmers flocking to cities as a result of the dam project and the appearance of HIV/AIDS.

To add insult to the injury of goodwill, in the 1980s, Haitian farmers suffered again because their Creole pigs, upon which they depended, were destroyed. Because Americans were fearful that an outbreak of African swine fever in the Dominican Republic would wreak havoc on the pork industry in the United States, "the United States led an effort to destroy all the Creole pigs in Haiti" (Kidder, 2003, p. 38). This one single act further complicated the miserable life of Haitians, and one tragedy begat another tragedy. For example, because there were no pigs, there was no money for Haitian pig farmers to support their children's education. As a consequence, student enrollments in the valley around Cange decreased. What is hauntingly telling about these sorrowful, gloomy stories is that individuals who worked for the U.S. Army Corps of Engineers and Brown & Root of Texas prospered while the poor shouldered one miserable burden after another, creating a chain of human-altering events that will shape generations of Haitians to come.

When one stops seriously to process the relationship that obtains between decision making, acts of intended human kindness, and large consequences, one can see why justice is unhappily disturbed. To use the Creole phrase *pa semp*, which, in loose translation, means that things are not always what they seem but rather full of complexities, I now turn to another issue that stands stalwart in the domain of injustice: trust.

Trust in the Individual

At bottom, the wretched stories detailed earlier of giving gone wrong also relate specifically to levels of trust. To what extent do Westerners trust individuals in developing countries to manage their own affairs? As noted, even under the rubric of the public good in Zaire, NGOs failed to hire local workers. Too often, professionals are outsourced to developing countries with insufficient thought about consequences of human and intellectual capital. There is, as Fukuyama (1995) argues, a "close relationship between moral virtue and habit" (p. 35), and I extend his comment to include a relationship between giving and levels of trust.

Trust in matters of charity has a great deal to do with who succeeds and who fails economically, socially, and intellectually. "Communities depend on mutual trust and will not arise spontaneously without it" (Fukuyama, 1995, p. 25). Microcredit works well in Bangladesh and other places primarily because norms that produce "truth-telling, meeting obligations and reciprocity" are evident in cultural systems (Fukuyama, 1995, p. 99). As Yunus (2006) notes, "Microlending has already helped millions reach a better life through their own initiative. It has also given them valuable skills as well as crucial financial back-up in case they ever face a disaster like

Katrina" (p. A6). The point is that a lack of trust in poor people serves as barriers to mobility. This lack of trust is fostered when CARE and other NGOs, however well intentioned, spend inordinate sums of money helping the poor and then sit back and congratulate themselves on a job well done!

Matters of trust are also implicated when scholars such as Stephen Ellis (2005, p. 135) recommend international trusteeship control over African countries, undermining not only uncomfortable assumptions about state sovereignty but also faith in individuals. Even in the most heartfelt but scorching communitarian tradition, these paternalistic recommendations implicitly argue that Africans are deviant and lack administrative decision-making skills; they also undermine the equal dignity rule of humanity. At the same time, however, the recommendations gnaw at the edges of 19th-century philosopher Jeremy Bentham's notion of the greatest good for the greatest number. In other words, even if the aforementioned principles of trust are undermined, should charitable international trusteeships be implemented for enormous economic and moral survival of the masses in Africa and elsewhere?

Such concerns move us to the center of worrying, complex issues regarding the relationship that obtains between charity, economics, and trust in the individual. One might be able to reduce poverty, for example, through constraints on charity but at the same time violate ethical norms pertaining to trust in the individual. Economists place such nettlesome issues in the special domain of "moral growth" (Stiglitz, 2005, p. 130)—that is, growth and helping that are "sustainable, that increase living standards" not just today but for future generations as well, leading to a more tolerant, open society. In efforts to create social justice, erosion of trust in individual responsibility can and does occur.

It would be a mistake to suggest that no good comes from charitable organizations and people, but humanity's obligation is to trust and help poor people learn valuable skills and create healthy civil and economic societies. Greg Mortenson's (Mortenson & Relin, 2006) story of helping people in impoverished villages in Pakistan, exquisitely told in the book *Three Cups of Tea*, is one moving example. Mortenson, a daring adventurer, finds himself in dangerous situations as he tries and succeeds in building schools for poor children in Pakistan and in Afghanistan.

An Empathetic Place Beyond Catastrophes

So far, I have been arguing that some charities, in the name of the good, do no long-term good. If we consider some stereotypes and negative thinking that are cited as reasons why people in poor countries are poor, we can further understand the need for an "empathetic place beyond catastrophes."

Chang (2008) and other scholars note that one of the most often cited reasons to explain why people in developing countries are poor is "laziness!" The characteristic of laziness is no newcomer to the realm of reasons that hover over the poor like a huge, sprawling tent. Even during slavery, Black slaves were labeled lazy, shiftless, and irresponsible because they failed to speed up their cotton picking, cotton hoeing, and other "ing" acts deemed both worthy and necessary by their masters. For malingering, language was co-opted, and Blacks were soon defined as "lazy," not the slave masters who appropriated the labor of the slaves!

Masters were not viewed as lazy because they got to define, because they were in control of symbolic capital. As a parallel, the poor today are also beset by such negativity, which fails to explain matters. Chang (2008) argues, for example, that "many poor people in poor countries actually work long hours in backbreaking conditions" and that "what makes them *appear* lazy is often their lack of an 'industrial' sense of time. When you work with basic tools or simple machinery, you don't have to keep time strictly" (p. 194). Furthermore, as Chang notes, "If you are working in an automated factory, it's essential. People from rich countries often interpret this difference in sense of time as laziness" (p. 194). Inherent in such stories is the belief that poor people "bear some responsibility for their troubles" (Williams, 2006, p. A19). After all, as Williams (2006) reminds us, "The suspicion that the poor cause problems for themselves was at the heart of President Clinton's effort to 'end welfare as we know it'" (p. A19).

Williams (2006) further notes that nonprofits and foundations "encourage individual responsibility by rewarding the poor for getting high school diplomas, finding jobs and being good parents" (p. A19). Such efforts not withstanding, we must confront the "poverty of spirit. Because that's what was tearing down the city, long before Hurricane Katrina" (p. A19). Is it far easier for countries to avert such anguish and catastrophes by being more inclined to help others? And by tailoring human efforts to the work of such organizations as the International Monetary Fund and the World Bank? Have they new proposals for addressing issues of poverty?

7

"I Didn't Do It for You"

Organizations, Class, and Poverty

Openings: Inclined to Help

In 1998, an image of Michael Camdessus of France, head of the International Monetary Fund (IMF), leaning over helpless president Sukharto of Indonesia as the latter is forced to turn over his country's sovereignty to the IMF, stirred controversy worldwide. For some, the picture symbolized business as usual between hegemons and former colonies. "Hapless president" is the term that renowned economist and Nobel laureate Joseph E. Stiglitz (2002, p. 41) used to describe the picture, because for him and other critics of the IMF, too often, in efforts to improve the fortunes of the poor, the organization has commandingly dictated economic policies to developing countries.

Supporters of Camdessus, however, argue that the photograph was taken out of context and seriously distorted relations between Camdessus, the IMF, and developing countries. Nevertheless, a sophisticated viewer could not help but observe a central iconic argument that inheres in the photogenic evidence, and it is that the IMF, World Bank, nongovernmental organizations (NGOs), and other organizations are investing huge sums of money in emerging countries. At the same time, however, the picture raises rather disturbing questions: To what extent are inclinations to help the poor recover from poverty, natural disasters, rubble-strewn earthquake scenes, inadequate education, environmental destruction, malaria-infested waters, and overall material damage to their lives bearing fruit from those inclined to help? And is the guise of public duty, in style, tone, and substance, cloaked in garments of self-interested world bureaucrats?

Despite criticism of the World Bank and the IMF, their founding in 1944 was rooted in deeply held values and possibilities of making substantive changes in the human condition. Although an articulated, empathetic mission of the IMF and World Bank today is to narrow harsh wealth inequalities between rich and poor nations, it emerged on the rubble of physical and emotional devastation during World War II, as policy makers of both social and economic change in the United States and Europe vied for ways to strengthen postwar economies.

Thus, after World War II, as a consequence of "ransacked economies of its victims" (Judt, 2005), the World Bank and the IMF emerged to benefit people and to rebuild international commerce and financial institutions. Plans for the IMF and the World Bank were begun in July 1944 "while fighting was still raging in the European and Pacific theatres" (Judt, 2005). Currently, there are 179 members of the IMF, and the largest contributors to the fund are the United States, United Kingdom, Germany, France, and Japan. Vocal critics of the IMF and the World Bank argue that donor nations are less than transparent in the way in which they conduct the business of the organizations—usually behind closed doors and away from the clicks of cameras.

Although the ostensible, publically articulated goals of the IMF and the World Bank were to "grant loans to rebuild Europe after the war" in conjunction with the Marshall Plan for the "redevelopment and economic stabilization of Europe," others argue that the goals of the organizations (including other institutions such as the Organisation for Economic Cooperation and Development [OECD] and the free trade organization, GATT) were "consciously to promote capitalism and contain Communism" (Chua, 2003, p. 20). There is, of course, some truth in the assertion that the United States and Western Europe made conscious attempts to thwart the growth of communism in Third World countries, creating a carefully nuanced reason for public good works. Nevertheless, at the July 1944 conference at Bretton Woods in New Hampshire, led by Harry Dexter White and John Maynard Keynes—a chief dynamo behind the idea of new international organizations—economists and statesman set up an International Monetary Fund "to facilitate the expansion and balanced growth of international trade." Then, as today, major donor countries included the United States, United Kingdom, and France.

The public good works philosophy helped to solidify the West and the rest. Later, at the end of World War II and prior to the collapse of the former Soviet Union in 1989, the world was divided geopolitically. Huntington (1996, p. 21) argues that the cold war consisted of a bipolar world with three major parts. The first group comprised rich countries in the West led by the United States; the latter was militarily and economically very strong. The second group consisted of the Soviet Union and communist satellites such as former Yugoslavia; Ukraine; "Stan" countries (e.g., Kazakhstan, Uzbekistan, Turkmenistan, and Kyrgyzstan); the Baltic states of Estonia, Latvia, and Lithuania; and other countries. And the final group was composed of poor Third World countries that both the Soviet Union and the "West and the Rest" vied for in terms of who would give what to impoverished, former colonial countries.

In light of such geopolitical arrangements and competition, the consequences of who would give what to what nation and people were huge indeed. These points are raised here to illustrate that geopolitical arrangements, economics, and "isms" are all intertwined and arrayed in terms of giving because in the bipolar world of the cold war, both capitalist and communist countries were inclined toward empathic solidarity. As Dallaire (2004, p. A29) observes, today, when Western nations make decisions regarding giving aid to such countries as Darfur, Sudan, or Rwanda, they typically ask, "What's in it for us? Is it in our 'national interest'?" (p. A29). Rightly or wrongly, such questions are consistent with diplomacy and inclinations to help developing countries. Whether the requirements for helping are centered in self-interest or pure altruism, some scholars argue that "whatever the culture, man certainly will seek his advantage" (Wilson, 1993, p. 122; see also Bourdieu, 1999; Geertz, 1973), while other social scientists maintain that because humans are a product of specific symbolic worlds, culture, identity, and "webs of significance" spun by both familiar and communal bonds, self-interest is bound to occur.

Contested Giving

Given humans' penchant for struggling to reconcile the giving part from the self-interested part, we still should not overlook the fact that people and countries are willing to employ the guiding principle that poor people need help—a nasty necessity or otherwise. Clearly, issues of what constitutes doing the right thing and statistical equations for helping are implicated in nation-states' willingness to promote the general welfare globally. Morally, should both donor and recipient countries worry about motives for giving, or should the latter merely be grateful that giving has occurred?

In any case, with the breakup of the former Soviet Union and the emergence of newly freed countries such as Croatia, Slovenia, and Kosovo, capitalism was seen around the world "as triumphant and inexorable" (Chua, 2003, p. 21). Newly constituted conditions paved the way for economic and

neoliberal globalization and for intellectuals to trumpet the goodness of foreign policy and economic coffers that affected contributions to developing
countries. A key promoter of economic globalization is Thomas L. Friedman
(2005), who argues that the "world is flat." Friedman paints a positive
picture of the economic impact of globalization on poor nations.
"Collaboration in poverty alleviations is not just for NGOs," according to
Friedman. "It is also for multinational corporations. The rural poor in India,
Africa, and China represent a huge market, and it is possible to make money
there and serve them—if countries are willing to collaborate horizontally
with the poor" (p. 389). With these words, Friedman frames helping the
poor not in terms of the vertical dimension but rather in horizontal terms.
We know from scholars who study power arrangements (Duncan, 1985;
Hofstede, 2001) that vertical dimensions of culture focus on statusful matters such as position, income, and education.

Friedman (2005), as well as his edicts about helping the poor, fore-
grounds the point that empathy-minded economic arrangements should flow
from a consultation between such rich global companies as Hewlett-Packard
and local citizens wherever they might be. In fact, Friedman praises Hewlett-
Packard as a company, which, in its dealing with poor people, began with
the humane question: "What do poor people need most that we could sell to
them?" (p. 389). Although the question clearly reflects capitalist, market-
driven discourse, it nevertheless tilts in the direction of "the user-customer
beneficiary" (p. 389). As Friedman notes, Hewlett-Packard with a mission-
oriented zeal created a "public-private partnership" with both local and
national governments of India.

Where Friedman and Hewlett-Packard see a "user-customer" symbiotic
relationship between the poor and Hewlett-Packard, global activists
Arundhati Roy and Vandana Shiva question whether such arrangements
promote the collective good in India and other developing nations. In a
stinging criticism of Friedman's (2005) overarching metaphor, "the world is
flat," Shiva (2005) indicts "projects of corporate Globalisation" as means
for "polarising and dividing people—along axis of class and economic
inequality" and other such axes as gender, religion, culture, and geographies
(p. 1). Shiva says, "When you look at the world perched on heights of arrogant, blind power, separate and disconnected from those who have lost their
livelihoods, styles, and lives," especially farmers and workers worldwide, "it
is easy to be blind both to the valleys of poverty and the mountains of afflu-
ence. Flat vision is a disease" (p. 1).

The picture that Shiva (2005) paints with her lively up/down and light/
dark metaphors, personification, and inside/outside juxtaposition reinforces
the assertion held by some that the world is not flat but rather composed of

policies that are designed to assist those already materially and economically advantaged. Furthermore, writes Shiva, Friedman's flat world metaphor conceals more than it reveals, including such matters as "walls of insecurity and hatred and fear—walls of 'intellectual property,' walls of privatization" (p. 1).

Shiva (2005) indicts and enlarges her interrogation of Friedman and other globalists. She questions whether Friedman's snapshot views of economic globalism actually serve the interests of poor people around the world. "Laws, regulations and policies" of neoliberals and other globalizers shut out the light of "freedom and democracy, rights and justice, peace and security, sustainability and sharing of the earth's precious and vital resources," Shiva asserts (p. 1).

Novelist Arundhati Roy (2002) also weighs in on who is inclined to help the poor and in what manner. And she wonders whether globalization is about "eradication of world poverty" or whether it is about "a mutant variety of colonialism remote controlled and digitally operated" (p. 1). Furthermore, Roy denounces the World Trade Organization as a keen example of how the business of helping the poor is suffused with experts who appear to be a world away from the interests and concerns of the dispossessed. Eagleton (2003) declares that "the rich are global and the poor are local," emphasizing again a division between those who have and those who have not, as Shiva's and Roy's discourses underscore. Shiva, Roy, and Eagleton all raise concerns of great importance: whether the extraordinary economic dominance of the West and its claims of helping the poor, uprooted, scattered, transplanted, and disposed are dramatic and compelling instances of rhetoric trumping reality.

In the next section, I examine to what extent such self-help but self-interested organizations such as the IMF, NGOs, World Bank, and World Trade Organization have joined rhetoric and practice by using empathy in superior ways or whether the organizations are alchemy of another elixir.

Who Gets What?

Sachs (2005) declares that his book, *The End of Poverty,* "is about ending poverty in our time" (p. 1). And he offers chilling words and statistics to support his claim that we should end poverty in our time: "Currently, more than eight million people around the world die each year because they are too poor to stay alive" (p. 1). Sachs argues that our generation can "choose to end that extreme poverty by the year 2025" (p. 1).

Under the auspices of the United Nations Millennium Project, well-meaning people and nations are, at least, verbally dedicated to the proposition that extreme poverty is an incriminating blight on our collective humanity. Clearly, a "fierce sense of urgency" governs many people's views on excruciating poverty. More than 2 million community-based NGOs worldwide, 20,000 in poor countries, and about 275,000 in the United Kingdom alone are devoted to altering the economic and education equation that exists between poor and rich nations. An NGO is "any non-profit organization that is independent from the government" (Bhagwati, 2004, p. 37).

The average person is familiar with such humanitarian NGOs as CARE, World Vision, Oxfam, and others because they bombard media airwaves daily with pitiful pictures of starving, malaria-infested, matchstick-thin children from barrios in Brazil to "huts" in "dusty places" in Burkina Faso. And yet, poverty, impoverishment, and disease persist. So if there are so many people inclined to help, why is there still so much poverty in the world? Theories abound to explain this anomaly, from the interference of traditional attitudes and beliefs to corrupt leaders to a lack of instrumental values that foster economic development.

"Progress-Prone" Versus "Progress-Resistant" Cultures

Grondona (2000), professor of government at the Law Faculty of the National University of Buenos Aires, in a classic piece in the book *Culture Matters*, lists 20 contrasting variables that determine whether cultures are "progress prone" or "progress resistant" to economic development. The factors are religion, trust in the individual, the moral imperative, concepts of wealth, views of competition, notions of justice, the value of work, the role of heresy, the role of education, the importance of utility, the lesser virtues, time focus, rationality, authority, worldview, life view, salvation from or in the world, views on utopia, the nature of optimism, and visions of democracy. Let me focus on two variables to give the reader a sense of Grondona's arguments about the role of values in promoting or retarding economic progress.

In discussing notions of justice, Grondona (2000) argues that in resistant societies, "distributive justice is concerned with those who are alive now," whereas favorable societies are more likely to "define distributive justice as that which also involves the interests of future generations" (p. 49). By focusing on those who are yet unborn, progressive cultures temporally harness their creative powers toward generations of computers to come, for example. Concepts of wealth matter because societies resistant to development focus too much on "what exists"; favorable societies concentrate on "what does not yet exist" (p. 49). The former value resides in land, whereas the second value finds force in innovation. These orientations toward justice and wealth, Grondona maintains, are in the realm of instrumental values because the latter encourages attention to values that are a means to an end. For example, in the realm of economic development, the ends are such values as freedom, religion, and happiness.

Toward this end, in trying to determine who gets what in the economic realm and why, Grondona (2000) and other scholars such as Harrison and Huntington (2000), Montaner (2000), and Edgerton (2000) recommend a stiff paradigm shift in the way we view poverty, which includes cultural injection or infusion programs designed to change traditional cultures. The scholars call for particular Western-oriented ideologies, activities, and resources that will facilitate these ends.

Despite often quoted grim statistics (e.g., 75% of people in Africa subsist on less than $2 a day) regarding poverty in terms of how many people actually die daily from poverty, "the share of U.S. GNP devoted to helping the poor has declined for decades, and is a tiny fraction of what the United States has repeatedly promised" (Sachs, 2005, p. 1). Sachs (2005) and others fight mightily for a "much safer world based on a true reverence and respect for human life" (p. 2). Regardless of how we view the dire circumstances of the poor in the world, the concern, first and foremost, should be "about reverence and respect for human life" (p. 2). Concerning bonds of humanity and caring, the issue also pertains to how we harness our caring in the present, the immediate future, and the distant future. Each temporal focus that we embrace carries a specific empathic logic of its own, moving from lukewarm responses to a fierce sense of urgency, with accompanying resources, skills, knowledge, education, and structural changes. Using this divisible rod of temporally dealing with poverty, whether we are fortunate enough to meet Sachs's and the United Nations' timetable should tell us much about how rich countries and people can abide such extreme poverty in the midst of oceans of plenty. In this way, humanity is yoked to time.

NGOs, World Bank, and IMF

Hard Empathy Versus Soft Empathy

We should gain some knowledge of such logics by examining the collective role and function of NGOs, the IMF, and the World Bank in alleviating poverty. NGOs, the World Bank, and the IMF are much maligned, and it is hard to find scholars, pundits, laypeople, and intellectuals who are lukewarm about whether such organizations do much good or harm in developing countries. Based on literature, views toward the work of NGOs tend to cluster in two major areas that I will label here as *soft empathy* and *hard empathy*. *Soft empathy* refers to NGOs and other organizations that do mostly obligatory work that eventuates in short-term relief of suffering and poverty regardless of noble intent. Comparatively speaking, soft empathy enters the sanctuary of poverty and renders its place of stay relatively undisturbed in regards to long-term, durable changes in such areas as education, food, nutrition, shelter, wealth, program work, and women's empowerment.

Hard empathy, in contrast, enters the sanctuary of poverty and significantly alters the livelihood of the people being serviced. It brings to the scene an attitude of mindfulness, attentiveness to local concerns, an understanding of the social setting, trustworthiness, and visions of independence for poor people.

Hard Empathy: Grameen Bank

The story of the Grameen microcredit bank (literally, "Bank of the Villages") in Bangladesh started by Muhammad Yunus, a PhD from Vanderbilt University in the United States, is the prototype of what I mean by hard empathy. Although Yunus was educated in the United States and steeped in theories of Milton Friedman and the economics of capitalism, he was inspired to try a different approach to alleviating poverty. Motivated by the 1974 dreadful famine in Bangladesh, Dr. Yunus decided to make a small, out-of-pocket loan of U.S.$27 to 42 craftspeople who had suffered in the famine in the town of Jobra (BusinessWeek, December 26, 2005). Yunus was interested in testing a hypothesis that he had hit upon while professor and head of the Rural Economics Project at Bangladesh's University of Chittagong. Specifically, he wanted to know what benefits would accrue to poor people who had no collateral to offer in securing even small loans.

Onto something pretty powerful, Dr. Yunus provided credit and banking services to the families, with an understanding that the borrowers would repay the loan. The experiment was a big success. Stiglitz (2006) writes that Yunus's schemes "have been so successful because they entail groups of women who take responsibility for one another" (p. 51). BusinessWeek (December 26, 2005) notes that Yunus "turned traditional banking on its head." There are, however, more equally significant reasons why Yunus's bank succeeded.

First, using a synthetic mind oriented toward economic and social development, Yunus believed that people would repay the loan. And the trust was passed along to borrowers like a chromosomal imprinting mechanism. Fortunately, Yunus provided a climate of freedom that worked reciprocally and, as a consequence, left small loan borrowers in control of their own destiny. Implicitly, Yunus, the "microcredit missionary," communicated values of human dignity and respect to borrowers. Many people are trapped in poverty because formal financial lending institutions use the bogeyman of fear of no repayment as reasons for denying them loans. Fukuyama (1995) and other scholars are adamant about what happens when climates of trust pervade human relations and disturb settled ways of thinking about who gets to decide who gets what in civil society. Fukuyama argues that trust is the glue that holds civil societies together. So in a moment of human caring and giving, Yunus simultaneously fostered not only trust but also goodwill for human beings.

Second, Yunus, being other directed, crafted his humane experiment out of *what was present* there in Jobra, the first site of his experiment, and other places in Bangladesh. Later, other-regarding behavior extended outward to other sites in Bangladesh like ripples in the proverbial tranquil, serene pond. By 2005, according to *Business Week* (December 26, 2005), Grameen Bank had lent more than $5.1 billion to 5.3 million people.

Third, Grameen Bank communicated to poor people that they also have the entrepreneurial spirit and skills necessary to make the world better off than they found it upon entering. In this regard, Yunus and the people tapped into a reservoir of human behavior that not only strengthened community but also served as a *public announcement* about what it is possible for human beings to think and do. In a special, empowering way, this is probably the most critical of all variables that are subsumed under the rubric of *hard empathy*. And it is the fact that Grameen Bank set in motion habits of mind necessary for transformative economic development to occur from the bottom up instead of from the top down. Without overstating the matter, microcredit is indeed a resilient mechanism because of its far-reaching consequences.

Like a giant colossus, in parts of Bangladesh, microcredit stands astride almost every meaningful aspect of everyday living in areas such as education, food, shelter, good roads, justice, self-help, hard work, beliefs, attitudes, and habits of investing and innovating. And all because one man dared to see the world and people in it in a different light—free of tired, musty old stereotypes!

Sixteen Decisions of Grameen Bank

The "16 Decisions of Grameen Bank" further reveal Yunus's appreciation of the poor, and they are instructive for what they teach about pride, hope, faith, beauty, and elegance of spirit. The 16 principles focus on respect for hard work, fine living standards, familial duty and responsibility, agrarian activities of cultivating vegetables, what is to be planted and when, instructions about not accepting marriage dowries, educating children, and taking care of one's health.

In addition to the above persuasive complex of elements that diagnose reasons for the eradication of poverty, Yunus also couches the solution portion of the 16 decisions in collective homilies that could be right out of the pages of a Horatio Alger sermon or book. And Yunus uses the principles to capture the mind and imagination of the rural poor that is so exemplary of hard empathy. Because the homilies are compellingly congruent with modes of hard empathy, I list five of them here—out of numerical order:

1. We cause harm to no one and will not tolerate that anyone should do us harm.

2. To increase our income, we make important investments in common.

3. We are always ready to help each other. When someone is in difficulty, we all give a helping hand.

4. If we learn that discipline is not respected in a centre, we go along to help and restore order.

5. We are introducing physical culture in all centres. We take part in all social events. (Grameen Bank, Bangladesh, n.d.)

Principles 12 through 16 seem to me a pretty inclusive listing of what it means to be part of a community. A community is tolerant, makes investments in common, is ready to help others, and is disciplined, orderly, and sociable. Grameen Bank recognizes rural poor people's need for employment of the powerful, reassuring communal "we," and for this reason, it permeates all 16 principles—not just the ones listed here. More than this, the 16 principles reinforce one another in a kind of symbiotic harmony. Furthermore, the use of *we* impels Bangladeshis to recognize not only causations of poverty but also what can be done about it with sufficient right efforts and right attitudes, as well as hope. The principles argue for unabashedly human pride and individual effort and not for government help, although the Bangladeshi government has, of course, aided rural poor.

Finally, the 16 agenda-driven principles are articulated in active, can-do attitudes, as if the work of eradicating poverty had already been done before it was begun. This engenders optimism and empowers the poor to behave in sturdy and uplifting ways.

The sister organization of Grameen Bank (the Bangladesh Rural Advancement Committee) offers still another way of understanding how human empathy can relieve human stress. The establishment of a university, mortgage financing, and health and legal services demonstrates what happens when human beings offer a proper course of treatment for poverty.

Hard Empathy: Malawi

Still another example of what I mean by *hard empathy* comes from the president of Malawi. Before I elaborate on the Malawi example, it is necessary to reiterate that the IMF and the World Bank originated in World War II as a means of dealing with the financial crisis that occurred during and following the war. The two organizations were founded at a conference at Bretton Woods, New Hampshire, in July 1944. At the time of founding, India, Africa, and most of the countries in the developing world were still under colonial rule (Stiglitz, 2002, p. 11). This means that developing countries were not factored into the equation of how the IMF and the World Bank functioned at the time of founding.

Although the IMF was assigned the crucial task of ordering global stability, directors and heads of the IMF and the World Bank as well as governments that ran the organizations later determined that the economic net should be cast wider. For this reason, because of growing poverty in developing countries, economic interconnectivity fueled by globalization, and new economic policies driven by Ronald Reagan and Margaret Thatcher of the United States and the United Kingdom, respectively, in the 1980s, the IMF and the World Bank instituted measures that came to be known as structural adjustment programs (SAPs).

Stiglitz (2002) and others argue that under the newly instituted structural adjustment programs, the IMF and the World Bank became "the new missionary institutions" through which policies were "pushed on the reluctant poor countries" (p. 13). In this regard, the IMF and the World Bank have employed *soft empathy;* this will become more apparent later when I detail Malawi's president's response to such measures. Structural adjustment programs refer to IMF and World Bank policies of "free market ideology" that have been forced upon developing countries (Stiglitz, 2002, p. 13). Free market ideology is driven by democratization, market efficiency, unrestrained laissez-faire policies, and trade liberalization (Chua, 2003; Stiglitz, 2002).

With the spread of new markets, the IMF and the World Bank "purged" their old policies and, under the rubric of reducing poverty in developing countries, sought solutions that, in effect, had a one-size-fits-all approach. It is here that *soft empathy* is most apparent. Instead of taking time and using resources to be attentive to specific, local needs of countries in Africa, Asia, and South America, the IMF and World Bank together felt key reasons for global poverty were lethargic markets in developing countries. This new economic missionary zeal is reminiscent of characters in Barbara Kingsolver's (1998) novel, *The Poisonwood Bible,* a tale of an evangelical Baptist minister, Nathan Price, and his wife and four daughters, who travel to the Belgium Congo in 1959.

In a well-meaning fashion and with preconceived cultural notions that had been formed in Georgia, the characters try to transform the African soul with hardly any knowledge of the customs and traditions of Congo. To African soil, Price family members took garden seeds, cake mixes, cans of deviled ham, and other items, expecting them to function as they had in Georgia. As a result of inattentiveness, the Price family's stay in postcolonial Africa was a series of disasters!

The new ideological fervor, under the auspices of doing good and employing *soft power,* also caused the IMF and World Bank to make tragic mistakes in their efforts to alleviate poverty in emerging countries. Now to the case of Malawi, which fell under IMF and World Bank rules of free market efficiency. In 2005, Malawi witnessed a severe food crisis borne of drought, lack of sufficient foreign exchange, and other factors. Three months before the crisis occurred, the World Bank urged Malawi "to keep foreign exchange instead of storing grain" (www.mindfully.org). Malawi complied because it is impossible to pay foreign debts without foreign exchange. Furthermore, creditors were not keen to accept Malawian Kwachas or grain but rather wanted hard currency—most notably at the time, American green dollars.

As a consequence of market-driven, one-size-fits-all policies, according to Malawi's president, the country had no option but to "sell maize in order to repay commercial loans taken out to buy surplus maize in previous years" (www.mindfully.org). So Malawi sold 28,000 tons of corn to Kenya and "under pressure from her creditors, led by the World Bank and the IMF . . . exchanged maize—her people's staple diet—for dollars" (www.mindfully.org). Malawi hovered for years at the brink of famine as a result of advice and actions by the IMF and the World Bank, according to Dugger (2006). Three years later, in 2008, Malawi, "a nation that has perennially extended a begging bowl to the world is instead feeding its hungry neighbors" (Dugger, 2006, p. A6) more than any other country in southern Africa, according to the World Food Program of the United Nations. Why? Because Malawi's newly elected president, Bingu wa Mutharika, "decided to follow what the West practiced, not what it preached," writes Dugger (2006, p. A6).

Where the former president of Malawi followed the advice of the IMF and the World Bank, Mutharika decided to trust his own knowledge base and instincts and pressed his advisers and the country's agricultural officials to distribute state-subsidized fertilizer to farmers; this was done over the advice of Britain and the United States. "As long as I'm president, I don't want to be going to other capitals begging for food," Mr. Mutharika declared. More than this, Mr. Mutharika had felt great humiliation over his country having to beg for charity—a strike at the very center of what constitutes human dignity. One should not lose sight of this as a galvanizing force behind

Mr. Mutharika's decision not to follow the advice of the IMF and the World Bank. "Our people are poor because they lack the resources to use the soil and the water we have," Mr. Mutharika argued (Dugger, 2006).

Mr. Mutharika's allies and admirers agree that he followed the proper course of action by "ignoring the experts." But Mutharika's words are also significant for what they reveal about his talent for *synopsizing empathy*. His keen vision showed itself in three ways. First, like the Stoics of old, by keeping his eyes on the local context as well as on the universal context, Mr. Mutharika demonstrated a sharp ability to both diagnose and determine what Malawians needed in the very center of southern Africa. Second, he felt the sting of what recognition and its absence can do to human fiber. "Use the talents you have," "cast down your bucket where you are," and "there are diamonds in Malawians own backyard" became his implied mantras. Third, he had a knack for understanding that even governments that depend on the largess of the IMF and the World Bank should play a commanding role in deciding their own fate.

Most explicitly, strains of *soft empathy* inhered within IMF and World Bank policies toward Malawi and other developing countries in the following ways: (a) in their failure to understand economic policies peculiar to the cultural, social, and agrarian demands of countries; (b) in their turning inward instead of outward; and (c) in using the paradigm: the pursuit of free markets at any cost as a panacea for what ails developing countries. Of course, the paradigm of the West is not to be indicted wholesale because its ideology is driven by a quasi-logical style of reasoning; that is, statistics, testimony from experts, and objective witnesses are used as key evidence to support decisions about economic success or failure (Cooper, Calloway-Thomas, & Simonds, 2007, p. 217).

Lessons From Hernando De Soto

These modes of reasoning also help to explain why in 2005, U.S. President Bush also declared that in granting loans to developing countries, the IMF and the World Bank should "tie support more directly to clear and measurable results" (*The Wall Street Journal*, January 11, 2005, p. A20). Bush's thinking was facilitated by a common belief that some loans go to governments that waste, squander, and steal funds that are intended for poor people. For example, Meredith (2005) reports that "some two-thirds of IMF and World Bank adjustments lending to African governments between 1989 and 1991 was directed towards parastatal reform" and that "donors kept no close control over the process" (p. 374).

This lack of transparency gave African leaders a "golden opportunity to sell off governments assets to political cronies and select businessmen at minimum prices on favorable terms" (p. 374). In another instance, President Biya of Cameroon used the absence of transparency to "strengthen the economic power of his Beti kinsmen" (p. 374). These cases also tell a story of inattentiveness to the common good, "the good we share in common."

There are also other cultural and economic constraints that scholarly speeches, interviews, and presentations fail to capture in the arena of *soft empathy,* and it is a finding that comes from the work of Nobel laureate Hernando De Soto (2000). According to De Soto, "Charitable organizations have so emphasized the miseries and helplessness of the world's poor that no one has properly documented their capacity for accumulating assets" (p. 11). The "mystery of capital," De Soto and a hundred researchers explain, is that Western capitalism is anchored in "formal property," the kind that relies on "titling, recording, and mapping assets—it is an instrument of thought representing assets in such a way that people's minds can work on them to generate surplus value" (p. 218).

De Soto (2000) finds that 80% of developing countries have no way of identifying "who owns what, addresses cannot be easily verified, people cannot be made to pay their debts, resources cannot conveniently be turned into money" (p. 15). Contrary to what many Westerners assume, as De Soto notes, people in such countries do have wealth but no fully developed systems of representation. To illustrate his thesis, De Soto and his research team conducted a fascinating experiment that also links to empathy capital. They opened a small garment factory on the outskirts of Lima, Peru, with the goal of "creating a new and perfectly legal business" (p. 18). In the process, however, De Soto and his research team were stunned to learn how much was involved: filling out forms, standing in the lines, making bus trips into Lima to get certification, and other such things.

Altogether, De Soto and his team spent 6 hours a day trying to secure the business, and 280 days later, they finally registered the business! The same process was repeated in other countries with similar results. For example, in Haiti, De Soto found that Haitians can settle legally on government land only if they (a) first lease it from the government for 5 years and (b) buy it. De Soto and his team had to go through "65 bureaucratic steps— on average more than two years" to complete the steps (De Soto, 2000, p. 21). As a result of such awful, time-consuming, energy-defeating steps, poor people give up or find other nonlegal means of conducting business because "it is very nearly as difficulty to *stay* as it is to *become* legal" (p. 21).

The moral of the stories is that many poor citizens in developing countries have little alternative other than to live and work outside the "legal" system. They do not have "representational systems" or a "store of inventories . . . in a property document that is the visible sign of a vast hidden process that connects all these assets to the rest of the economy" (De Soto, 2000, p. 6). Although "the poor inhabitants of these nations—five-sixths of humanity—do have things, they lack the process to represent their property and create capital" (De Soto, 2000, pp. 6–7). This is the "mystery of capital." And this mystery also has embedded within it a calculus that helps to explain why the poor worldwide are generally perceived as lacking postmodern values and having static values: "a dislike of work, suppression of individualism and irrationality," "low priority of education," "fatalism," and "mistrust of those outside the family" (Sachs, 2005, p. 315). Such attributions are not of recent origins.

Cultural Interpretations of the Poor

In the early 20th century, Max Weber tried to explain the economic success of Northern Europe as growing out of entrepreneurial Protestant values; Catholic countries and places in Southern Europe and Ireland privileged more static values. Sachs (2005) goes even further; he argues that such cultural representations "are usually made on the basis of prejudice rather than measurable evidence" (p. 317). He notes, for example, that "the arguments tend to be circular. People are poor because they are lazy. How do we 'know' they are lazy? Because they are poor" (p. 317).

These interpretations conceal the role of "a lack of capital inputs to production" (Sachs, 2005, p. 317). For example, Sachs (2005) argues compellingly that when one realizes that African farmers "lack soil nutrients, tractors, feeder roads, irrigated plots, storage facilities, and the like" (p. 317), then one begins to understand the primacy of systemic explanations as opposed to value-deficit reasons as explanations for poverty.

Furthermore, such mythic castigations of the poor hide a harsh cultural reality: the willingness of the rich and well heeled to attribute the absence of *their* values as *explanations* for why the poor behave as they do without looking outwardly sufficiently to understand comprehensively the thoughts and feelings expressed from the worldview of the other. In effect, *deficit model* explanations wipe out all differences instead of erecting "republics of hope" to reach the poor, to use Vandana Shiva's (2005) words. From these perspectives, opportunities for achieving insights from the other are woefully lacking, unlike the dazzling findings of De Soto (2000) and his colleagues; they phrased a powerful research question from the perspective of the other and shed light on a massive, dispossessed segment of humanity.

The World Trade Organization (WTO), with emphasis on free trade, rules governing imports and exports, investment, and competitive markets, is another arena that offers dramatic contrasts between haves and have-nots—poor and rich countries. Perhaps without realizing it, Friedman (2005) captures the debate over "the most obvious symbol of the global inequities and the hypocrisy of the advanced industrial countries" (p. 114) in metaphors of the lion and the gazelle. As the story goes, on December 11, 2001, when China finally joined the WTO, a few days later, an American working for a Chinese company that manufactured fuel pumps posted the following African proverb on his factory floor. It had been translated into Mandarin.

> Every morning in Africa, a gazelle wakes up. It knows it must run faster than the fastest lion or it will be killed. Every morning a lion wakes up. It knows it must outrun the slowest gazelle or it will starve to death. It doesn't matter whether you are a lion or a gazelle. When the sun comes up, you better start running. (Friedman, 2005, p. 114)

Such metaphors raise intriguing class questions. In the world of world trade, who is indeed the lion and who is the gazelle? Of course, there are advantages of free trade, including (a) market and resource specialization, (b) increased competition among nations, and (c) low prices for consumers. But there are also disadvantages, including (a) unemployment, (b) outsourcing and displacement of workers, and (c) constraints on developing nations that might find it more difficult to compete with wealthier nations. But, to extend the logic of the metaphors further, is it possible for one to be both a lion and a gazelle? Friedman (2005) concludes that "ever since the Chinese joined the WTO, both they and the rest of the world have had to run faster and faster" (p. 114). The WTO is one of the three main institutions that govern globalization. Created by the Uruguay Round between 1986 and 1994, the WTO "is the only global international organization dealing with the rules of trade between nations" (Bhagwati, 2004, p. 270). Although the WTO exists ostensibly to level the playing field between developing and advanced industrial countries, developing countries and social justice protesters have consistently lodged grievances against the United States and other Western nations over trade policies.

Domains of Grievances

Economic Grievances

Hardt and Negri (2004) group "global demands for democracy" grievances into four major domains, which I will adopt for purposes of analysis here since they are insightful tools for understanding the relationship between such grievances and empathy. They are grievances of representation, grievances of rights and justice, economic grievances, and biopolitical grievances (pp. 268–284). Because of the centrality of my mission, I have collapsed grievances of representation and economics into one category: economic representation.

Grievances of economic representation fall into dominant and subordinated divisions of humankind based on access to capital; grievances of rights and justice focus on civil and human rights, economic grievances focus on reasons why there is such dire poverty in the world, and biopolitical grievances focus on a medley of concerns. Uncomfortable with the old, standard categories of economics, politics, rights, and justice, Hardt and Negri (2004) employ the term *biopolitical* to include the major aspects of human activities that "are mutually implicated" in the basic ways that we give meaning to our lives. The term *biopolitical* is also capacious enough to include the field of ecology and struggles over air pollution, water pollution, and other aspects of the interconnected planet.

In a globalized world, economic representation spills over into the domain of empathy primarily because it raises important questions regarding whose interests are represented, that is, whether there exists in the WTO a Western, patriarchal control over systems of trade. Knowing this, it is not surprising that author and social activist Shiva (2005) should lament, "Poor people have no reason to exist in the future" since they are "not being given an option to live." Critics of the WTO claim further that there is a large distance between the promises that advanced industrial countries made about opening up their markets to developing countries and what has and is actually being delivered (Stiglitz, 2002, p. 244). In some instances, sermons fell on fallow ground in such areas as textiles and agriculture, which developed countries closed to developing countries.

Let us consider some important consequences of trade imbalances between poor and rich countries. Subsidized cotton in the United States, for example, gets dumped on Indian markets, lowering the prices in India. As a result of such "unfair" trade policies, it is impossible for many cotton farmers in India, Sudan, and other places to compete in the global marketplace. The problem of cotton is exacerbated further by the appearance of cheap imports into India. "Though India is technically free to export its agricultural produce, in practice most of it cannot be exported because it doesn't meet the First World's environmental" standards, argues novelist and activist Roy (2002). Parenthetically, and with biting irony about how rich countries, under the force of WTO policies, tell the poor how to conduct their business, Roy says, "You don't eat bruised mangoes or bananas with mosquito bites or rice with a few weevils in it, whereas, we don't mind the odd mosquito and the occasional weevil."

As I have argued, there is a crucial distinction to be made between tradition and postmodernity, and Roy's compact example of what is acceptable in developing countries and what is forbidden in pristine supermarkets in London or Paris stands in great contrast. In effect, Roy's (2002) comments invoke representatives of industrial countries' inclination, under the guise of public duty, of organizing the poor into one system, with elites at the center. Clearly, environmental standards notwithstanding, critics claim some leeway should be granted to local standards—without risk to life or limb, of course.

Rights and Justice

Furthermore, in the area of economics, grievances of rights and justice are intricately tied to issues of human rights. Many Indian farmers are committing suicide because the psychological burdens of imbalance are so great. Indians farmers cannot cope in an international system so heavily weighted against them. Over the past 2 years, 1,200 farmers have died as a result of frustration and fatigue over WTO, World Bank, and IMF procedures, policies, and modes of implementations (*The Economist,* January 20, 2007, p. 34). "Farmers who produce too much are in distress, farmers who produce too little are in distress and landless agricultural laborers are out of work, as big estates and farms lay off their workers," according to Roy (2002). These examples vividly illustrate the wretched situations the poor find themselves in because of an imbalance of representation. Fortunately for Indian farmers, Shiva and Roy have heard farmers' and others' frustrations and taken up their causes.

One of the strongest examples of appeals to justice comes from poor Indians' fight against Enron, the Houston-based company. Before its demise in 2006, Enron had managed to gain control of power plants in India, much to the distress of its citizens. Under the framework of justice, the Maharashtra Electricity Regulatory Committee (MERC) fought back and declared that "no power should be bought from Enron." Earlier in their struggle, this was to no avail, however, because according to Roy (2002), "President George W. Bush warned India about vitiating the 'investment climate' and running the risk of frightening away future investors." Roy trenchantly framed the human rights issue involved in the Enron takeover and President Bush's entrance into the debate this way: "In other words: Allow us to rob you blind, or else we'll go away."

A tragedy of the violation of human rights is the sharp argumentative tactic that developing countries use in elevating their economic and social missions over developing countries. For example, Stiglitz (2002) points out that even when advanced economies recognized inequities in the system, they merely "agreed to discussion; just to discuss redressing some of these imbalances was viewed as a concession!" (p. 245). Like the proverbial "let us discuss it later" stalling tactic that some organizations use, industrialized economies employ process discrimination as a way of addressing human inequities.

Speth (1999) calls attention to other measures that weigh heavily on the poor. According to Speth, as late as 1999, "some 150 million people—equal to the combined populations of France, the United Kingdom, the Netherlands, and the Nordic countries—were pushed into poverty when the Soviet Union collapsed" (pp. 13–14). Today, "Ethiopia needs about $70 per person per year in development assistance" (Sachs, 2005, p. 267). "If West Africa has a population of some 250 million people, $4.4 million over three years would be *less than a penny per year,* enough perhaps to buy a Dixie cup, but probably not enough to fill it with water!" (Sachs, 2002, p. 267).

As humans, we love glass half-empty/half-full stories; however, to see the glass of human rights issues as only half empty would fully miss the good that derives from economic globalization. In 2008, during his trip to five African countries, President George W. Bush called attention to enormous aid that is going to Africa in the form of HIV/AIDS packets. In 2005, the Group of 8 countries (Britain, Canada, France, Germany, Italy, Japan, Russia, and the United States) played a critical, caring role in canceling $18 billion in Nigeria's debt (Dugger, 2006, p. A6). This level of generosity, in turn, will permit Nigeria to save less than $1 billion in debt payments a year over 20 years. According to Oxfam, Group 8 debt relief to developing countries helped 19 poor countries invest in health and education (Bhagwati, 2004; Dugger, 2006).

Oxfam's acknowledgment speaks to advantages that accrue to citizens in recipient countries as a result of broad-based economic support. Clearly, poverty reduction plans are tied to quality-of-life issues. Ronald Inglehart (2000), who conducts a great deal of research on world values, argues that reducing poverty also "tremendously reduces the likelihood that people will die prematurely from starvation and disease," and when "economic development takes place, human expectancy rises" (p. 215). When humans are free from starvation, they are then free to create in other innovative ways. It is no small wonder that so much beautiful art and literature came out of Florence, Italy, during the 16th century! This is one reason why people despair when human rights are violated in egregious ways: Violations point toward a future or no future!

Biopolitical Grievances

A final domain of grievances is biopolitical. Grievances in this area question whether land, water, and other resources in poor and indigenous populations are being exploited to the detriment not only of people but of the good earth. Save the Narmada Movement is a very specific example of biopolitical disturbances. Narmada is a river in India whose project was funded by the World Bank starting in 1980. The argument centered on wholesale displacement of Indian citizens as a result of the big dam project. Although protesters were certainly interested in saving their land, they claimed that building the dam would endanger fish species, change farming practices in the country, and change the natural flow of the river.

Critics of the Narmada Dam Project were mindful that poor Indians should benefit from new forms of electricity, irrigation, safe drinking water, and the like but that they would also suffer disproportionately. Most of the profits would have gone to the rich. Hardt and Negri (2004) argue that the dam "functions as a powerful vehicle for privatization, transferring the common wealth of the river and the land to private hands" (p. 283). Indeed, this is a central grievance of biopolitical issues; the imbalance between empathy for the poor and empathy for the rich. Moreover, the real issue is whether "consent of the governed" is also part and parcel of the decision-making apparatuses that pertain to projects funded by the World Bank and governments—in this instance, the Narmada Dam Project. Consistent with foundational communitarian principles, there must be "the integrity of decision making" by "the people as a whole." I will discuss this issue in more detail later. Meanwhile, it must be noted that biopolitical struggles occur because the voices of poor and indigenous people are muted by economic powers and giant corporations.

Another example of biopolitical struggle that worked in empathy's favor took place in November 1999 in Seattle, Washington, in the United States. As do many global protest organizations, the Seattle protest movement combined issues such as "dumping," justice and fair play, and inequalities in the global system under one gigantic narrative of grievances against the WTO. During the first global protest, activists arrived from foreign countries and inside the United States to focus attention on the plight of the poor. The world media accommodated protesters by painting "an idyllic, tranquil image of Seattle, the Emerald City, forgetting the violence of its radical past," including activities of the International Workers of the World (Hardt & Negri, 2004, p. 286).

The protest in Seattle served as a heady reminder that all was not well with the World Bank, IMF, and WTO; the latter organization comprised delegates and heads of state from 135 countries who had convened in Seattle to discuss issues such as subsidies and consumerism. As a result of the Seattle protesters, WTO officials were unable to finish their meeting. Thus, for the first time in the 20th century, a concerned group of global citizens demonstrated what can happen when empathy is fully operative in human affairs. The actions of Seattle protesters are all the more powerful and instrumental when one considers the power of the global class. Who are members of the global class, and why do they matter so much?

Governing Class: "Party of Davos"

The introduction to Jeff Faux's (2006) book, *The Global Class War*, features a dazzling story that tells us a great deal about the compelling power of elites in the world. And it has a significant bearing on the subject of empathy today. In 1993, Jeff had a lively conversation in the corridors of the U.S. Capitol with a corporate lobbyist who was trying her best to make him "see the virtues of the proposed North American Free Trade Agreement" (NAFTA) that her company was supporting (p. 1). After some exasperation over her failure to make Jeff understand the weighty significance of the treaty, the lobbyist finally said to him, "Don't you understand? We have to help Salinas. He's been to Harvard. He's one of us" (p. 1). The lobbyist, of course, was referring to Carlos Salinas, who was president of Mexico at the time.

The lobbyist's reference to "one of us" hugely magnifies the difference between those who belong to an elite class and those who do not. As far as I can determine, political scientist Huntington (1996) first coined the term *Davos man* to refer to a global citizen who exists in a borderless world. Later, the words morphed into the term *Party of Davos* to signify the "politics of the global economy" that is "dominated by a virtual network" of influential people worldwide but mainly from Western countries (Faux, 2006, p. 4). Marginalization of the poor in global society can best be seen through the prism of a class system that privileges elites. The subordination occurs for many reasons; chief among them, from a global perspective, are (a) promotion of a worldwide agenda designed to facilitate the mission of corporate capital, (b) strategic ideologies and benefits emanating from the stance of a ruling class, and (c) class divide in terms of lines of power derived from elites who "run the major nation-states of the world," the U.S. superpower being the most important (Chang, 2008; Rothkopf, 2008).

In discussing the governing class, I am mindful of the complexities associated with class. Aronowitz (2003) details some of the complications, from "struggles that lead to the formation of alliances" to the role of radical social movements to power blocs that may not have anything to do with material modes of production. Aronowitz's caveat heeded, it is the case that globally, class is conflated with the rich and the powerful and with money and position (Lapham, 1998). I have already noted that a feeling of "one of us" pervades identity and alignments among the rich and "best people." An extension of the argument is that well-connected people end up inhabiting similar public space and imbibing through their mother's milk an agenda of issues that confirms who they are and their place in the world.

Makeup of the Governing Class

Let us focus specifically on one example of how this can and does occur by noting who constitutes the governing class. Domhoff (1998) was one of the first researchers to publicize the fact that many political appointee positions in the United States—both Democratic and Republican—"are corporate executives and corporate lawyers, and hence members of the power elite" (p. 151). Faux (2006) dramatically illustrates the resonance of external measures of success:

> George W. Bush owned an oil company, as well as a being a former owner of the Texas Rangers. His vice president, Richard Cheney, is known world-wide as the former CEO of Halliburton. Lesser known is his service on the board of directors of Electronic Data Systems, Procter & Gamble, and Union Pacific. Bush's chief of staff, Andrew Card, had been General Motors' chief Lobbyist in Washington for seven years. His secretary of state, Condoleezza Rice, formerly provost of Stanford University, was on the board of directors of Chevron and Transamerica. Former secretary of state Colin Powell had been Director of Gulfstream Aerospace and America Online. (p. 43)

This brief citation (there are many other examples) is presented not to denigrate the powerful and rich or to suggest that merely being a member of the governing class ipso facto ensures that members will dupe the poor. Rather, it underlines the point that reference groups hold tremendous sway over such matters as images of ourselves; whom we value; chumminess with one group as opposed to another; whether we wear Prada, Chanel, or Brooks Brothers designer clothing; what we read; and whether we are inclined toward avarice or generosity.

NAFTA and the Global Class

With regard to NAFTA, which was created during the Clinton administration, let us focus on some interesting governing class variables associated with the group that affect empathy. During his 1992 campaign, President Clinton pledged to support NAFTA with social protections for working-class people; when he took office, he soon found himself shifting priorities. One of the reasons was that Clinton's first budget was less than sanguine for his democratic constituents. But Clinton heeded the advice of Robert Rubin and Treasury Secretary Lloyd Bentsen and placed social spending on the back burner and deficit reduction on the front burner. In this way, President Clinton's support of NAFTA trumped his social agenda of health care for many Americans (Faux, 2006).

That turn of events both surprised and disappointed Clinton's most ardent supporters, who later mobilized against him. But despite the mobilization and the fact that citizens in the United States, Canada, and Mexico opposed NAFTA, the measure passed in Congress. According to a Gallup Poll, 65% of Americans opposed the agreement, while 28% favored it. Third party candidate Ross Perot also added his voice to a chorus of responses against NAFTA. It later passed despite warnings from Clinton staff and aides George Stephanopoulos and Mickey Kantor. Finally, in early September, Robert Rubin and Mack McLarty, Clinton's chief of staff, presented a tough option to Clinton: support NAFTA or health care. And Clinton chose the former (Faux, 2006, pp. 19–20).

Other people present at the meeting included Secretary of State Warren Christopher, Secretary of Treasury Lloyd Bentsen, and a roster of well-heeled globalists. Not to offer an "after this, therefore because of this" mode of reasoning, but it must be noted that "Rubin while at Goldman Sachs, had had extensive dealings as underwriter of several of Mexico's privatization schemes and had personally known Carlos Salinas since the 1980s" (Faux, 2006, p. 20). The point is that President Clinton placed NAFTA ahead of health care at a time when Robert Rubin privately believed that the measure would not create many jobs. Who, then, benefitted from NAFTA? Although many North Americans have lost their jobs following NAFTA, there is still great debate over causal and correlational renderings of the decisions made by the governing class over the wishes of the American, Canadian, and Mexican people.

Stiglitz (2006) maintains that "it is clear that NAFTA has not succeeded"—"it has not been the disaster that its critics predicted, neither has it brought all the benefits that were claimed by its advocates" (p. 62). Despite Stiglitz's fair and balanced reading of the effects of NAFTA, there still are critics who argue vigorously that a "commodified world" is working against the interests of poor people. My point is that supporters of NAFTA moved outside the public space of a general consensus from the people and toward their agenda—functioning at the level of attitudinal irrelevance and disregard for the poor. The general opinions of the people appeared to have been irrelevant and focused almost exclusively on concerns for the governing class. What are the limits to the tolerance of such elites?

Farmers in Mexico City provided an answer in 2002 by protesting farm prices. They "opened the elaborately carved wooden doors of the lower house of the Mexican Congress and rode horses through its lobby, denouncing NAFTA and demanding that the Mexican government renegotiate the treaty" (Faux, 2006, p. 129). The forceful, vocal, and lively nature of the protest spoke volumes about subordinate people. Farmers set loose big and small animals—cows, horses—on the legislative grounds to symbolize resistance and power, and to symbolize that something was woefully lacking in governing class decision-making spheres of influence: human rights considerations and respect for the dignity and honor of the dispossessed. NAFTA decisions reveal further that members of the governing class sometimes behave as if there are no poor people "out there."

The Party of Davos

Faux and others refer to the global class as the "Party of Davos" primarily because "the politics of the global market reflect a virtual one-party system" (Faux, 2006, p. 163). Having set globalist at ease, the breakup of the former Soviet Union ensured transnational membership mediated by time and space. The Party of Davos includes professors, doctors, lawyers, technocrats, media moguls, consultants, representatives from NGOs, and others.

To further complicate the class relations that obtain between the Party of Davos and other members of the superclass, it is noteworthy that we are talking about 6,000 people in a world that comprises 6 billion people (Rothkopf, 2008)! The scale and distance between who gets to say what, when, how, and with what effect are indeed enormous. This small cadre of people, ex cathedra-like, have empowered themselves to speak on behalf of humanity. And even though they do not meet in secrecy (media are invited), they convene in Davos, a small, exquisite ski resort nestled in the beautiful Swiss Alps, where the air is both cheerful and refreshing.

Even though the cabal is referred to as a party, it is not sanctioned by a party in the way the Democratic and Republican Parties are sanctioned, nor in the sense of the Socialist Party of France. Rather, Davos meetings have taken tools and activities from political parties: There are flyers, speeches, Web sites, receptions, dinners, food, conviviality, workshops, and other accoutrements of organizations. As I noted previously, religious officials, movie stars, singers, and other popular figures are extended an invite; one must be invited to attend privileged and special meetings at Davos!

To keep the hoi polloi at bay, the meeting site is protected by razor-sharp wire and soldiers with standards of war like missiles and tanks. Pulitzer Prize–winning writer Laurie Garret, who attended a Davos meeting in 2003, sent a detailed e-mail to Faux describing the goings-on there. Of the meeting, she wrote,

The world isn't run by a clever cabal. It's run by about 5,000 bickering, sometimes charming, usually arrogant, mostly male people who are accustomed to living in either phenomenal wealth, or great personal power. A few have both. . . . They are comfortable working across languages, cultures and gender, though white Caucasian males outnumber all other categories. They adore hi-tech gadgets and are glued to their cell phone. Welcome to Earth: meet the leaders. (Faux, 2006, p. 165)

Garret's electronic missive suggests several things: (a) a bifurcated world—privileged pitted against the voiceless masses; (b) exalted content-rich people in terms of education, language (feel and flair), and access to technology; (c) the special rhythms of power and all they entail in terms of the resonance of wealth: jets, limousines, vintage wines, mansions; and (d) an exclusive atmosphere where the poor are considered mostly in terms of abstractions. Now I do not wish to promote the assumption that the above mentioned things absolve many of the rich from compassion, caring, and the like. But I do want to highlight the fact that such pristine settings away from the concrete, lived experiences of ordinary people can constrain the range of human consideration, agendas, and decision making and, by extension, bring forth wittingly or unwittingly human exploitation and indifference.

Constraining Empathy: Behavior of Elites

The real challenge to the Party of Davos and the governing class is for its members to find consultative voice with the people whose lives are affected by their decisions. How, then, do members of the governing class constrain empathy? Let us start with a captivating advertisement that appeared in several magazines featuring Warren Buffet and Bill Gates—the number 1 and 3 richest men in the world, respectively, as of this writing—on a Boeing Business NetJets. In the superclass signifying advertisement, the two men are in a convivial, cheerful pose, both dressed in white shirts with open collars and black pants. Gates is on the left side and avuncular Buffet is seated on the right side on a cushy, light brown sofa that could be straight out of someone's elegant living room. Buffet wears braces or suspenders, with a gold watch clearly visible on his wrist.

Gates's head is tilted to the left with his right hand resting on a lever that positions the seat-like sofa; his legs are apart, while Buffet's left leg crosses his right leg. In front of the two seated rich men is a lacquered brilliant butternut table displaying playing cards, a china plate with two cookies on it, a fruit cheese tray (with purple grapes, honeydew melon, a strawberry, and kiwi), and a medley of what appears to be M&Ms. A flat contraption (perhaps a computer) is in front of Gates with a neatly folded newspaper on top. Three bundles of napkins complete the ensemble of displays of wealth. Without consciously intending to do so, the advertisement of the two wealthy but generous men is iconic for what it symbolizes about the governing class. Their comfortable, happy-appearing lifestyle, however far away, juxtaposes itself strikingly against "the lifestyle of Mexican immigrants and the specter of an enduring underclass" (*The New York Times,* May 25, 2005, p. 1) caught up in a nightmarish, on-the-run existence.

The problem is not the wealth of the two men, because the poor and rich have lived in relative proximity at least since Croesus. Rather, the point is that such pristine, well-appointed insular splendors incline the rich to imagine and envisage a different role for the poor. This evolves largely from a constraint of separation that inhibits *hard* empathy. Although humans have an infinite ability to imagine what it would be like to live by someone else's light, it is also the case that proximity matters. Whether humans are close or distant can determine "how they divide up their world, assign values to its parts, and measure them" (Tuan, 1977).

Geographic Distance: East Timor

In short, geographic distance reinforces hierarchical decision-making apparatuses that place the poor in an uncomfortable position of not being allowed to tell their stories. Instead, the poor are viewed as universal abstractions with scarcely any attention paid to their arguments, modes of reasoning, and opinions. As a result, the poor lose their economic, social, and cultural agency, and the decisions of the governing class take precedence over their collective voices.

In an interview with Matt Lauer of NBC's *TODAY Show,* New Jersey Governor Jon Corzine, in discussing whether hedge-fund managers were "out of touch with America," acknowledged that "some people, based on the size of the houses I see built and the automobiles and the things that people accumulate, there are some who might be drifting away from reality" (*The Wall Street Journal,* May 18, 2007, p. W2). A drifting away from reality is clearly revealed in what happened to East Timorans from 1999 to 2002, when the United Nations administered the country (Perlez, 2006). East Timorans received "gifts of tractors" from well-meaning donors, who, because of insularity or a failure to do the lovely work of othering, did not stretch their minds far enough to process whether East Timorians would have sufficient money to pay for fuel to run the tractors or to maintain them. Furthermore, during the same period, "more than half the foreign assistance was spent on salaries and consultant fees of the foreign advisers" (Perlez, 2006, p. A3).

The situation in East Timor signifies what happens when elites in one geographic space talk to elites in another. Assumptions about what works and what does not are too often governed by the mind-set of elites. Traditionally, in both the West and the rest, decisions that affect many poor people are based on consulting experts who are supposed to know what is in the best interest of the other. With these views, the governing class in one country relies on the governing class in another.

Structural and Social Ease: Africa

And this leads to a second factor that constrains empathy: the structural and social ease of talking to and identifying with other cosmopolitan members of transnationals.

Africa is a typical case. Moeletsi Mbeki (2005), writing in *The Wall Street Journal,* suggests that the governing class of Africa has firm notions of who is to get what. And the governing class reasserts its sense of entitlement and disregard for the poor by exploiting the natural resources of their countries, transferring "profits, taxes, and aid funds into their own foreign bank accounts" (Mbeki, 2005, p. A20). Jeffrey Herbst (2005), in explaining the workings of postapartheid South Africa, claims that efforts to help the poor there "have largely failed, serving mainly to enrich a small black elite" (p. 94).

The structural, symbiotic relationship between the governing class in the West and the governing class in Africa has also done a great deal to perpetuate poverty on the African continent and to create an immense divide between rich and poor. While Africa is constrained by many things such as drought, bad roads, malaria, inadequate education, and ethnic strife, nowhere is the constraint on empathy more visible than in the political class that governs the continent. Mbeki (2005) refers to the actions of elites as "predatory policies" (p. A20). To ferret out all the complicating variables that help to explain motivations for predatory policies, suffice it to say, historically, competition between communism and capitalism played a role. And so did the machinations that evolved after many African countries gained independence, starting with Ghana in 1960. "The political elites that took over African countries in the 1960s thus saw government as a source of power and personal enrichment" (Mbeki, 2005, p. A20).

A question of great significance regarding the behavior of audacious African political officials who make up the governing class is this: What habits of mind are at work that would allow them to display pageantry while millions starve? A former president of Liberia, Samuel Doe, is a case in point. "Credited with the power not only to be impervious to bullets" and maintaining "a coterie of juju men from all over Africa, notably Togo," Doe also managed to amass a huge fortune for himself and his cronies (Meredith, 2005, pp. 549–550). It is reported that during his reign in the 1980s, Doe amassed something akin to $300 million (Meredith, 2005, p. 550). Doe used his ties to such state organizations as the Liberian Petroleum Refining Corporation and the Forestry Development Authority as vehicles for generating wealth. From this perspective, in the process of consulting and talking to like-minded members of the governing class, both symbolically and in reality, Doe ignored a large segment of humanity.

Of course, there are also variations on the continent of Africa in terms of the distribution of empathy. Earlier, I described the classic case of Malawi's president and his fidelity to the well-being of his people. Time constraints will not allow a discussion of the role of Great Britain, France, and the United States in selecting and propping up African leaders who have done harm to their citizens. Joseph Mobutu in the Belgium Congo is the classic example. With the intrigue of a John LeCarre spy novel, Belgians and U.S. Under-Secretary of State Douglas Dillion orchestrated the political situation in Congo and replaced Patrice Lumumba, who was considered to be "an irrational, almost 'psychotic' personality," with Mobutu (Meredith, 2005, p. 104). Lumumba was declared unfit to rule Congo; of course, a big part of the political action revolved around whether Communists would take over the Congo. It should not go unnoticed that following Congolese demands for freedom, Lumumba told former colonial King Baudouin of Belgium, "We are no longer your monkeys" (Meredith, 2005, p. 102).

The point of this truncated story is once again to illustrate the role of elites in determining the fate of many. And never before have inequalities between rich and poor been so great. The Grand Rapids, Michigan, newspaper recently ran the following headline: "Filthy rich own half of world's wealth" (qtd. in *The Wall Street Journal*, May 5, 2007, p. W2) to underscore some startling statistics about the great divide: "The richest 1% of Americans now control 33% of the nation's wealth, up from 30% in 1989" (p. W2). As I noted earlier, more than 8 million people die each year because of dire poverty. Some good news is that the rich and other members of the governing class are beginning to respond to some of the stupendous challenges of our global age, including HIV/AIDS, global warming, food distribution, agriculture, the physical environment, safe drinking water, malaria, inadequate education, and allocation of other resources.

The United Nations Millennium Project

What, then, are some promises and fulfillments regarding empathy in light of haves and have-nots worldwide? One of the most promising programs ever undertaken by the United Nations is the Millennium Project, under the leadership of economist Jeffrey Sachs of Columbia University in the United States. The project grapples with some of the most complex and far-reaching problems confronting the planet "by building a consensus around a shared vision and understanding" of the collective task necessary to implement the work (Sachs, 2005, p. 222). For once, the world is beginning to come together with greater intensity to shoulder the burdens of the poor in an edifying way. Through the process of fact finding, analysis, debate, and discussion and, most critically, with great empathy, world leaders are promising bold and innovative initiatives to help eliminate poverty by 2025.

The magnitude and timings of these projects are daunting. To accomplish these hoped for miracles, rich countries will have to rethink the way they do global business and concentrate on seeing things from the perspective of the poor—using both a top-down and a bottom-up approach. As Sachs (2005) notes, rich countries will also have to move beyond "the platitudes of helping the poor, and follow through on their repeated promises to deliver more help" (p. 266). In pushing bold efforts to eradicate poverty among the poorest of poor, Sachs and the UN Millennium Project have been confronted by some pretty vexing questions and issues. For example, will attention to people who earn just $2.70 a day, as is the case in India, "break the bank" of wealthy countries? Is it possible for rich countries to take responsibility for the billions of poor out there? And haven't G-7 countries already done enough to help the poor with small returns in some countries? In other words, is there a point of diminishing returns when it comes to alleviating poverty? And what role do natural disasters continually play in the persistence of poverty?

Using a pointed and empathetic question, Sachs (2005) embodies the series of aforementioned questions into one succinct but moving statement: "The more one looks at it, the more one sees that the question isn't whether the rich can afford to help the poor, but whether they can afford not to" (p. 288).

Despite Sach's (2005) beautifully value-laden and haunting question, another question of equal significance emerges: Is it possible for industrially rich countries to become so overburdened by aiding the poor in other countries that they will also suffer? At this writing, the United States, Great Britain, France, and other places are being challenged by a foreclosure crisis. *The New York Times* (2007), under the banner heading "Spreading the

Misery," noted that "in the third quarter, there were 635,000 foreclosure filings, a 30 percent increase from the previous quarter and nearly double from a year ago" (p. A26). The point is if American citizens are busily engaged in their own misery, will there be enough to go around? And will Hume's concentric circle of empathy revert back to its center position exclusively?

Of course, Sachs's (2005) trenchant comment is designed to focus attention on the interconnectivity of the globe. It just might be the case that my misery is your misery and that our miseries are so tightly joined that it is almost impossible to separate one misery from another. In the area of health care, for example, Laurie Garrett (2007), in a scary scenario, states, "More money is being spent on global health than ever before, but because the efforts are narrow, uncoordinated, and heedless of the 'brain drain' on local health systems, the current age of generosity might actually make things worse instead of better" (p. 14).

Garrett (2007) focuses world attention on a point that I made earlier with regard to the governing class, and that is an inclination to define things from their own perspective. She urges us to focus on local issues. If we go backstage, we can see how giving to poor countries is intimately tied to who will be alive in developing countries to offer aid. For example, will the over $6.6 billion that the Bill and Melinda Gates Foundation has already given away cure ills if there are few nurses, doctors, and other practitioners in Ghana, for example?

A survey found that in Ghana, "72 percent of all clinics and hospitals were unable to provide the full range of expected services due to a lack of sufficient personnel" (Garrett, 2007, p. 26). Furthermore, "a study by the International Labor Organization estimates that 18–41 percent of the health-care labor force in Africa is infected with HIV" (p. 27). These mind-boggling statistics are designed to illustrate further that the general, universal idea of helping the poor needs to be coupled with attention to structural and systemic forces that are operative in the countries receiving aid.

Consider other crucial factors in the area of health care that constrain the relationship between promises and fulfillment, such as (a) who is dying, how many, and why; (b) how HIV/AIDS medicines are secured and delivered; (c) how many nurses and doctors are being trained; (d) the inability to track the operations of foreign organizations operating on the soil of donor countries; (e) where drugs can and will be stored in places where there is little or no sustainable electricity; (f) job opportunities; (g) donors' priorities, politics, and values; and (h) recruitment activity inside poor countries. The latter issue is fraught with deep, hidden dimensions of global empathy because the brain drain clearly is a specter that haunts rich donor countries.

On one hand, rich countries are giving aid for health care, and on the other hand, they are accepting a steady and forceful stream of doctors and nurses coming from such poor countries as the Philippines, Ghana, and Kenya. How do rich donor countries reconcile the dissonance? And how, in turn, do leaders in recipient nations cope with the dissonance, knowing that their countries gradually are being emptied of qualified workers whose very absence helps to ensure meager returns on the health front? There appears, then, to be a symbiotic relationship between rich donor countries and organizations and poor recipient countries and organizations. Without sufficient scrutiny of "backstage" issues, to use Erving Goffman's phrase, beautiful giving and receiving just might not be what they purport to be. This is indeed a moral, humanitarian emergency that should summon the best in empathy itself. Are there breakthroughs? Can humans more competently employ empathetic fluency in looking to the future?

8

Empathetic Literacy

Come, Shout About It?

Breakthroughs and Empathy

Sinah Matlou, who works in a poor section of Johannesburg in South Africa, is no typical, ordinary volunteer. "Every day," she says, "I have to cross a river of sewage to see my patients who are too sick to leave their beds" (*Index of Global Philanthropy*, 2007, p. 58). In commenting on the sad plight of her patients, Matlou notes further that "I've often brought them just enough drinking water from the PlayPump so that they can at least stay hydrated or swallow their medicine" (*Index of Global Philanthropy*, 2007, p. 58).

Matlou's work is no small endeavor and is made more palatable by the PlayPump, an innovative way of hauling clean water to nearly 2 million people in South Africa. The PlayPump is the brain child of retired advertising executive, Trevor Field. Combining his expertise and reputation in commercial advertising with a moral zeal to promote clean water and good health for citizens of South Africa, Field will certainly be numbered among the many who are changing the face of empathy worldwide, and his work also signifies breakthroughs in empathy.

Field's method of bringing clean water to South Africans and others operates on one human concept, the interplay between play and advertising. To ensure the presence of clean water, Field, in a truly innovative moment, wed the idea of pumping clean water to a children's merry-go-round and placed it on a school playground. The mechanical process of the pump is this: As children play on the merry-go-round, they activate the pump, making it turn, as gallons of clean, fresh water are pumped above ground in a large storage tank. The free-flowing water is then assessable to families, schools, and communities. To ensure economic sustainability of the pumps for at least 10 years, Field leased out sides of the tank for commercial billboards. Today, more than 736 pumps are operating in South Africa at a cost of $14,000 per pump (*Index of Global Philanthropy*, 2007). Field's philanthropic method symbolizes infinite possibilities of ways to address a myriad of global issues that confront international communities: disaster relief, health and social issues, agricultural and environmental improvement, political unrest and poverty, clean water, transportation, illiteracy, individual and social improvement, housing, and economic development.

Not surprisingly, today there are thousands of humanitarian organizations and governments worldwide ready and willing to help alleviate pain and suffering in developing countries. According to the *Index of Global Philanthropy* (2007), there are approximately 62,000 foundations in the European Union alone. Based on 2002–2005 data of remittances from Organisation for Economic Cooperation and Development (OECD) donor countries, contributions from European countries to the developing world totaled $34.98 billion by 2005 (*Index of Global Philanthropy*, 2007, p. 30). Contributions from the United States totaled $61.70 billion, with the United States being the largest donor. Other countries that made the list in the category of remittances, from highest to lowest, are the United Kingdom, Canada, Japan, Spain, France, Germany, Italy, Australia, the Netherlands, Switzerland, Austria, Sweden, Greece, Denmark, Belgium, Portugal, Norway, New Zealand, Ireland, Finland, and Luxembourg (*Index of Global Philanthropy*, 2007, p. 31).

As these data suggest, as the world's wealth is steadily increasing, attitudes toward giving have become embodiments of a universal value. Jim Holt (2008) questions whether this season of altruism ("ostentatious giving") might also be motivated by traits deeply rooted in a Darwinian philosophy of trying to "bankrupt one's rivals" (p. 12). In this section, I do not wish to debate the reasons for giving; rather, I wish to follow philosopher Thomas Nagel's moral edict that "the conception of oneself as merely a person among others equally real" as a way of thinking about other remarkable breakthroughs in empathy.

Although clearly much more needs to be done to set things right in the world, Nagel's philosophy is congruent with my research.

Reasons for Generosity

Based on my analysis of empathy in the global age, evidence suggests that something potent, but insufficient, is happening internationally in the arena of giving, and four major reasons for the generosity are the following:

1. *Increasing recognition that a world divided cannot stand.* We are all interdependent now. Human typography has changed! We are no longer physically and emotionally separated one from another, even if we willed it so. As a result of globalization, there is a recognition that what affects one affects all; this interdependent relationship requires more collective action. This means that we must be committed to global justice and the global public good. Unlike primeval times, and even during Roman times, it is no longer possible for humans to have virulent forms of infectious diseases today without them affecting the entire planet. As I noted previously, human beings could go in the opposite direction—destroying the ozone layer, polluting oceans, preventing vaccines against malaria for the poor, denying literacy to millions, and turning away from a general caring for others. But we do so at the peril of the entire planet.

2. *A reign of true believers.* There exists among us a cadre of people and organizations who believe deeply that economic and social injustices should disappear from the face of the earth. Like moral abolitionists of 19th-century England and North America, these dedicated individuals are driven by zeal and fervor. They work most successfully through local and national organizations but also have a global reach. M. S. Swaminathan (father of India's green revolution), Shiva, Roy, and Tavis Smiley (author of *Contract With Black America*) comprise this group.

3. *Contagious stars and high-profile celebrities.* Bono, Angelina Jolie, Oprah, former President Clinton, Sharon Stone, and others have taken a passionate stand against ills in the world. Using their bodies and mind as public announcements, they are driving home the point that we must care about social issues and matters of economic justice. As a consequence, facilitated by a general, emotional contagion that comes from high-profile humans, plus electronic mailboxes, television, film, and other forms of media, stars have enormous human capital and an ability to stir people to action.

Stars are crucial to the spread of empathy worldwide: They hold fundraisers, have access to the airwaves, generate articles about generosity and philanthropy in newspapers and magazines, and create interests among ordinary people.

The rhetorically resonant stance of stars and high-profile celebrities echoes Hochchild's (2005) message regarding empathy that I mentioned in Chapter 1: "There is always something mysterious about human empathy, and when we feel it and when we don't" (p. 5). Increasingly, we feel empathy, and it is being facilitated by stars' acumen in delivering a powerful message to young and old and rich and poor across continents. The message is this: It is embarrassing and shameful in the extreme to witness the great contrasts between plenty and poverty in the world and not do something about it. With these implicit and explicit goals, by creating hope, stars are sewing ideas of empathy into international consciousness. Stars are bringing the far and the distant together, creating a multiplier effect by helping write the poor into history.

The three facilitating attitudes have helped set in motion a cast of characters that would be worthy of emulation by the Medicis of 15th-century Florence, Italy, lenders and investors who were instrumental in sponsoring goodly causes in such areas as arts and humanities. Although the more than 150 years that the Medicis used their grand wealth for great causes differ significantly from what is happening today, even then, there were among the human population people who were symbols of generosity.

Next, I offer a few mini case studies of breakthroughs in cooperative empathy to underline the spectrum of activities operating locally and internationally.

"Help on Wheels"

In 1986, in a remote village in the tiny country of Somalia, villagers greeted guests Randy Mamola and Andrea and Barry Coleman, who were there under the sponsorship of Save the Children international charity to witness firsthand the nature of health care in Somalia. What the three guests witnessed astonished them: Pregnant women about to deliver children were being "carted to hospitals in wheelbarrows" (*Index of Global Philanthropy*, 2007, p. 53). Mamola and the Colemans also witnessed something that matched their skill set beautifully: junkyards filled with rusty cars that were in need of minor repair. Soon after seeing a pretty brand-new $30,000 Land Cruiser that had been abandoned for lack of a $3 part and aided by a marvelous idea, the Colemans and Mamola, a well-off Grand Prix motor racing star, created a way to assist human productivity in Somalia. What do we learn from such animating forces?

Reviewing the powers of attentiveness that drove Mamola and the Colemans, it is striking how closely their sensibilities mesh with a humanitarian impulse. Their clear goal was to help the preexisting state of Somalians and create conditions for change that would approximate the local environment— what was already there, waiting to be galvanized, both agency and empowerment. Another instructive aspect of the story is the absence of a "blame the Somalians" narrative that too often disturbs projects in developing countries. Instead, one sees a measure of respect for the dignity of "Riders for Health." The metaphor "Riders for Health" clearly embodies robust optimism that potentially created cohesion and camaraderie among workers.

Eventually, the trio raised sufficient sums of money to help citizens in Somalia, Uganda, Gambia, and Lesotho learn the rudiments of car repair. With the skills obtained from the generosity of Mamola and the Colemans, women are now transported to hospitals in vehicles. From 1991 to 1996, there was not a single breakdown of vehicles in one country, Lesotho. Operating under the delightful and official charitable title "Riders for Health," the organization now has a fleet of 1,200 vehicles in Nigeria, Gambia, Zimbabwe, and Gambia (*Index of Global Philanthropy*, 2007, p. 54).

Finally, this story is magical because it reveals that a quick, moving idea can be as powerful as any idea poured over in board rooms, parliaments, and halls of congress. Furthermore, the case study demonstrates what happens when caring is embodied in concrete form.

"Rugs to Riches: How Fair Trade Matters"

A second success story has its origins in Cairo, Egypt, on the heaps of a garbage dump! On the edge of town, a huge trash pile sustains the livelihood of millions of poor Egyptians. Meticulously, and undoubtedly with much bathos and humiliation, the poor sort through stuff that has been tossed away; children get up in the morning and go to the dump routinely while better-off children wend their way to elementary school. Needless to say, conditions there are distressing.

But help arrived in the form of the Association for the Protection of the Environment (APE), in conjunction with a local nongovernmental organization (NGO). In 1988, through single-mindedness and determination to give the children a better future, APE and the local NGO had a compelling idea. Why not teach the mothers of the children who sift through garbage bins a trade?

Employing the dynamism of capitalism based in a recognition of natural self-interest and in vivid microcosm, agents from the two groups taught mothers how to weave and sew rugs, as well as make bedspreads and other handicrafts. The effects were stunning (*Index of Global Philanthropy*, 2007). The human gesture of creating vibrant jobs from a garbage heap—a largely unthinkable idea—surely aided empathy's work. Furthermore, a central point is that changes in the mothers' pool of talent not only altered family incomes but also fostered economic specialization, a key to skill production in a globalized world. In this crucial way, a local NGO magnified human possibilities.

Noticeable also in this story is a blending of local habits of mind and markets. APE showed no disdain for the plight of poor Egyptians, which is a barrier to trampling on the dignity of others.

Today, with help from United Nations Educational, Scientific and Cultural Organization (UNESCO), at least 250 women are participating and learning the basics of mathematics, family planning, and other forms of literacy. As a result of this breakthrough in empathy and through Ten Thousand Villages, an American fair trade organization, poor Egyptian women as well as women in 30 other developing countries are becoming entrepreneurs, selling their crafts in more than 160 retail stores in America (*Index of Global Philanthropy*, 2007).

The "Rugs to Riches" story is also significant because it dramatizes how the poor can be helped through a flow of capital goods, labor, and plain old-fashioned ingenuity.

"The Mount Kenya Academy: Strings Attached"

A final narrative of breakthroughs in empathy is closely interwoven with civic virtue, reading, and the arts—clearly, values that are essential to a beautifully engaged world. The impetus for the story is Gillian Clements, who teaches violin at Mount Kenya Academy in Nyeri, Kenya. As a student at Rice University in Houston, Texas, Clements recalls the exquisite joy that she received from her violin lessons. She noted, for example, that violin lessons increased her self-confidence and gave her a better vision of self.

While studying for her doctoral degree, Clement also tried to think of ways that she could sustain the musical lives of students as she had done through a program called "String Fling" at Rice University. Later, she met Scott Hawkins, who was diligently involved in fundraising for Mount Kenya Academy, a sister school of one in Atlanta. Their friendship grew, culminating in wonderful insights about the joining of ideas with reality. Hawkins reported to Clement that Mount Kenya Academy was confined to teaching "academics, but it's important to the leaders of the Academy to provide a variety of learning opportunities" (*Index of Global Philanthropy*, 2007).

Fortunately for children at Mount Kenya Academy, Clement wrote her dissertation on the academy. In the process of writing, she hit upon a vivacious idea embodied by mounds of empathy: Why not begin a strings program at the academy? And she did! What Clements was getting while writing her dissertation was a lesson in how to engage the mind and imagination in the service of others. And for her, there was an ecological relationship between getting and giving in the pursuit of achievement that she wanted to share with others. With strong echoes of Stage 2 empathy that I discussed in Chapter 1, Clement moved from self to empathic openness. Like Cicero and Immanuel Kant, she clearly aspired to justice and goodness, sources of great richness in life. As a result of Clement's recognition of the humanity of others, she has captivated the minds of over "85 children ages six to 19 in August 2006" (*Index of Global Philanthropy*, 2007, p. 60).

Once again, a program had a particular impact because creativity and caring meshed well. For Clement, what remained was for her to find ways of sustaining the program through donor enlistments—actions also at the heart of empathetic lives.

There are many other stories that I could cite more fully, including the narrative of Divine Bradley of Team Revolution, New York, who "opened his family's front porch and basement as a makeshift community center for drifting young people" (*The New York Times,* March 9, 2008, p. 46), and the story of Becca Robison, creator of AstroTots, a "space and science camps for girls 4 to 10 years old" (p. 53). As a result of Bradley's efforts, he raised more than $25,000 in about 2 weeks. Robison's AstoTots is helping to disturb the myth that girls are only interested in the humanities and not hard sciences.

A Common Empathetic Agenda

Despite the outpouring of creativity and compassion worldwide by a host of NGOs, the World Bank, the International Monetary Fund, private and voluntary organizations (PVOs), the Melinda and Bill Gates Foundation, Warren Buffett, George Soros, Oprah, Alfred Mann Medical, David Rockefeller, the Packard Foundation, the Ford Foundation, Wal-Mart, Google Foundation, the Charities Aid Foundation, World Vision, Oxfam, Caritas, Kokusai Volunteer Chokin, universities, the Red Cross, and government aid, it still is the case that more than 2 billion human beings worldwide live on less than $2 a day.

As I have noted, now we have an opportunity to create an empathetic agenda. But what should a global empathetic agenda be and do? Although there are no magic bullets for a common empathetic agenda, here are some ideas that, with some planning and attentiveness, just might help us do more morally right things.

1. *Increase Interaction Between Rich and Poor*

The rich have loved lots of space since ancient times. And they have used it to sustain opulent lifestyles, build extraordinary manor houses, sustain honorific monarchies, dine on nouvelle food, wear designer clothes, and craft gilded ceilings. Machmud of Ghazni, Mansa Musa, Jacob Fugger, John Law, Louis the XVI, the Rothschilds, the Guinnesses, the Vanderbilts, and Bill Gates are examples of wealthy individuals whose impact on society has been striking, whether for good or ill. "And yet," Crook (1999) observes, "historically speaking, as individuals, the rich often remain invisible" (p. 4).

With the possible exception of Bill Gates, Warren Buffett, Donald Trump, Bono, and Oprah, few individuals could identify pictures of the rich and superrich, even if offered a thousand dollars.

And herein lies a fundamental human problem for the distribution of empathy, knowledge, skills, and other forms of capital. To a remarkable extent, physical and moral proximity between rich and poor is too large. As a consequence, the "echelon of deciders" remains secure in stately offices, making decisions that affect humankind without having sufficient knowledge of how the other half truly lives. We have a responsibility to share not only money but also mental resources with others. In his *Meditations* (8.9), Marcus Aurelius (1983) advises that people who live what he terms a "palace life," meaning a life of wealth and privilege, cannot be exempt from doing good. Above all, Marcus believed that even in a palace, one can live a virtuous life, one that radiates outward toward a common purpose. What can those who live "a palace life" do?

To ensure that more cultural, intellectual, and symbolic capital circulates among the general population, local governments and communitarian organizations should encourage the building of physical zones of and for living. This would be a major change in the way we use space, distribute human skills, and reorder human relations. We already know that access to power and knowledge is an integral part of learning and that "being there" (in decision-making zones) is a pedagogical tool. "Being there" is one way that humans gain intellectual and cultural capital from others. Reducing physical distance between middle-class and rich "insiders" and poor "outsiders" could make a big difference in perspective and in the acquisition of skills. Such arrangements need not be driven by a "trickle-down" theory of denigration. I remember growing up in the one traffic light, blink and it's gone kind of southern town of Bernice in Louisiana, where teachers (major owners of symbolic and economic capital) lived next door to working-class families. In that setting, the conduct of teachers served as rich sources of knowledge that empowered others. Unless we narrow the skills gap between the rich and the poor, I fear there will continue to be a diminution in both intellectual and economic capital globally. What is moral about the great physical, cultural, and intellectual separation that is taking place today based on wealth?

2. Treat the Poor With Intellectual and Moral Seriousness

Rich countries, NGOs, the International Monetary Fund, the World Bank, and other organizations should consult with the poor before embarking on projects that influence the latter's standard of living and well-being. While there are some organizations that do this, too often decisions are made from top to bottom. As I have noted before, shockingly, too often charities and economic aid benefit practitioners rather than recipients. We should not only give money but also ensure that charitable giving is making a significant difference in such areas as education, health care, global environment, trade agreements, debt relief, poverty reduction, improvements in essential infrastructures, disease control, and agronomic practices.

Opening up the decision-making process paves the way for consultative empathetic practices, empowers the poor, and reduces despair, hopelessness, and even death. The more than 1,200 illiterate cotton farmers who committed suicide in India because of policies implemented by the World Trade Organization (WTO) might be alive today had they been involved in the decision making that so dreadfully affected their lives. *The Economist* (January 20, 2007) writes that Indian farmers "are the most poignant example of India's 'agrarian crisis'" (p. 34). And I add that they are "the most poignant examples" of what happens when the interests of the poor are not balanced against the interests of rich people and countries. Furthermore, according to Oxfam, a leading global charitable organization, the plight of farmers increased as a result of "indiscriminate and forced integration into an unfair global system" (*The Economist*, January 20, 2007, p. 34). Low prices of cotton, India's labor laws, farm subsidies, "biotech" cotton seeds, and other factors are also implicated here. However, encouraging a balance between decision makers and the poor should not only democratize human processes and modes of communication but also help rectify past grievances and harm. More crucially, by taking such action, we weave moral imperatives into the fabric of global society.

3. *Hold Grameen-Global Dialogues Between Rich and Poor People*

The United Nations should establish and convene regular meetings between rich and poor people. Apple Computer, Bristol-Myers Squibb, Bajaj Allianz, German Technical Cooperation (GTZ), the Coca-Cola Company, Wal-Mart, Mercy Corps, churches, synagogues, mosques, and other organizations and groups could help sponsor such events. This idea might strike some as both naive and revolutionary, but it is time for us to *unprivatize privilege* and human skill building and development. Consider this: *What happens* to poor people and why are logically implicated in what is *done to them* in terms of civil inattention and civic and social disregard. Details regarding power dimensions, procedures, protocols, vocal symmetry, and who says what and how long should, of course, be managed fairly. I have in mind here a *Grameen-Global Dialogue,* using the name Grameen to symbolize and dramatize human possibilities. In a previous chapter, I described some of the impressive empathetic features of Grameen Bank. By being inclusive and by encouraging individual accountability, Grameen Bank manifests one of the most stunning examples of Christ's and other religions' injunctions that we should help the poor among us.

By such acts of assertion and goodwill, the United Nations could give the poor distinctive voices in international affairs that affect many aspects of their lives. An offshoot of this, of course, is that we should be able to tap into wellsprings of human intellect that lie fallow, to use an agrarian metaphor, because half of global society is dismissed, disregarded, and vulnerable—whether by omission or commission—because their symbolic and practical capital options are not taken seriously. Think about the consequences of human capital and the transfer of knowledge, ideas, skills, and creativity! Too often we assume that the poor have little to give in the areas of human capital.

4. Foster a More Harmonious International Public Culture

At the beginning of the book, I identified some troubling aspects of humanity, from the attack on the World Trade Center to violent responses to the publication of photographs that "appeared" to impugn the Prophet Muhammad. To square principles of empathy with Kant's notion of human dignity, fostering a more harmonious public culture worldwide could occur by *changing the environment of public discourse.* Hunter (1991) argues sensibly that media technologies are primarily responsible for passing along the *content* of debates that flow between opposing groups. Because contending parties to geopolitical quarrels rely heavily on bits and pieces of information that flow back and forth via television, for instance, the parties rarely confront each other face-to-face.

Giving groups along the great divide an opportunity to confront one another face-to-face should resurrect old-fashioned modes of discursive discourse, which should encourage a serious and rational public conversation on empathy's behalf.

I have in mind here an environment that would discourage discourse excess. All of us know very well that television invites sound-bite and bombastic generalities. Changing the environment in which debates over ethnicity and race, poverty and welfare occur should help debaters to draw upon complex, rich sources of language, such as rebuttal, cross-examination, and presentation of evidence, in addition to predisposing individuals to civility. Would, for instance, a discussion between President Barack Obama's former pastor, Jeremiah Wright, and FOX television talk show host Sean Hannity concerning the relative merits of what constitutes racism degenerate in a face-to-face rhetorical environment free of television? Perhaps. However, rules governing what can and cannot be said, when, and where should mitigate the development of hostile rhetoric. And work to the benefit of empathy. My point is that a change from a media environment to an environment more conducive to discursive talk should promote civility, global community, and goodwill.

5. Hold Days of Empathy and Care Celebrations

Media and popular stars matter in today's postmodern international society because they shape arguments, influence conversations, modify beliefs and values, mobilize behavior, and use symbols to great effect. The symbolic capital of Bono, Oprah, Stone, and other members of the superclass is compelling—aided by others, of course. These *carriers of capital* (CCs) could also use their resources worldwide to hold days of empathy and care celebrations. Before doubting the effects of repetition on the human soul, consider how long racism has been nestled inside humanity's bosom. Then, ask how and why that nestling came to be and why it has lasted so long. Scholars reveal that historically, racism became a form of cultural expression and practice that was sustained aggressively by major human institutions such as churches, pulpits, courts of law, economic systems, and universities that contributed to its longevity. Through castigations, vile language, wealth and power, the Bible, fear, bureaucracies, corporatization, calculation, comparison and contrast, ideological consensus, and other expressive forms, racism triumphed.

Like the Stoics, who sat among painted colonnades and adopted strategies of "self-shaping," we, too, just might be able to "tone up" our souls and transform human behavior in exquisite and far-reaching ways. Again, the wisdom of Isabel, a character in Smith's (2004) novel, *The Sunday Philosophy Club,* resonates. Said Isabel, in discussing a hot topic that a group of philosophers in her club had wrestled with, "The whole emphasis of morality should shift from what we do to what we do not do" (p. 101). Isabel recognized almost immediately that the stance was "potentially burdensome" and "would be uncomfortable for those who sought a quiet life. It [the position] required vigilance and more awareness of the needs of others," which was a bit more than Isabel "felt that she possessed" (pp. 101–102).

But Isabel does possess more, and the entire global community can become more vigilant and more aware of the needs of others. Collective focus on a world of broader possibilities just might be helped via dramatizations of our moral obligation to people both near and far. Is this sufficient to hush global concerns? What would my gentle reader recommend? At the most basic level, of course, more things are required of humans on a daily basis to further the ends of empathy, including a movement toward empathetic literacy. Following are some things that we might collectively accomplish in this domain.

Toward Empathetic Literacy

In *Why Geography Matters,* Harn de Blij (2005) laments the fact that not enough high schools and universities today offer courses in geography. He notes, for example, that elite "Harvard University has not offered geography to students for about a half century" (p. 13). de Blij also claims that "geography is a superb antidote to isolationism and provincialism" (p. 21).

Increasingly, scholars in communication, geography, history, political science, and other disciplines decry North American students' inability to identify the Declaration of Independence, find Iraq on a world map, and place the Civil War in the correct half century. Empathetic literacy is also a critical way for us to provide articulate attention to the interior of humans—starting with families and with students in elementary school. Being human means that a person is attuned properly to the wishes and concerns of others in civil society.

In Chapter 1, I stressed the importance of moral attention in human affairs. Here, I will use another one of Smith's (2004) delightful characters to further underline the point, with an eye toward expanding definitions of what it means to be empathy literate in the 21st century. While discussing the role of manners in human relations, central character Isabel contrasts and ponders the "well-mannered" behavior of Paul Hogg and Toby, who had bad manners. "Good manners depended on paying moral attention to others; it required one to treat them with complete moral seriousness; to understand their feelings and their needs," says Isabel (p. 140). It was Isabel's discerning way of recognizing that people count and that they are owed human dignity and standing in community, as Kant and Aurelius pointed out years ago. "Accustom yourself not to be inattentive to what another person says," says Aurelius (6.53), and "as far as possible enter into his mind" (Aurelius, 1983).

But not all human beings are attentive enough, respectful, and caring toward others. And this is where a program of empathetic literacy can gain power. By empathetic literacy, I mean knowledge and information-based skills that help global citizens respond to and manage intercultural encounters caringly and competently. It focuses on skills that students and other citizens need to develop empathy, factors that influence empathetic competence, and approaches to improving empathetic effectiveness. Empathetic citizens should have the ability to understand, analyze, interpret, and communicate ideas, feelings, and behavior across a range of intercultural settings.

Although principles of empathetic literacy might vary cognitively, geographically, and educationally, I offer the following set of conceptual principles.

Global Respect

Global respect suggests that we must try our best to "acknowledge in a practical way, the dignity of humanity in every other man (or woman)" (see Kant, 1991). We should be inclined to show this respect both verbally and nonverbally. In communicating with a person from another culture, we should actively search for ways to elevate humanity and not denigrate it. A respectful person will consider how information and communication will affect the other.

Mutuality

Mutuality is the notion of trying to find common understanding within an intercultural encounter. We should expect that the shared experience with other people is guided by neither our cultural background nor theirs. In communicating with a person from another culture, we should actively search for some mutual ground that allows for an authentic exchange of ideas and feelings. We must be willing to entertain ideas and beliefs that might not be consistent with our own notion of things.

Trust

Trust is the glue that holds societies together. Leading scholar Fukuyama (1995) maintains that the drive for social capital is deep and meaningful. And he argues that the economic well-being of a nation is "conditioned by a single, pervasive cultural characteristic: the level of trust inherent in the society" (p. 7). Clearly, trust undergirds most aspects of society, including ethical habits, common purposes, norms, and values. Most crucially, the communitarian principle of trust tells another human being how much faith one has in his or her ideas and values and whether the person should be taken seriously. As I pointed out earlier, "doing things" for poor people and poor countries and telling them how to order their lives often stem from a lack of trust. One can, in some instances, judge the amount of trust that human beings have by the presence or absence of a huge police force in neighborhoods and by the number of human beings who are imprisoned. What is happening in your neighborhood or town? It is hard to build *trust-establishing* relationships when comments such as, "You can't trust Whites," "Beware of Jews," or "Italians are excitable" are part of our linguistic repertoire. Trust-establishing relationships move us toward empathetic attitudes and behaviors; *non-trust-establishing* relationships move us away from empathetic attitudes and behavior.

Knowledge Base

Because ideas, products, and their accompanying messages are extending beyond specific borders, we can expect these changes to challenge deeply held values and beliefs worldwide. Knowing this, we should adjust our empathetic communication practices and attitudes to reflect an ongoing, dynamic flow of ideas and meanings across borders. The saying, "no man is an island entire of himself" or herself, clearly resonates here. What are some things that a truly empathetic global citizen should do? First, one should be curious about the cultural other. Second, one should read both vertically and horizontally about other cultures, including materials about family practices, values, language, economics, sociocultural factors, religion, and geopolitical issues. Third, one should understand the role of media in promoting stereotypes and prejudices about other people and cultures. Prejudiced and stereotypical attitudes "sabotage trust" (Carr-Ruffino, 1996, p. 305).

So far, I have outlined principles that should encourage fidelity to empathetic communication practices. Next, I discuss some concrete practical things that we can do to become effective empathetic intercultural communicators. These are general rules and will, of course, vary from situation to situation and from person to person. Also, remember that sometimes it is most difficult to communicate with some individuals, despite our good and noble intentions. This can lead to a special kind of anguish when communicating empathetically.

Ten Basic Rules of Intercultural Relations

To improve relations with others, observe the following rules:

1. *Develop empathy.* Try to infer the feelings and actions of others.

2. *Give people the benefit of the perceptual doubt.* Assume goodwill. This rule assumes that most individuals seek psychological comfort and congeniality.

3. *In potentially confrontational or hostile encounters,* treat the question or comment from another "as if" the person is seeking information or knowledge.

In 2006, one of my colleagues and I traveled to Riga, Latvia, and Vilnius, Lithuania, to participate in a conference on democracy and civic engagement and to give lectures, respectively. In beautiful Riga, while my colleague and I were shopping for trinkets for family members, we were greeted by two young, enthusiastic Latvian high school women, who, judging from their youth, clearly should have been in school and not on the streets of gorgeous Riga—however engaging and fetching.

As my colleague and I approached the young women, we greeted them, only to be met with the following question: "Why your skin black?" In a nanosecond, I replied, "Our skin is black because we have more melanin in our skin than you have." And then I said, "But if you stay out in the sun long enough, you might get as dark as we are." My friend and I finished our obligatory-familial shopping, and upon leaving the product-laden vendor stalls, we encountered the same young women en route back to our hotel. The young woman who had put a question to us that might have been viewed by some as hostile, mean-spirited, and confrontational said, "Hello, we are out in the sun trying to get dark like you."

By employing a pleasing tone and a warm, cooperative verbal message, the young woman who had uttered the interrogative previously signified that she had asked the question earnestly and with no malice in her heart.

The story also has embedded within it an equally interesting and instructive point about "othering" behavior, however. The young woman's question was not why her skin was different but rather why was my skin different. The analysis suggests that she saw my colleague and myself as being different from a phenotypical standard! Despite this back story analysis, the point is that marvelous things can happen when we handle as many questions as possible in a "this (whatever *this* or *that* is) in a search for information" manner. Can you recount similar stories that hugely altered your human consciousness? Who sets a powerful example in your neighborhood?

4. *Learn how to distinguish between* things that happen to you *because* you are White, Latino, Chinese, male, or female and things that happen to you *in spite* of your sex or ethnicity.

As you consider your thoughts, actions, and feelings and how they relate to the thoughts, actions, and feelings of others, you can improve your overall empathetic competence by making distinctions between *because of* and *in spite of* thinking. *Because of* thinking is the assumption that A (one's race, sex, ethnicity, age, etc.) is responsible for B (whatever is happening as result of human interaction). For example, saying things like, "Amelie neglected to acknowledge

Semaj's presence because he is Japanese American," or "Chinese don't like Trae, A'Morion, and Tynasia because of their acquired Spanish accent."

There is a mathematical and social equation inherent in "because of" thinking because it assumes there is a one-to-one, direct causal relationship between A and B. "In spite of" thinking is accountability reasoning. It assumes that A (whatever is happening) might or might not cause B. It is symmetrical thinking because it promotes congenial relationships.

5. *When watching television*, viewing a film, or reading a book about other cultures, ask what information (ideas, concepts, etc.) is present and what is absent. This helps to focus attention on the nature and work of media, which is their capacity to leave out specifics, examples, stories, statistics, and the like that can give one a simplistic understanding of human behavior. Such omissions can influence how we see the other. In a previous chapter, I discussed my first trip to South Africa in 1999. And I noted that before I arrived there, television had given a distorted view of the place, emphasizing such things as poverty, disease, and denial of civil and human rights instead of offering more complexity. I also learned that media had omitted the fact that there were also rich Blacks in South Africa at the time. Daily, we are bombarded by heavily skewed views of cultures and people because of media presentations of the other.

6. *Be mindful that human beings are complex and various.* Our complexities are marked by several things, including gender, ethnicity, age, religion, regional factors, and organizational affiliations. To say that one is "Russian," "Middle Eastern," "Italian," or "Nigerian" is also to conceal whether one is a father or a mother or whether one enjoys perennial gardening, painting, traveling, dancing, listening to B. B. King, Buddy Guy, Mozart, or a range of other things that ethnicity would not automatically bestow. As Alba (1990) notes, "Individuals may be ethnic in their 'identities' and still consciously reject their ethnic backgrounds" (p. 22).

This sixth principle should also help overcome stereotyping, which can disturb empathy in powerful ways (Chen & Starosta, 1998; Jandt, 2004; Martin & Nakayama, 1997; Samavor & Porter, 2003).

7. *Imagine that the stranger is a friend!*

One of the ways that we can end nastiness and awful forms of human injustice in the world is to imagine strangers as friends. Our "moral neighbors" can be people who are close to us spatially as well as those who are removed from us in time and space. As Duncan (1985) notes, structures of relationships determine how we address each other; that is, "what kind of speech we make" to others has not only psychological implications but also implications for whether we treat a person as a friend or an enemy. Translation: We rarely, if ever, use such metaphors as "snake in the grass," "rat," "vermin," "cockroach," or "bacilli" to refer to family and friends. There is a keen relationship between thought and action.

As war and tribal violence in former Yugoslavia republics, Kenya, Sudan, East Timor, Iraq, Congo, Liberia, Lebanon, Rwanda, Middle East, Mozambique, and other places reveal, it is easy to kill, maim, hate, and even destroy others once we put them in the enemy category. "If I love another," said Isabel in Alexander McCall Smith's (2004) enticing novel, *The Sunday Philosophy Club*, "then I know what it is to be that other person. If I feel pity—which is an important emotion, isn't it?—then this helps me to understand the sufferings of others. . . . We develop a moral imagination" (p. 46).

8. *Use empathetic language.* Learn how to respond positively to conditions, people, and situations as they arise. This helps to create "a world of broader possibilities." The language of empathy includes such phrases as "I understand," "I see," and head nodding in agreement, appropriately, of course.

9. *Repeat the following mantra as often as necessary: "I have a moral obligation to others."* A similar rule guided young Clarkson as he caught sight of Wades Mill in Hertfordshire in 1785, following his realization of the awesome implications of the Latin/Greek essay that he had written on the subject, "Is it lawful to make slaves of others against their will?" (Hochschild, 2005, pp. 87–88). Recall from Chapter 1 that Clarkson's moral commitment was instrumental in helping abolish slavery in the British colonies and elsewhere. He and other abolitionists succeeded because they had a moral obligation to uphold the dignity of other human beings. En route from Cambridge after winning the prize, Clarkson turned the plight of the slave over and over in his head; this was tantamount to what I mean by a repetitive mantra. "If the contents of the Essay (stories about the evils of slavery) were true," said Clarkson, "it was time some person should see these calamities to their end" (Hochschild, 2005, p. 89). *Someone should see these calamities to their end,* Clark repeated, until he had translated his words into an awesome reality.

10. *Share empathy:* Pass it on.

Every time we have a moment to uplift humanity, we should do so, passing along stories that ignite and have an extraordinary impact on other people in edifying ways.

Epilogue: Where Do We Go From Here?

For empathy to become realized in more exquisite ways, we must not only know about the awful conditions of others, acknowledge that there is suffering in the world, explain huge gaps between the rich and the poor, have a deep insight into international economics, know that AIDS is destroying families in Africa, and be aware of the magnitude of horror in Darfur in Sudan, but we must also hate injustice and do something marvelous about it. Empathy must be transformed into everyday linguistic and behavioral practice. This is where we go from here. It is the way of empathy in the global age!

References

Preface

Obama, Elie Wiesel Buchenwald speech (text, video). (2009, June 5). *Huffington Post.* Retrieved June 10, 2009, from http://www.huffingtonpost.com/2009/06/obama-buchenwald-speech-t_n_211898.html

Washington, J. M. (Ed.). (1991). *A testament of hope: The essential writings and speeches of Martin Luther King, Jr.* New York: HarperSanFrancisco.

Chapter 1: A Global Imperative: The Unveiling of Empathy

Berlin, I. (1991). *The crooked timber of humanity: Chapters in the history of ideas.* New York: Knopf.

Berman, S. H. (1998, May). The bridge to civility: Empathy, ethics and service. *School Administrator Web Edition,* pp. 1–8.

Bhagwati, J. (2004). *In defense of globalization.* New York: Oxford University Press.

Blake, C. (1979). Communication research and African national development. *Journal of Black Studies, 10,* 225.

Carreyrou, J. (2005, November 11). Muslin groups may gain strength from French unrest. *The Wall Street Journal,* p. 1.

Depraz, N. (2001). The Husserlian theory of intersubjectivity as alterology: Emergent theories and wisdom traditions in the light of genetic phenomenology. *Journal of Consciousness Studies, 8*(5–6), 169–178.

Dictionary of the history of ideas. (2003). Retrieved May 10, 2006, from http://etext.virginia.edu/cgi-local/DHI/dhi.cgi?id=dv2-09

Eisenberg, N., & Strayer, J. (1990). *Empathy and its development.* New York: Cambridge University Press.

Fagan, B. (1984). *A clash of cultures.* New York: W. H. Freeman.

Fattah, H. M. (2006, February 9). At Mecca meeting, cartoon outrage crystallizes. *The New York Times,* p. 1.

Fisher, J. (2004, October 15). Italian woman's veil stirs more than fashion feud. *The New York Times,* p. A3.

Fontaine, P. (2001). The changing place of empathy in welfare economics. *History of Political Economy, 33,* 387–409. Retrieved May 25, 2005, from http://muse.jhu.edu/journals/history_of_political_economy/v033/33.3fontaine.html

Friedman, T. L. (2005). *The world is flat: A brief history of the twenty-first century.* New York: Farrar, Straus & Giroux.

Fukuyama, F. (1995). *Trust: The social virtues and the creation of prosperity.* New York: Simon & Schuster.

Gilroy, P. (2000). *Against race: Imagining political culture beyond the color line.* Cambridge, MA: The Belknap Press of Harvard University Press.

Glover, J. (2000). *Humanity: A moral history of the twentieth century.* New Haven, CT: Yale University Press.

Gourevitch, P. (1998). *We wish to inform you that tomorrow we will be killed with our families: Stories from Rwanda.* New York: Farrar, Straus & Giroux.

Hochschild, A. (2005). *Bury the chains: Prophets and rebels in the fight to free an empire's slaves.* Boston: Houghton Mifflin.

Holzwarth, J. (2004). *Liberty's horizons: Politics and the value of cultural attachment.* Unpublished doctoral dissertation, Department of Politics, Princeton University.

Johnson, C. (2004). *The sorrows of empire: Militarism, secrecy, and the end of the republic.* New York: Holt.

Kant, I. (1991). *The metaphysics of morals* (M. Gregory, Trans.). New York: Cambridge University Press.

Karmi, G. (2002). *In search of Fatima: A Palestinian story.* London: Verso.

Kitwood, T. (1990). *Concern for others.* London: Routledge.

Kohut, H. (1997). *The restoration of the self.* New York: International Universities Press.

Ridley, C. R., & Lingle, D. W. (1996). Cultural empathy in multicultural counseling: A multidimensional process model. In P. Pedersen, J. Drugans, W. Lonner, & J. Trimble (Eds.), *Counseling across cultures* (4th ed., pp. 21–46). Thousand Oaks, CA: Sage.

Rogers, C. R. (1951). *Client-centered therapy: Its current practice, implications, and theory.* Boston: Houghton Mifflin.

Rogers, C. R. (1975). Empathic: An unappreciated way of being. *The Counseling Psychologist, 5,* 2–10.

Rose, F. (2006, February 19). Why I published those cartoons. Retrieved January 1, 2007, from http://www.washingtonpost.com/wp-dyn/content/article/2006/02/17/AR2006/02/17/AR2006021702499.html

Singer, M. (1987). *Intercultural communication: A perceptual approach.* Englewood Cliffs, NJ: Prentice Hall.

Smith, A. M. (2004). *The Sunday philosophy club.* New York: Pantheon.

Stein, E. (1964). *On the problems of empathy.* The Hague, the Netherlands: Nijhoff.

Sullivan, H. S. (1945). *The interpersonal theory of psychiatry.* New York: W. W. Norton.

Thompson, E. (2001). Empathy and consciousness. *Journal of Consciousness Studies, 8*(5–7), 1–32.

Tichener, E. B. (1909). *A textbook of psychology.* Delmar, NY: Scholars' Facsimiles & Reprints.

Tuan, Y.-F. (1977). *Space and place: The perspective of experience.* Minneapolis: University of Minnesota Press.

Vetlesen, A. J. (1994). *Perception, empathy, and judgment: An inquiry into the preconditions of moral performance.* University Park: Pennsylvania State University Press.

Vico, G. (1968). *The new science of Giambattista Vico* (T. G. Bergin & M. H. Fisch, Trans.). New York: Cornell University Press.

Vischer, R. (1994). *Empathy, form and space: Progress in German aesthetics, 1873–1893.* Santa Monica, CA: Getty Center for History, Arts & Humanities, University of Chicago Press.

Wilson, E. O. (1998). *Consilence: The unity of knowledge.* New York: Knopf.

Wilson, J. Q. (1993). *The moral sense.* New York: Free Press.

Chapter 2: The Creation of Empathy: From Ancients to Moderns

Armstrong, K. (2001). *Buddha.* New York: Penguin.

Berlin, I. (1991). *The crooked timber of humanity: Chapters in the history of ideas.* New York: Knopf.

Bernal, M. (1987). *The Afroasiatic roots of classical civilization: Vol. 1. The fabrication of ancient Greece, 1785–1985.* New Brunswick, NJ: Rutgers University Press.

Bethell, T. (1998). *The noblest triumph: Property and prosperity through the ages.* New York: St. Martin's Griffin.

Bloom, A. (1987). *The closing of the American mind.* New York: Simon & Schuster.

Burke, J., & Ornstein, R. (1995). *The axemaker's gift: A double-edged history of human culture.* New York: Putnam.

Cicero. (2000). *On obligations (de officiis)* (P. G. Walsh, Trans.). New York: Oxford University Press.

Crossen, C. (2000). *The rich and how they got that way.* New York: Crown Business.

Diamond, J. (2005). *Collapse: How societies choose to fail or succeed.* New York: Viking.

Fukuyama, F. (1995). *Trust: The social virtues and the creation of prosperity.* New York: Simon & Schuster.

Gottlieb, A. (2000). *The dream of reason: A history of Western philosophy from the Greeks to the renaissance.* New York: W. W. Norton.

Hanson, V. D. (2001). *Carnage and culture: Landmark battles in the rise of Western power.* New York: Doubleday.

Herodotus. (1921). *The histories* (A. D. Godley, Trans., 4 vols.). London: William Heinemann.

Herodotus on ancient Egypt. (2002, December 11). Retrieved June 23, 2009, from http://everything2.com/index.pl?node_id=1400312

Hochschild, A. (2005). *Bury the chains: Prophets and rebels in the fight to free an empire's slaves.* Boston: Houghton Mifflin.

Kant, I. (1991). *The metaphysics of morals* (M. Gregory, Trans.). New York: Cambridge University Press.

Mill, J. S. (1884). *Principles of political economy.* New York: D. Appleton.

Mill, J. S. (1806–1873). (2009). University of Adelaide. Retrieved June 23, 2009, from http://ebooks.adelaide.edu.au/m/mill/john_stuart/

Murray, C. (2003). *Human accomplishment: The pursuit of excellence in the arts and sciences, 800 B.C. to 1950.* New York: HarperCollins.

Murray, O. (1972). Herodotus and Hellenistic culture. *The Classical Quarterly, 22,* 200–213.

Nussbaum, M. C. (1994). *The therapy of desire: Theory and practice in Hellenistic ethics.* Princeton, NJ: Princeton University Press.

Nussbaum, M. C. (1997). *Cultivating humanity: A classical defense of reform in liberal education.* Cambridge, MA: Harvard University Press.

Patterson, W. R. (2005). The greatest good for the most fit? John Stuart Mill, Thomas Henry Huxley, and social Darwinism. *Journal of Social Philosophy, 36,* 72–84.

Redfield, J. (1985). Herodotus the tourist. *Classical Philology, 80, 97–118.*

Rollo, W. M. (1937). Nationalism and internationalism in the ancient world. *Greece & Rome, 6,* 130–143. Retrieved June 6, 2006, from http://www.jstor.org/

Seneca. (1995). *Moral and political essays* (J. M. Cooper, Trans.). Cambridge, MA: Cambridge University Press.

Smith, A. (1776). *The wealth of nations.* London: Methuen.

Smith, A. (1790). *Theory of moral sentiments.* Retrieved April 13, 2007, from http://www.econolib.org/Libray/Smith/smMS1.html

Smith, H. (1958). *The world's religions.* New York: HarperCollins.

Van Doren, C. (1991). *A history of knowledge: Past, present, and future, the pivotal events, people, and achievements of world history.* New York: Ballantine.

Walsh, P. C. (2000) *Cicero on obligations (De Officiis).* New York: Oxford University Press.

Watson, P. (2005). *Ideas: A history of thought and invention, from fire to Freud.* New York: Harper Perennial.

Wells, J. (1907). The Persian friends of Herodotus. *Journal of Hellenic Studies, 27,* 37–47. Retrieved June 1, 2006, from http://www.jstor.org/

Wilson, J. Q. (1993). *The moral sense.* New York: Free Press.

Wolcott, E. O. (1995). *The art of fieldwork.* London: Altamira.

Wrong, M. (2005). *I didn't do it for you: How the world betrayed a small African nation.* New York: HarperCollins.

Chapter 3: Geopolitics: The Spoils of Empathy

Allen, D. S. (2004). *Talking to strangers: Anxieties of citizenship since* Brown v. Board of Education. Chicago: University of Chicago Press.

Ansari, M. (2004, May 9). Daniel Pearl 'refused to be sedated before his throat was cut.' *Telegraph.* Retrieved June 23, 2009, from http://www.telegraph.co.uk/news/

worldnews/asia/pakistan/1461368/Daniel-Pearl-refused-to-be-sedated-before-his-throat-was-cut.html

Anti-Defamation League. (2009). *Terrorism.* Retrieved June 16, 2009, from http://www.adl.org/terrorism/symbols/al_qaeda_iraq.asp

Berman, M. (2006). *Dark ages America: The final phase of empire.* New York: W. W. Norton.

Calloway-Thomas, C., Cooper, P., & Blake, C. (1999). *Intercultural communication: Roots & routes.* Needham Height, MA: Allyn & Bacon.

Chandrasekaran, R. (2006). *Imperial life in the emerald city: Inside Iraq's green zone.* New York: Knopf.

Daalder, I. H., & Lindsay, J. M. (2003). *America unbound: The Bush revolution in foreign policy.* Washington, DC: Brookings Institution Press.

Diamond, J. (2004). What went wrong in Iraq? *Foreign Affairs, 83*(5), 34–56.

Eagleton, T. (2003). *After theory.* New York: Basic Books.

Faux, J. (2006). *The global class war: How America's bipartisan elite lost our future and what it will take to win it back.* New York: John Wiley.

Friedman, T. L. (1989). *From Beirut to Jerusalem.* New York: Farrar, Straus & Giroux.

Gilroy, P. (2000). *Against race: Imagining political culture beyond the color line.* Cambridge, MA: The Belknap Press of Harvard University.

Glover, J. (2000). *Humanity: A moral history of the twentieth century.* New Haven, CT: Yale University Press.

Hezbollah. (n.d.). Retrieved June 16, 2009, from http://en.wikipedia.org/wiki/Hezbollah

Hourani, A. (1991). *A history of the Arab peoples.* Cambridge, MA: The Belknap Press of Harvard University.

Human Rights Watch. (2006, July 24). Israeli cluster munitions hit civilians in Lebanon. *ReliefWeb.* Retrieved June 23, 2009, from http://www.reliefweb.int/rw/RWB.NSF/db900SID/EKOI-6S2458?OpenDocument

International reaction to the September 11, 2001, attacks in New York City and the Pentagon in Washington. (2001). Retrieved June 23, 2009, from http://www.september11news.com/InternationalReaction.htm

Janis, I. (1972). *Victims of group think.* Boston: Houghton Mifflin.

Johnson, C. (2004). *The sorrows of empire: Militarism, secrecy, and the end of the republic.* New York: Holt.

Joint resolution to authorize the use of United States armed forces against Iraq. (2002). Retrieved October 30, 2007, from http://www.iraqwatch.org/government/US/WH wh-house-jointresolution-100202.htm

Klein, N. (2007). *The shock doctrine: The rise of disaster capitalism.* New York: Holt.

Knowlton, B. (2009, May 30). Image of U.S. falls again—Americas—International Herald Tribune. *The New York Times.*

Lewis, B. (2004). *From babel to dragomans: Interpreting the Middle East.* New York: Oxford University Press.

The lost year in Iraq: Interviews. (2007, June 13). *Frontline* [Television broadcast]. New York and Washington, DC: Public Broadcasting Service. Retrieved from http://www.pbs.org/wgbh/pages/frontline/yeariniraq/interviews.html

Makiya, K. (1998). *Republic of fear*. Berkeley: University of California Press.

Marquand, R. (2001, September 17). Global empathy: Will it last? From Paris to Pakistan, a new perspective on the lone superpower. *Christian Science Monitor.* Retrieved June 23, 2009, from http://www.csmonitor.com/2001/0917/p4s1-wogi.html

Mylroie, L. (1998, November 1). Clinton signs Iraq Liberation Act. *Iraq News.*

Packer, G. (2005). *The assassins' gate: America in Iraq.* New York: Farrar, Straus & Giroux.

President delivers "State of the Union." (2003). Retrieved April 26, 2007, from http://www.whitehouse.gov/news/releases/2003/01/20030128–19html

Public diplomacy by the numbers. (n.d.). Retrieved September 15, 2007, from http://www.publicdiplomacy.org/14.htm

Ricks, T. E. (2006). *Fiasco: The American military adventure in Iraq.* New York: Penguin.

Selznick, P. (1992). *The moral commonwealth: Social theory and the promise of community.* Berkeley: University of California Press.

Think progress: A timeline of the Iraq war. (n.d.). Retrieved September 9, 2007, from http://Thinkprogress.org/iraq-timeline

Tuan, Y.-F. (1977). *Space and place: The perspective of experience.* Minneapolis: University of Minnesota Press.

Tyler, P. E. (1992, March 8). U.S. strategy plan calls for insuring no rivals develop. *The New York Times.* Retrieved June 23, 2009, from http://www.nytimes.com/1992/03/08/world/us-strategy-plan-calls-for-insuring-no-rivals-develop.html

U.S. Secretary of State Colin Powell addresses the U.N. Security Council. (2003). Retrieved April 26, 2007, from http://www.whitehouse.gov/news/releases/2003/02/20030205-1.html

Wilson, J. Q. (1993). *The moral sense.* New York: Free Press.

Chapter 4: Immigration: Empathy's Flickering Flames?

Ali, A. H. (2007). *Infidel.* New York: Free Press.

Bercovitch, S. (1978). *The American jeremiad.* Madison: University of Wisconsin Press.

Berlinski, C. (2006). *Menace in Europe: Why the continent's crisis is America's, too.* New York: Crown Forum.

Bissett, J. (2007, October 29). Kosovo and the Westphalian order. *Chronicles: A Magazine of American Culture.* Retrieved December 13, 2007, from http://www.chroniclesmagazine.org/?p=375

Bloom, A. (1987). *The closing of the American mind.* New York: Simon & Schuster.

Boyer, P. S., Clark, C. E., Kett, J. F., Salisbury, N., Sitkoff, H., & Woloch, N. (1996). *The enduring vision: A history of the American people* (3rd ed.). Lexington, MA: D. C. Heath.

Brooks, D. (2006, February 9). Drafting Hitler. *The New York Times,* p. A27.

Burke, J., & Ornstein, R. (1995). *The axemaker's gift: A double-edged history of human culture.* New York: Putnam.

Buchanan, P. (2006). *State of emergency: The Third World invasion and conquest of America*. New York: St. Martin's.

Buchanan, P. J. (2007). *Day of reckoning: How hubris, ideology, and greed are tearing America apart*. New York: St. Martin's.

de Beer, P. (2005). *The message in France's explosion: Open democracy*. Retrieved January 13, 2007, from http://www.opendemocracy.net/globalization_intitutiions_government/banlieues_3021

de Blij, H. (2005). *Why geography matters: Three challenges facing America: Climate change, the rise of China, and global terrorism*. New York: Oxford University Press.

Demographic tear. (2007, October 27). *The Economist*, p. 66.

Eagleton, T. (2003). *After theory*. New York: Basic Books.

Farr, J. (2005). Point: The Westphalian legacy and the modern nation state. *International Social Sciences Review, 80*, 1–6.

Fattah, H. M. (2006, February 9). At Mecca meeting, cartoon outrage crystallized. *The New York Times*, pp. 1, A13.

French sissies. (2005, November 11). *The Wall Street Journal*, p. A10.

Friedman, T. L. (1999). *The Lexus and the olive tree*. New York: Farrar, Straus & Giroux.

Fukuyama, F. (1995). *Trust: The social virtues and the creation of prosperity*. New York: Free Press.

Gannon, M. J. (2003). India: The dance of Shiva. In L. A. Samovar & R. Porter (Eds.), *Intercultural communication: A reader* (pp. 65–77). Belmont, CA: Thomson/Wadsworth.

Granitsas, A. (2006, November 11). Europe's next immigration crisis. *YaleGlobal Online*. Retrieved October 30, 2007, from http://yaleglobal.yale.edu/display.article?id=7243

Hargreaves, A. G. (2007). *An emperor with no clothes*. Retrieved January 13, 2007, from http://riotsfrance.ssrc.org/Hargreaves/printable.html

Higgins, A. (2004, November 11). A brutal killing opens Dutch eyes to threat of terror. *The New York Times*, pp. A1, A11.

Horne, A. (2005). *La Belle France: A short history*. New York: Knopf.

Huntington, S. P. (2004). *Who are we?* New York: Simon & Schuster.

Italy: Behind the crackdown on the Roma. (2007, November 30). *The Week*, p. 15.

Judt, T. (2005). *Postwar: A history of Europe since 1945*. New York: Penguin.

Kimball, R. (1990). *Tenured radicals: How politics has corrupted our higher education*. New York: Harper & Row.

Lewis, B. (2002). *What went wrong? Western impact and Middle Eastern response*. New York: Oxford University Press.

Locke, J. (1689). *Essay concerning human understanding* (collated by A. C. Fraser). Oxford, England: Clarendon.

Murray, C. (2003). *Human accomplishment: The pursuit of excellence in the arts and sciences, 800 B.C. to 1950*. New York: Perennial.

Preece, J. J. (1997). Minority rights in Europe: From Westphalia to Helsinki. *Review of International Studies, 23*, 75–92.

Pullella, P. (2007). Italy politicians urge Nazi policies for immigrants. http://ww.reuters.com/article/worldnews/id/us10563062920071205?feel tyol+RSS&fe

Rifkin, J. (2004). *The European dream: How Europe's vision of the future is quietly eclipsing the American dream.* New York: Penguin.

Salins, P. D. (1997). *Assimilation, American style.* New York: Basic Books.

Sciolino, E. (2007, November 28). In French suburbs, some rage, but new tactics. *The New York Times,* p. 1.

Starr, P. (2004). *The creation of the media: Political origins of modern communications.* New York: Basic Books.

Steele, S. (2003, November). Yo, Howard! Why did Dean have to embrace the confederate flag? *The Wall Street Journal.* http:www.opinionjournal.com

Steyn, M. (2006). *America alone: The end of the world as we know it.* New York: Regnery.

Taheri, A. (2006, February 8). Bonfires of the vanities. *The Wall Street Journal,* p. A16.

Takaki, R. (1990). *Iron cages: Race and culture in 19th century America.* New York: Oxford University Press.

Taylor, C. (1992). *Multiculturalism and "the politics of recognition": An essay.* Princeton, NJ: Princeton University Press.

Wilson, J. Q. (1993). *The moral sense.* New York: Free Press.

Chapter 5: Crafting Images: Media and Empathy

Allen, D. S. (2004). *Talking to strangers: Anxieties of citizenship since* Brown v. Board of Education. Chicago: University of Chicago Press.

Al-Marashi, I. (2004). Iraq's hostage crisis: Kidnappings, mass media and the Iraq insurgency. *Middle East Review of International Affairs, 8*(4), 1–11.

Appiah, K. A. (2008). *Experiments in ethics.* Cambridge, MA: Harvard University Press.

Barlow, M. H. (1998). Race and the problem of crime in *Time* and *Newsweek* cover stories, 1946–1995. *Social Justice, 25,* 149–183.

Bhagwati, J. (2004). *In defense of globalization.* New York: Oxford University Press.

Brown, C., & Waltzer, H. (2004). Organized interest advertorials: Responding to the 9/11 terrorist attack and other national traumas [Electronic version]. *Harvard University Journal of Press/Politic, 9,* 25–45.

Buying the war. (2007, April 25). *Bill Moyers Journal.* http://www.pbs.org/moyers/journal/btw/transcript1.html

Calloway-Thomas, C. (2007, spring). Barbed wire enclosed spaces and places: Elites, ethnic tensions and public policy. *Forum on Public Policy Online: A Journal of the Oxford Round Table,* pp. 1–19.

Chiricos, T., & Eschholz, S. (2002). The racial and ethnic typification of crime and the criminal typfication of race and ethnicity in local television news [Electronic version]. *Journal of Research in Crime and Delinquency, 39,* 400–420.

Chomsky, N. (2003). *Media control: The spectacular achievements of propaganda.* New York: Seven Stories Press.

Clawson, R. A., & Trice, R. (2000). Poverty as we know it: Media portrayals of the poor. *Public Opinion Quarterly, 64,* 53–64.

Fenton, F. (2005). *Bad news: The decline of reporting, the business of news, and the danger to us all.* New York: ReganBooks.

Gerbner, G. (1997). *Television demography: What's wrong with this picture?* Unpublished manuscript.

Glover, G. (2001). *Humanity: A moral history of the twentieth century.* New Haven, CT: Yale University Press.

Gourevitch, P. (1998). *We wish to inform you that tomorrow we will be killed with our families: Stories from Rwanda.* New York: Farrar, Straus & Giroux.

Hannerz, U. (1992). *Cultural complexity.* New York: Columbia University Press.

Hanson, V. (2001). *Carnage and culture: Landmark battles in the rise of Western power.* New York: Doubleday.

Herman, E. S., & Chomsky, N. (1988). *The propaganda model: A retrospective.* New York: Pantheon.

Holtzman, L. (2000). *Media messages: What film, television, and popular music teach us about race, class, gender and sexual orientation.* New York: M. E. Sharpe.

Iraq dominates PEJ's first quarterly NCI report. (2007, May 25). Journalism.org. http://www.journalism.org/node/5712

Kaiser daily HIV/AIDS report. (2006, January 27). Retrieved June 23, 2009, from http://www.kaisernetwork.org/daily_reports/rep_index.cfm?DR_ID=35025

Kaplan, R. D. (2002). *Warrior politics: Why leadership demands a pagan ethos.* New York: Random House.

Kirkpatric, D. D. (2003, April 7). Mr. Murdock's war: Global news empire marches to chairman's political drum. *The New York Times,* p. C1.

Koselleck, R. (2004). *Future past on the semantics of historical time.* New York: Columbia University Press.

Kurtz, H. (2003, April 28). For media after Iraq, a case of shell shock. *The Washington Post,* p. A01.

Lakoff, G. (2008). *The political mind: Why you can't understand 21st-century American politics with an 18th-century brain.* New York: Viking.

Lukaszewski, J. E. (1987, March 19). *The media and the terrorist: A dance of death.* Paper presented at Joint Meeting of the Airport Operators Council of America and the American Transport Association, Clearwater Beach, FL.

Lull, J. (2000). *Media, communication, culture.* New York: Columbia University Press.

Lynch, M. (2006, March 1). Al-Qaeda's media strategies. *The National Interest.* http://www.nationalinterest.org/PrinterFriendly.aspx?id=11524

Mitchell, J. (2007). Rwandan genocide: Reconsidering the role of local and global media [Electronic version]. *Global Media Journal, 6*(11), 1–30.

Park, J., & Wilkins, J. (2005, spring). Re-orienting the Orientalist gaze. *Global Media Journal, 4*(6). Retrieved on December 28, 2007, from http://lass.calumet.purdue.edu/cca/gmj_sp05-park-wilkins.htm

Pérez-Peña, R. (2007, November 28). Grim view of Iraq dangers in survey of journalists. *The New York Times.*

Roberts, D. (1993). Crime, race and reproduction. *Tulane Law Review, 67*, 1945–1977.

Robinson, R. (2007). *An unbroken agony: Haiti, from revolution to the kidnapping of a president.* New York: Basic Books.

Sachs, J. D. (2005). *The end of poverty: Economic possibilities for our time.* New York: Penguin.

Schama, S. (2006). *Rough crossings: Britain, the slaves and the American Revolution.* New York: HarperCollins.

Starr, P. (2004). *The creation of the media: Political origins of modern communications.* New York: Basic Books.

Taylor, C. (1992). *Multiculturalism and "the politics of recognition": An essay.* Princeton, NJ: Princeton University Press.

Welch, K. (2007). Black criminal stereotypes and racial profiling [Electronic version]. *Journal of Contemporary Criminal Justice, 23*, 276–287.

Wilson, J. Q. (1993). *The moral sense.* New York: Free Press.

Chapter 6: Catastrophes, Tsunamis, and Katrinas

Aronowitz, S. (2003). *How class works.* New Haven, CT: Yale University Press.

Barry, D. (2006a, June 9). In the bayou, 100-ton symbols of a recovery still suspended. *The New York Times,* p. 1.

Barry, D. (2006b, August 27). A city's future, and a dead man's lost past. *The New York Times,* p. 1.

Bourdieu, P. (1999). *Language and symbolic power.* Cambridge, MA: Harvard University Press.

Burkhalter, H. (2004). The politics of AIDS. Engaging conservative activists. *Foreign Affairs, 83*(1), 8–14.

Chang, H.-J. (2008). *The myth of free trade and the secret history of capitalism.* New York: Bloomsbury.

de Blij, H. (2005). *Why geography matters: Three challenges facing America: Climate change, the rise of China, and global terrorism.* New York: Oxford University Press.

Eagleton, T. (2003). *After theory.* New York: Basic Books.

Egeland, J. (2005, January 1). Press briefing on tsunami disaster on Monday 3, January. United Nations. Retrieved April 4, 2005, from http://www.un.org/News/briefings/docs/2004/egelandbrf050103.doc.htm

Ellis, S. (2005). How to rebuild Africa. *Foreign Affairs, 84*(5), 135–148.

Foner, P., & Branham, R. J. (Eds.). (1998). *Lift every voice: African American oratory 1787–1900.* Tuscaloosa: University of Alabama Press.

Fukuyama, F. (1995). *Trust: The social virtues and the creation of prosperity.* New York: Free Press.

Gannon, M. J. (2003). India: The dance of Shiva. In L. A. Samovar & R. Porter (Eds.), *Intercultural communication: A reader.* Belmont, CA: Thomson/Wadsworth.

Garrett, L. (2000). *Betrayal of trust: The collapse of global public health.* New York: Hyperion.

Gilroy, P. (2002). *Against race: Imagining political culture beyond the color line.* Cambridge, MA: The Belknap Press at Harvard University.

Hall, E. T. (1959). *The silent language.* New York: Doubleday.

Hall, E. T. (1976). *Beyond culture.* Garden City, NY: Anchor.

Herbert, B. (2006, December 25). The ninth ward revisited. *The New York Times,* p. A23.

Hume, D. (1751). *An enquiry concerning the principles of morals.* London: Printed for A. Millar.

Johnson, P. (1997). *A history of the American people.* New York: HarperPerennial.

Kidder, T. (2003). *Mountains beyond mountains: The quest of Dr Paul Farmer, a man who would cure the world.* New York: Random House Trade Paperbacks.

Krugman, P. (2006, December 22). Helping the poor, the British way. *The New York Times.*

Leonhardt, (2008, March 9). What makes people give? *The New York Times Magazine,* pp. 44–49.

Lull, J. (2000). *Media, communication, culture.* New York: Columbia University Press.

Maren, M. (1997). *The road to hell: The ravaging effects of foreign aid and international charity.* New York: Free Press.

Mehta, S. (2004, December 28). Now we hate seeing this sea. *The Wall Street Journal,* p. A10.

Morley, J. (2005, January 18). Tsunami wipes Darfur off priority list. *The Washington Post.* Retrieved December 5, 2007, from http:www.washingtonpost .com/w-dyn/articlesA17744–2005.Jan18.html

Mortenson, G., & Relin, D. O. (2006). *Three cups of tea: One man's mission to promote peace . . . one school at a time.* New York: Penguin.

Rich, F. (2006, August 27). Return to the scene of the crime. *The New York Times,* p. 10.

Rothkopf, D. (2008). *Superclass: The global power elite and the world they are making.* New York: Farrar, Straus & Giroux.

Safire, W. (2005, January 1). Where was God? *The New York Times,* p. A23.

Scott, B. (2005). Tsunami coverage: Slow to start, left us wanting more. *Global Journalist, 11*(1), 15–17.

Sherman, D. (1999). Aristotle and the problem of particular injustice. *The Philosophical Forum, 30,* 235–248.

Stiglitz, J. (2005). Review essay: The ethical economist: Growth may be everything, but it's not the only thing. *Foreign Affairs, 84*(6), 128–134.

Stiglitz, J. (2006). *Making globalization work.* New York: W. W. Norton.

Strom, S. (2006, June 9). Relief rift persists, report says. *The New York Times,* p. A23.

Traub, J. (2008, March 9). The celebrity solution. *The New York Times Magazine,* pp. 38–43.

Wilson, J. Q. (1993). *The moral sense.* New York: Free Press.

Williams, J. (2006, September 1). Getting past Katrina. *The New York Times,* p. A19.

Wrage, E. J., & Baskerville, B. (Eds.). (1960). *American forum: Speeches on historic issues, 1788–1900.* Seattle: University of Washington Press.

Yunus, M. (2006, October 14). A hand doesn't always require a handout. *The New York Times,* p. A6.

Chapter 7: "I Didn't Do It for You": Organizations, Class, and Poverty

Aronowitz, S. (2003). *How class works*. New Haven, CT: Yale University Press.

Bhagwati, J. (2004). *In defense of globalization*. New York: Oxford University Press.

Bourdieu, P. (1999). *Language & symbolic power*. Cambridge, MA: Harvard University Press.

Chang, H.-J. (2008). *The myth of free trade and the secret history of capitalism*. New York: Bloomsbury.

Cooper, P. J., Calloway-Thomas, C., & Simonds, C. (2007). *Intercultural communication: A text with readings*. Boston: Pearson Allyn & Bacon.

Chua, A. (2003). *World on fire: How exporting free market democracy breeds ethnic hatred and global instability*. New York: Doubleday.

Dallaire, R. (2004, October 4). Looking for Darfur, seeing Rwanda. *The New York Times*, p. A29.

De Soto, H. (2000). *The mystery of capital: Why capitalism triumphs in the West and fails everywhere else*. New York: Basic Books.

Domhoff, G. W. (1998). *Who rules America? Power and politics in the year 2000*. Mountain View, CA: Mayfield.

Dugger, C. W. (2006, June 9). Some nations slow with pledged aid. *The New York Times*, p. A6.

Duncan, H. D. (1985). *Communication and social order*. New Brunswick, NJ: Transaction.

Edgerton, R. B. (2000). Traditional beliefs and practices: Are some better than others? In L. Harrison & S. Huntington (Eds.), *Culture matters: How values shape human progress* (pp. 126–140). New York: Basic Books.

Eagleton, T. (2003). *After theory*. New York: Basic Books.

Faux, J. (2006). *The global class war: How America's bipartisan elite lost our future— and what it will take to win it back*. New York: John Wiley.

Friedman, T. L. (2005). *The world is flat: A brief history of the twenty-first century*. New York: Farrar, Straus & Giroux.

Fukuyama, F. (1995). *Trust: The social virtues and the creation of prosperity*. New York: Simon & Schuster.

Garrett, L. (2007). Do no harm: The global health challenge. *Foreign Affairs, 86*(1), 14–38.

Geertz, C. (1973). *The interpretation of cultures*. New York: Basic Books.

Grameen Bank, Bangladesh. (n.d.). Retrieved October 5, 2007, from http://www.gdrc.org/icm/grameen-16.html

Grondona, G. (2000). A cultural typology of economic development. In L. Harrison & S. Huntington (Eds.), *Culture matters: How values shape human progress* (pp. 44–55). New York: Basic Books.

Hardt, M., & Negri, A. (2004). *Multitude: War and democracy in the age of empire*. New York: Penguin.

Harrison, E. H., & Huntington, S. P. (Eds.). (2000). *Culture matters*. New York: Basic Books.

Herbst, J. (2005). Mbeki's South Africa. *Foreign Affairs, 84*(6), 93–105.

Hofstede, G. (2001). *Culture's consequences: Comparing values, behaviors, and organizations across nations* (2nd ed.). Thousand Oaks, CA: Sage.

Huntington, S. P. (1996). *The clash of civilizations and the remaking of world order.* New York: Simon & Schuster.

Inglehart, R. (2000). Globalization and postmodern values. *The Washington Quarterly, 23,* 215–228.

Judt, T. (2005). *Postwar: A history of Europe since 1945.* New York: Penguin.

Kingsolver, B. (1998). *The poisonwood Bible.* New York: Harrper Flamingo.

Lapham, L. H. (1988). *Money and class in America.* New York: Weidenfeld & Nicolson.

Mbeki M. (2005, July 5). Liberate Africa from its political elites. *The Wall Street Journal,* p. A20.

Meredith, M. (2005). *The fate of Africa: From the hopes of freedom to the heart of despair, a history of 50 years of independence.* New York: Public Affairs.

Montaner, C. A. (2000). Culture and the behavior of elites in Latin America. In L. Harrison & S. Huntington (Eds.), *Culture matters: How values shape human progress* (pp. 56–64). New York: Basic Books.

Perlez, J. (2006, May 31). Poverty and violence sink grand plans for East Timor. *The New York Times,* p. A3.

Rothkopf, D. (2008). *Superclass: The global power elite and the world they are making.* New York: Farrar, Straus & Giroux.

Roy, A. (2002). *Interview with Arundhati Roy.* Retrieved January 5, 2008, from http://www-english.tamu.edu/pers/fac/andreadis/474H_ahapw/Arundhati_Roy_Interview.html

Sachs, J. D. (2005). *The end of poverty: Economic possibilities for our time.* New York: Penguin.

Shiva, V. (2005, May). *The polarised world of globalisation.* http://www.tamilnation.org/oneworld/shiva.htm

Speth, J. G. (1999). The plight of the poor: The United States must increase development aid. *Foreign Affairs, 78*(3), 13–18.

Stiglitz, J. E. (2002). *Globalization and its discontents.* New York: W. W. Norton.

Stiglitz, J. E. (2006). *Making globalization work.* New York: W. W. Norton.

Tuan, Y.-F. (1977). *Space and place: The perspective of experience.* Minneapolis: University of Minnesota Press.

Wilson, J. Q. (1993). *The moral sense.* New York: Free Press.

Chapter 8: Empathetic Literacy: Come, Shout About It?

Alba, R. (1990). *Ethnic identity: The transformation of white America.* New Haven, CT: Yale University Press.

Aurelius, M. (1983). *Meditations* (G. M. A. Grube, Trans.). Indianapolis, IN: Hackett.

Carr-Ruffino, N. (1996). *Managing diversity: People skills for a multicultural workplace.* London: International Thomson Publishing.

Chen, G.-M., & Starosta, W. J. (1998). *Foundations of intercultural communication.* Needham Heights, MA: Allyn & Bacon.

Crook, M. J. (1999). *The rise of the nouveaux riches.* London: John Murray.

de Blij, H. (2005). *Why geography matters: Three challenges facing America: Climate change, the rise of China, and global terrorism.* New York: Oxford University Press.

Duncan, H. D. (1985). *Communication and social order.* New Brunswick, NJ: Transaction.

Fukuyama, F. (1995). *Trust: The social virtues and the creation of prosperity.* New York: Simon & Schuster.

Hochschild, A. (2005). *Bury the chains: Prophets and rebels in the fight to free an empire's slaves.* Boston: Houghton Mifflin.

Holt, J. (2008, March 9). Good instincts: Why is anyone an altruist? *The New York Times Magazine.*

Hunter, D. J. (1991). *Culture wars: The struggle to define America.* New York: Basic Books.

Index of global philanthropy. (2007). Washington, DC: Center for Global Prosperity. http://gpr.hudson.org/files/publications/IndexGlobalPhilanthropy2007.pdf

Jandt, F. E. (2004). *An introduction to intercultural communication: Identities in global community.* Thousand Oaks, CA: Sage.

Kant, I. (1991). *The metaphysics of morals* (M. Gregory, Trans.). New York: Cambridge University Press.

Martin, J. N., & Nakayama, T. K. (1997). *Intercultural communication in contexts.* London: Mayfield.

Samavor, P., & Porter, R. (Eds.). (2003). *Intercultural communication: A reader.* Belmont, CA: Wadsworth/Thomson Learning.

Smith, A. M. (2004). *The Sunday philosophy club.* New York: Pantheon.

Index

About the Author

Carolyn Calloway-Thomas is an Associate Professor and Director of the Preparing Future Faculty program in the Department of Communication and Culture at Indiana University. She is coauthor of *Intercultural Communication: A Text With Readings* (2007) and *Intercultural Communication: Roots and Routes* (1999), as well as coeditor of *Dr. Martin Luther King, Jr. and the Sermonic Power of Public Discourse* (1993). Her teaching and research areas are intercultural communication, public dialogue in America, civic engagement, pedagogy, and communication in Black America. In 2007, Professor Calloway-Thomas was invited to participate in the Oxford Round Table conference on diversity and public policy at Oxford University in England. Her national awards include a Ford Postdoctoral fellowship; a Fulbright scholarship to Nigeria, West Africa; a Carnegie scholarship; the National Communication Association's Robert J. Kibler award; and the Distinguished Alumni award from Grambling State University. She holds a BS degree from Grambling College, an MA degree from the University of Wisconsin, and a PhD degree from Indiana University.